Men and Music

in Western Culture

William R. Sur

ADVISORY EDITOR IN MUSIC EDUCATION

Men and Music
in Western Culture

Don C. Walter
WESTERN WASHINGTON STATE COLLEGE

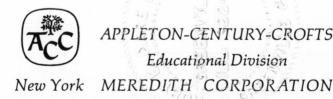

APPLETON-CENTURY-CROFTS
Educational Division
New York   MEREDITH CORPORATION

Preface

Several years ago I was called upon to develop a series of twenty-five lectures tracing the influence of music upon the lives of men from the time of antiquity to the present. These lectures—along with others on art, literature, and philosophy—were a part of a general studies course which was paced by the presentation of world history designed for college freshmen. The entire story of music cannot be told in so short a time, so it was necessary to select the men and the music which seemed to have had the greatest impact upon Western culture. This book develops further the material of those lectures. At the end of each chapter is a list of the recorded music that illustrates the musical concepts discussed in that chapter. Many new recordings are constantly being made available, and these should be carefully studied in order to keep the lists up to date. The text includes few examples of musical notation, since these seem to form a psychological block for the large number of students who are unskilled in reading music. For those who would find the examples meaningful, the scores are not difficult to obtain.

The world's great libraries are well stocked with books devoted to music and with books that tell about the master musicians who have taken an active part in its development. Why then should this book be written? In the first place, it was prepared to meet the needs of the reader who has neither time nor opportunity to spend long hours in research and reading and yet has a curiosity about music that can lead to an interest in it. Its second purpose is to point out the role music has played in Western culture and to show our age to be one of many ages, each of which has mirrored through its music the life of its people, their habits, their accomplishments, and the most profound expressions of their minds. We must carefully avoid the idea that the music of former ages was unsatisfactory, crude, or even preparatory to the accomplishments of our generation.

Finally, the purpose of this book is to chart a path through the maze of mythology, tradition, and fact which has been tempered by political, religious, and economic forces. It is hoped that, regardless of his musical background, the reader may travel this path with interest and confidence. He is encouraged to stop from time to time and acquaint himself with music and musical personalities that do not come within the scope of this work. Most of all, it is hoped that the reader will be helped to see music as a forceful art rather than a mere amusement—a force capable of affecting human thought and conduct.

Special acknowledgments are due A and C Black, Ltd., 4, 5 and 6 Soho Square, London, England, W 1, for their permission to reproduce the photographs of historical and antique instruments; to Dover Publications, Inc., 180 Varick Street, New York, N. Y., for their permission to reproduce the pictures of ancient and medieval instruments; and to Oxford University Press, 200 Madison Avenue, New York, for their permission to reproduce the Delphic Stone.

Of the many friends and colleagues who have helped in the preparation of this book, special acknowledgment and thanks are due Robert Carlton, Department of English, Western Washington State College, for reading the manuscript and making valuable suggestions; Mark Flanders of the VICOED program, Western Washington State College, for his expert photography; Miss Joyce Dabney, research staff artist, Department of Research, Western Washington State College, for her excellent illustrations; James Sjolund, State Supervisor of Music, Olympia, Washington, for his encouragement in the work; the very efficient secretaries in the Department of Research, Western Washington State College: Mrs. Dayle Jordan and Mrs. Jane Clark; and most of all to my wife, Ada Gambrell Walter, who served as typist and proofreader, and furnished inspiration for the entire project.

D. C. W.

Contents

Part Four: The 20th Century

Men and Music
in Western Culture

Part One ∽ *3000 B.C. = A.D. 1400*

1 ∿ The Music of Antiquity

There seems to be no single origin for an art whose primitive forms include singing, whistling, speaking, and shouting. Pitched and unpitched sounds are produced from every conceivable form of instrument, from hollowed gourd to scientifically built violin or pipe organ.

Who can say where a mother hummed the first lullaby to her child or where a man first expressed in song his feelings of joy or sadness? From earliest history men have recognized the power of music to express feelings, stir emotions, and influence thoughts and actions. By means of music, primitive man communicated with others. He found delight in work and exercise; he expressed his love and fear; he grew in bodily strength and grace and with music he went to fight his battles. From ceremonial song and dance, primitive communities drew physical strength, and as they advanced in the ways of civilization, their music became more varied and complex.

A study of the early history of music is confronted with a unique problem. Although we know music has been practiced since the dawn of history and although we know a great deal of what men thought about it and how they reacted to it, we know much less of how the music of antiquity sounded, since an adequate symbolism representing pitch and the quality of musical sounds is a comparatively recent development. Every civilized or semi-civilized country has traveled a path of musical progress that has been long and not always well marked. However, events of history usually reflect a country's music and we depend upon them for much of what we know about the music of antiquity. The most significant musical developments in early history took place in the cultures of the Egyptians, Chinese, Hebrews, and Greeks. In tracing the progress of early music, then, most of our concern will be with these people.

3

Egypt

The year 3000 B.C. marks an important period of culture for the Egyptians. Paintings left by them on the walls of their tombs and temples serve to show us the everyday life of the people. Some pictures show slaves singing songs as they carry their master in a chairlike conveyance; others reveal a family listening to a mother play a harp; and still others depict groups of entertainers playing pipes,

(a)   *(b)*   *(c)*   *(d)*

Fig. 1–1.   Artist Drawing of a Painting on an Ancient Egyptian Tomb at Thebes: (a) Arched Egyptian Harp; (b) Lute; (c) Aulos; (d) Lyre

lutes, and harps of various kinds. The musical devices of this early Egyptian culture seem remarkably well developed. The instruments and drawings found by archeologists have shown that Egyptian harps ranged from small shoulder harps with seven strings to elaborate standing harps of twenty-two strings, inlaid with mother-of-pearl and precious stones.

Wealthy Egyptians often maintained a household orchestra which provided concerts, musical displays, and daily entertainment for family and friends and which assisted in impressive ceremonial

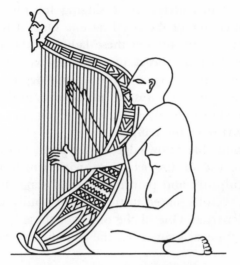

Fig. 1–2. Small Egyptian Harp

Fig. 1–3. Great Egyptian Harp

occasions. The superintendent of singing for the royal court was also usually in charge of the royal harem. One of his duties, as one writer suggests, was to instruct these ladies in the art of singing so they could "rejoice the heart of the king with beautiful songs." The early Egyptians achieved quite a high degree of organization in their music: large groups of musicians, numbering into the hundreds, are known to have performed together at festivals and at some of the rites of the temple.

Our considerable knowledge of Egyptian musical instruments is possible because of the exactness with which they have been depicted in sculpture and painting. Several songs have been found among papyrus scrolls placed in the ancient tombs for the entertainment of the departed. One of the oldest of these is the "Song of the Oxen." We will never know what the melody was, but the words are these:

> Thresh for yourselves,
> Thresh for yourselves!
> Straw for your fodder,
> Grain for your masters;
> Give yourselves no peace!

Thirty centuries before Christ, the Mesopotamians had developed their music to a level comparable with that of the Egyptians. By the year 2000, the Babylonians, Assyrians, and Chaldeans were all using music in their religious services as well as in their folk culture. We stress the music of the Egyptians, however, because we have more evidence of what they did and how they did it. Their close association with the Greeks at a later time in history resulted in some important contributions to Greek and Roman culture.

China

The ancient Chinese held remarkable views concerning music. They believed the essence of music was not in its sound alone but in a transcendent power. In their thought the whole universe was "One"; hence, the tones of their five-tone scale, which we call *pentatonic* (Fig. 1–4), were associated with elements such as direction, color, seasons of the year, taste, office or position, planets, and many other forces which they felt were carefully organized in a

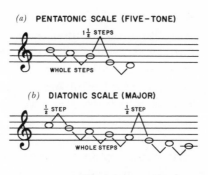

Fig. 1–4

smooth-working universe. All of these coordinates were written down in their "Book of Rites." In their thinking, it could be disastrous to use a wrong combination of musical elements, since it might endanger the harmony of the universe.

The Chinese pentatonic scale corresponds to the pattern of the black keys on the piano. We can also demonstrate it by singing the syllables as we know them, *do, re, mi, sol, la;* but the pitch of their *do*—the starting note—differed from one month to the next. At the first of each month, instruments had to be retuned to the assigned pitch for that month.

A sample of Chinese coordinates are these: When *do* is assigned to the pitch of our F on the piano, the month should be February; the season, winter; the direction, north; the color, black; the taste, salt; the favored position, prince; and the favored instrument, the drum.

Legend tells us that Ling-Lun, a young man, was given the task of finding the true tone of music. This was finally decided to be the pitch of the middle tone of his speaking voice when he spoke with no degree of passion. This true tone of music was called the Note of the Yellow Bell and was comparable to what the Greeks much later in history called a *Mese.* Contemporary music still maintains a fixed pitch, which we call a *key note* or *key feeling.*

Our understanding of Chinese music is derived only partly from a familiarity with legend. Historical facts are also important. Huang Ti was Emperor of China in 2697 B.C. In that year, he ordered that music be organized into *lu's,* or pitches. Bamboo tubes, equally thick, were cut in lengths of ratios of two-to-three, two being the numerical symbol of earth and three being the symbol of heaven. A five-to-two ratio was also brought in—five being the number of directions, north, south, east, west, and center. Regardless of the veil of mythology surrounding this period of history, there seems to have been some well-defined ideas of the science of sound which we know as acoustics, ideas which were later verified by the Greeks. The interval of the fifth was definitely established as a measurement of music.

It would seem that music would be greatly restricted by using only the pentatonic scale, but many songs in our culture have adopted this pattern. We find it most often in Scottish songs such as "Auld Lang Syne" and "Bonnie Doon," which can be played entirely on the black keys of the piano.

Most of the ancient Chinese studies of music dealt with acoustical principles. However, we know that a usable system of notation was not available to Confucius; in his lifetime he collected five hundred songs of the people but lamented the fact that he had no way of writing down their manner of singing them.

Considerable research has been done in finding and recording ancient music. One available recording is of a very old Chinese song played on a zither of thirteen strings: "An Old Man Strumming a Zither in a Refined State of Intoxication." We do not know the date of this composition, but it is probably about 900 B.C., well before the time of Confucius; it is a sort of program-music typical of the Chinese culture.

Jewish Music

The ancient music of the Hebrews was mostly made up of free-flowing melodies of four to six tones such as a shepherd might play on his harp or pipe. It was much like that of any pastoral people until after their four-hundred-year period of bondage in Egypt. This ended about 1400 B.C. when they returned to Palestine. The symbolism of Hebrew music was developed to a point of considerable accuracy. Signs which indicated pitch, interval, and rhythmic patterns were placed above the word syllables of a text. The first great Hebrew song in this form is known as "The Song of Moses" and is recorded in the Bible (Exodus 15:1–21). This is a song of praise and thanks for the deliverance of the Israelites from Egyptian bondage.

The manner of their singing, which involved large crowds of people, was quite simple. It used either an ancient chant with repetitious phrases or a call-and-response pattern in which the leader would sing a phrase, and the congregation would repeat it. If the phrase were too long or too complicated for the congregation to repeat, they at times would answer with an Amen, and the leader would continue the song. We have never gotten entirely away from this audience-participation kind of music; it was an especially popular way of singing ballads in sixteenth-century England.

About 1000 B.C., King David of Israel established music in the regular liturgy of the church. He also established an orchestra using several types of harps and lyres made of wood, ram's horns, and cymbals of bronze. Also, according to the Biblical account, King David "caused trumpets to be made of silver." He also "set apart men who were trained in music," and provided for this training to be perpetuated.

David is well remembered as the author of songs and psalms for the worship service. They are held in the highest esteem as poetry and literature, but they were written to be sung. Many of them have explicit directions regarding their performance. Hebrew religious traditions are strong and the ancient practices of chanting seem to have been preserved unspoiled. An available recording is the *Cantillation of Psalm 8,* subtitled *For the Leader Upon Gittith, a Psalm of David.*

One chant, *Ani Mamin,* dates from the Babylonian captivity, 596 B.C. *Ani Mamin* literally means "I believe" and is an assertion of the belief in the coming of the Messiah and of the resolution to await his coming though he delay.

The Greeks

The Greeks claimed nine beautiful goddesses as patrons of the arts and sciences. These beautiful ladies were daughters of the great god, Zeus, and were called Muses. Schools devoted to the disciplines of art and science were, therefore, called "Music Schools." We will name only the Muse, Euterpe, who was the patron of music

Fig. 1–5. Hebrew Kiner Player

A musician from an Egyptian wall painting at Beni Hasan. The instrument depicted is somewhat different from those seen on other paintings of the period; it is probably the Biblical "kinnor," played with a plectrum.

and lyric poetry. A musician of ancient Greece was a highly educated person who was familiar with the "language of the Muses." It was not until after the decline of Greek culture that music became the special discipline we know today.

Ancient Greek poets, philosophers, and historians have written so enthusiastically about their music that its high artistic quality must be accepted without doubt. However, with the collapse of the Hellenic world, nearly all of the documents of Greek music disappeared. Today, we have only about six hundred bars of ancient Greek music, mostly chiseled on tablets of stone (see Chapter 2).

Long before the earliest Greeks could write, they learned of their world, their history, and their religion through epic poetry chanted by bards or singers. The patterns were standard musical phrases repeated over and over again. Their greatest bard was Homer, a poet, singer, and master of the lyre. Tradition describes him as a wandering minstrel, journeying from place to place chanting stories of gods and heroes. In his *Iliad* he kept alive the tale of the Greek war with Troy; in his *Odyssey* he sang of the exploits and courage of Odysseus, the King of the Island of Ithaca. Sappho, a famous poetess, singer, and lyre player of ancient Greece, turned her home into a school for girls of noble birth where she taught them the arts and graces of music along with poetry and dancing.

All of the Greeks' instruments were used to accompany singing. Although the instruments were played in unison with the singer, the Greeks called this practice harmony. The Greeks borrowed most of their musical instruments from their neighbors. The lyre was a general name applied to any of several stringed instruments, but the model most commonly used by amateurs and beginners was made with a tortoise shell as a resonator; two arms of myrtle wood, ex-

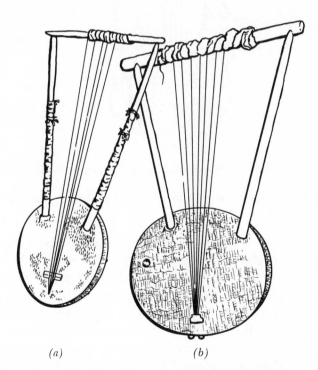

(a)   (b)

Courtesy of Dover Publications

*Fig. 1–6. (a) Five-String Lyre and (b) Seven-String Lyre,
Used Throughout the Middle East*

tended from the shell, supported a crossbar. Five, six, or seven silk strings extended from the edge of the shell to the crossbar, where they were tightened by means of a key (Fig. 1–7). The instrument was held in an inclined position and strummed with a plectrum in the right hand while the fingers of the left hand dampened strings not meant to be heard. The system was much like that of today's autoharp.

The Showcase of Musical Instruments, *Dover Publications*

Fig. 1–7.   Greek Lyre With a Tortoise Shell Resonator

The *kithara* was a lyre of quite elaborate proportions, handsomely made, with thirteen or more strings. This was the instrument of the professional, who often received large fees for his services. The *aulos* is often mistranslated as flute. It was, in fact, a pair of pipes, both placed in the mouth and blown with a double reed somewhat on the principle of the modern oboe (Fig. 1–8).

The *syrinx* was an instrument made by binding several aulai together; the performer blew first upon one and then another, selecting the pitch he wished. The syrinx was not important as a Greek instrument; but in the third century B.C., Ctesibius of Alexandria devised a means of supplying air to the syrinx with a

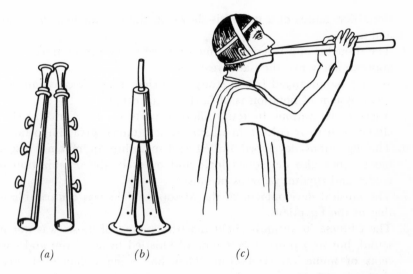

Courtesy of Dover Publications

Fig. 1–8. (a) Double Aulos, (b) Joined Aulos, (c) Greek Aulos Player, Wearing a Headstall to Assist in Blowing the Instrument

hydraulic pump. More pipes were added, wax was used to stop them in order to produce the right pitch length, a key system was attached, and a water organ called a *hydraulis* was produced. This instrument became extremely popular in the Roman world where it often furnished background music for pageantry. The effects, however, were more often striking and colossal than they were artistic.

Greek music, like Greek culture in general, had its roots in the Orient. Its theoretical system, the development of instruments, and even its magical association which were later refined and incorporated into the doctrine of *ethos* (ay'-thos) are evidence of an Oriental heritage. *Ethos* may be simply defined as the innate characteristic in music, poetry, drama, and the dance which influences human behavior.

Summary

1. There seems to be no single origin for music in its primitive forms.
2. The practice of music assisted men to advance in the ways of civiliza-

tion. The genius of a nation is shown in the development of its art and music.

3. The thoughts and reactions of men toward music can be traced back approximately five thousand years.
4. We are handicapped in the study of ancient music because an adequate system of notation is of fairly recent origin.
5. Ancient civilizations in four different parts of the world reached climaxes in their culture in which music attained great importance.
6. The Egyptians developed skilled craftsmanship in making instruments; they also developed logic and order in the organization of modes and rhythm patterns of music.
7. The musical development of the Mesopotamians was comparable to that of the Egyptians.
8. The Chinese in antiquity held that the essence of music was not in sound, but in a transcendent power. This led to mysticism and concepts of numerical symbolism. They had some well-defined ideas about the science of sound.
9. The Hebrews were founders of the Jewish-Christian religious traditions, which included music as a major part of worship.
10. The Hebrews devised the first functional symbolism of music, which was dependent upon a text.
11. The Greeks showed their genius in developing new concepts of beauty through their ability to discern and embody logical relationships in material things of art.

Examples of Music

1. *Ancient and Oriental Music,* Vol. I of *History of Music in Sound.* RCA Victor (Red Seal LM 6057).
2. *Jewish Holidays in Song.* TIKVA (T 60).
3. *Hebraic Chants for the Holy Days.* Parliament (PLP 133–2).
4. *2000 Years of Music,* compiled by Curt Sachs. Folkways (FT 3700).
5. Pindar (c. 522–c. 448 B.C.), "First Pythic Ode" (song), in *Music, The Universal Language* (Silver Burdett Co., 1941), p. 248.

2 ∿ Music as an Art and a Science

The Greeks inherited their music from Egypt, from Asia, and from their neighbors, the Hebrews, and they enjoyed their inheritance with wisdom and discrimination. Their tastes were simple—they had little liking for noise or ostentation. Instead they admired clearness, subtlety, and exquisite precision in their music. This information comes through their philosophic and literary writing together with a few samples of their version of notation carved on fragments of stone. Two of these fragments, the First Delphic Hymn (known as A Hymn to the Sun) and Skolion of Seikilos, have been reconstructed according to the best musical research, and recordings of each are available.

The place of music and the time it first appeared in performances of Greek drama cannot be established accurately, but it seems the drama itself was an outgrowth of the dithyrambs or choral hymns performed in honor of the Greek god Dionysus, son of Zeus and patron of choral song and drama. The famous Theater of Dionysus, in Athens, built in 500 B.C., testified to the importance that the Greeks placed upon their drama. It was situated on a hillside to take advantage of the natural slope, and hollowed to a semicircle and equipped with stone benches to accommodate 30,000 patrons. An open space below was a large flat piece of ground called the *orchestra*. In the center of this space was an altar where aromatic gum was kept burning. The actors each wore an oversized mask inside of which was an apparatus resembling a speaking trumpet. When they recited, it was in a sort of exalted monotone, often to the accompaniment of flutes. After the dialogue, the chorus entered through the wings with the promptness of a mimic army. Their leader stood on steps to lead their songs. The women's chorus entered in a less military manner. The action of the tragedy was diversified with various chorus dances and songs; the lyre was generally used to accompany them.

Fig. 2–1.   The Delphic Stone

The Delphic Stone showing the first Delphic hymn was discovered by a French archaeological expedition in 1893. The stone is broken and damaged so all of the words and signs of musical notation are not legible, but most of the song can be deciphered by using the explanation of music found in a treatise by Alypius, a Greek theorist of late antiquity. A translation of the words of the first section are: "Hearken, fair-armed daughters of Zeus the loud Thunderer, who have your appointed home on deep-wooded Helicon; come that you may honour with dance and song your brother, Phoebus of the golden tresses, who comes up to his abode on the twin peaks of this rock of Parnassus here, in the company of the far-famed women of Delphi, to visit the streams of Castalia with its fair waters, frequenting his prophetic hill upon the Delphic crag."

Dialogues and monologues were probably spoken while exciting or dramatic passages were sung. The chorus combined singing with acting and dancing, and in the works of the three great dramatists, Aeschylus (525–456 B.C.), Sophocles (495–406 B.C.), and Euripides (484–406 B.C.), the chorus and its music dominated the drama. Euripides introduced florid solo passages, a development which had far-reaching effects. About the middle of the fifth century B.C., professional musicians and virtuoso performers began to dominate the fields in both vocal and instrumental music; and although we have little information concerning the quality of music performance during this period, the artistic level seems to have gradually declined.

The ancient Greeks demonstrated a remarkable ability to as-similate the knowledge of other cultures and explain it in a meaning-ful way. They demonstrated that when a string of any length is tuned it will vibrate at a certain rate per second and produce a certain pitch. When the string length is divided in half, the pitch will be raised one octave. Also, a string twice as long will vibrate at half the frequency and will sound one octave lower. The twelve semitones into which Western music divides the octave constitute what is known as the *chromatic scale.* The method of dividing the octave into tones and semitones determines the kind of scale and the character of the musical system.

Under the leadership of Pythagoras and his followers, the Greeks were able to systematize a group of scales called *modes. Mode* is the manner of playing music and indicates the pattern in which the tones and semitones are to be placed within the octave. They also found the interval which we call a *fourth* to be an important one. This is equal to the interval from C to F on our piano keyboard. Two such intervals, one below the other, make up one octave. Four-note scales were called *tetrachords, tetra* meaning four and *tetrachord* referring to the group of four notes included in the in-terval of a fourth (Fig. 2–2).

If we start from the highest tone and place a half step between the first and second notes, a whole step between the second and third, and a whole step between the third and fourth, we would have the most common tetrachord pattern. If two tetrachords of this pattern are placed one below the other, we would have a *diatonic scale* (also known as a major scale), which would sound familiar to all of us. The tetrachord, then, is a half scale with the

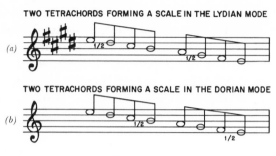

Fig. 2–2

possibility of arranging its four notes in a variety of ways. It should be noted that ancient Greek scales always started on the highest note and proceeded downward. It was not until the Renaissance that scales were built upon their lowest note.

Plato, Aristotle, and Aristoxenus exalted the aesthetic qualities of music. Pythagoras and his associates established a scientific basis for the study of acoustics. Their research was carried on largely with the aid of a one-stringed instrument called a *monochord* which Pythagoras invented (Fig. 2–3).

Acoustics is the study of the production and control of sounds. A study of acoustics must develop an understanding of the quality or *timbre* of sound. It is said that Pythagoras undertook this study in order to determine the physical difference between the sound of a plucked harp string and that of a hammered anvil. His studies were quite technical, but the principles involved may be understood by means of the common illustration of a playground swing. Suppose we watch an old-fashioned swing with iron posts, chain, and swing-board. Two children who are laughing and talking climb in and start swinging. Each back-and-forth movement we will call a cycle or vibration, and at a normal speed we can hear a number of different sounds such as the rattling of the swing-board and chain, the squeaking of the hinges, and the laughter of the children. If we can imagine the swing going faster and faster until it attains thirty or more cycles per second, the several sounds which were heard separately will fuse with the rush of air made by the moving swing and our ears will interpret the result as a low hum rising in pitch as the speed of the swing increases. Imagine now that the children become frightened and shrill screaming takes the place of their laughter. The quality

Fig. 2–3. Monochord

This Monochord is correctly shown being bowed above the point where the string is touched. The instrument existed in classical Greek times when it was used in the study of acoustics. In medieval times, it was revived in Western Europe as a musical instrument.

of the composite tone which could be heard would be changed because some of the partial tones, also called overtones, are changed. We may say then that the quality of a musical tone is determined by the relative strength of its constellation of partial tones.

Tone-quality and tonal relationship were considered by the Greeks to be the essence of music. There can be a wide variation in the arrangement of notes within a tetrachord. Each arrangement is best expressed in its own particular timbre or quality of tone. The timbre and tonal relationships result in the mood or mode of music, although some musicologists hold that a change of pitch also causes a change in mode.

The Greeks were greatly concerned with the quality in music which they called *ethos* (see p. 13). All of the transcendent powers of music were included in this concept of ethos, which will be discussed later. Today the melody in music is very important; it must maintain at all times the same tonal relationships. To the Greeks, melody was much less important, and interval changes within the melody were quite acceptable.

The basic Greek modes were named after provinces of Greece. The special ethos of each was thought to represent the characteristics of the people who lived in a particular province. The people of Lydia were considered thoughtful, tender, sincere, and sometimes sad: the Lydian mode tends to reflect those characteristics. The people of Phrygia were thought to be passionate, sensual, enthusiastic, and quick-tempered: the music of the Phrygian mode was much more exciting. The Dorian people were thought to be strong, honest, virile, and courageous: music in the Dorian mode reflected stability and helped one to be resigned to fate. Modes with compound names, such as *Mixolydian* or *Hypodorian,* used mixed tetrachords of two different kinds to make up their eight-tone scale. In this way, greater variation could be achieved.

In our culture we use two modes of music—major and minor. If we play our national hymn, *America,* as it is usually set—in the *key* of F—it is in the major mode; but if we were to raise the pitch of certain tones, the half-steps would be adjusted differently and the music would be in the minor mode. We then would say the melody was incorrect because of this alteration, but the Greeks would have seen nothing out of the way in this. They would have accepted it as the same melody in a different mode.

The Greeks stressed vocal music rather than instrumental, so from all of this early activity there developed no clear-cut scale system, such as instrumentalists need. Scale patterns developed later as instrumental music became more important (see Chapter 9).

In spite of the scientific insight into music of Pythagoras and his followers, the Greeks were mostly concerned with the ethos of music—that magic in music which can hold people spellbound and cause them to react in various ways. Writers of the time thought that music could affect the will and the character of human beings in many ways. It could (1) spur action; (2) strengthen the whole being; (3) undermine mental and spiritual balance; and (4) suspend will power. They argued further that, since it was possible for musicians to make an audience laugh or cry almost at will, surely their moral behavior, which stemmed from the emotions, could be controlled in somewhat the same manner. The doctrine of ethos explained the important role which music played in the Greek system of education and government. When Plato wrote the *Republic* and the *Laws,* he assigned a vital role to music and carefully explained the types of music to be used in education.

Modern science has demonstrated that the effects ascribed to music by the Greeks do exist in some measure. Music has proved effective in relieving pain, lessening fatigue, preserving mental health, and increasing workers' efficiency. A recent study made by a chain of department stores revealed that customers purchased approximately six percent more merchandise when a certain kind of background music was played than they did in the absence of background music.

Greek music served both social and religious functions. It was looked upon as a sort of supernatural means of communication between men and gods. All Greek festivals were religious in nature; that is, all festivals were dedicated to one or more of their many gods, so it was natural that music was closely associated with all important aspects of their culture. The Greeks organized their musical resources differently from the way we do today, but their purposes were well served. By way of Rome, they furnished a foundation upon which Western Europe built the complex art of music as we know it today. The collapse of Greek culture was due to inadequate economic and material planning. Their artistic glory ended in an era of sensuousness and sentimentality, but their Golden Age remains the culture which has not been equaled for its devotion to truth and beauty.

At the time that the Romans finally achieved dominance over Greek culture, about 200 B.C., the characteristics of the established music were:

1. Music was always monophonic, a lone vocal melody. Exceptions were solo pieces to be played upon instruments of the time.
2. Music was dependent upon poetry for its form and style.
3. Rhythm was determined by the poetic meter of the text.
4. Melodic line was determined by the inflection of the speech.
5. Since there was no harmony in the modern sense, concord and discord were not considered.
6. Notation, based upon letters of the alphabet, was limited and vague.

By about 200 B.C., the cultural center of the world had shifted to Rome, where it was felt that the function of music was to serve the people in war and pleasure. Thus the Romans' music tended toward the spectacular rather than toward the balanced lyricism of the Greeks. The trumpet and drum were more useful than the harp and lyre. Greek tragedies deteriorated into dance pantomimes, which became more popular with the Romans as they became more vulgar and obscene.

The Christians who were burned or killed by wild animals in Roman arenas died to the accompaniment of hydraulis and trumpet music. This association was probably a major reason why instrumental music was so strongly resisted in the Christian churches at a later time.

It should be noted that the Romans cultivated music as a mark

Courtesy of Dover Publications

Fig. 2–4. Tuba

The Tuba player was a common subject of Roman sculpture. This figure appears on the Arch of Titus.

of education. There was extensive amateur musical activity. The favored instrument seemed to be the Greek aulos, called *tibia* in the Latin language, which was commonly played in Roman middle- and upper-class homes. The Roman Emperor, Nero, who ruled from A.D. 54 to 68, considered himself a musician of great skill; and in the year A.D. 66, he traveled to Greece to take part in the singing and lyre-playing competition in the Olympic games. Needless to say, he rated very highly.

Music played an important role in the routine life and organization of the Roman army. They realized the psychological effect of musical tone and designed a set of war trumpets, each with its own set of signal calls. The *tuba* (Fig. 2–4), a long cylindrical instrument with a shrill, clear, piercing sound, was used to urge the

Courtesy of Dover Publications

Fig. 2–5.   Cornu

This Cornu has a wooden crossbar which supported the eleven-foot-long tube on the player's shoulder. The bell of the instrument is shaped like the head of a dragon.

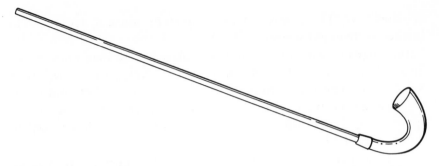

Musical Instruments *by A. J. Hipkins:*
A & C Black, Ltd., London

Fig. 2–6. Lituus

This Lituus is drawn from a reproduction in bronze of the original which was found in the tomb of a warrior discovered in 1827 at Cervetri, the Etruscan Cacre, and preserved in the Museum of the Vatican. The tube length of the instrument is five feet, four inches.

troops forward. The *cornu* (Fig. 2–5), a larger, curved, conical type of instrument with a more resonant and lower pitched voice was used to signal retreat and to calm the soldiers after battle. The *buccina* (which is the Latin word for the horn of an animal) was usually the horn of a water buffalo, although later copies were made in brass. This horn was used for sounding camp-calls and for short-distance signaling. The *lituus* (Fig. 2–6) was a small, high-pitched, curved bugle which was suitable for playing on horseback and was used extensively by the Roman cavalry.

It is generally assumed that Rome added little to the music they adopted from Greece, except to supply it with some Latin terminology and to create a variety of instruments particularly suitable for military and festal occasions. However, it is unthinkable that Rome, the center of a highly nationalistic empire, would not be aware of the influence of the musical styles from Western and Northern Europe, from Asia, and from Africa. The decline of Roman culture has probably obscured many of the artistic highlights in the lives of these musically gifted people of Italy. Nothing resembling the Greek doctrine of ethos appeared in Rome, nor do we know of any treatise or musical theory to come from the Romans. They practiced music widely but on an amateur scale. The finer things of art suffered at this time, since they were busy building and maintaining a political empire.

Summary

1. The Greeks assimilated knowledge from all over the world and explained it in a meaningful way.

2. Plato, Aristotle, and Aristoxenus exalted the aesthetic in music while Pythagoras and his associates established a scientific basis for it. Pythagoras (582–500 B.C.) was a Greek philosopher and mathematician from the island of Samos; he is credited with discovering the ratios of musical tone and developing the concept of simple and complex vibration. There is no record of Pythagoras' writings, but his theories were developed by his followers.

   Plato (427–347 B.C.) was a Greek philosopher whose concern with music was almost entirely with ethical values. His concepts of music and its place in society are stated in the *Laws* and the *Republic.*

   Aristotle (384–322 B.C.) was a pupil of Plato, also concerned with the ethical values of music, notably in the *Politics.*

   Aristoxenus (354–? B.C.) was the most important Greek writer concerned with the details of music. Two works have come down to us, *Harmonic Elements* and *Elements of Rhythmics;* the first is in a complete form.

3. Timbre or quality of sound results from the relative strength of partial overtones.

4. Mode is the manner of playing music.

5. Tetrachord is a group of notes within the interval of a fourth. Two tetrachords comprise an octave.

6. The basic patterns of Greek modes were called Lydian, Phrygian, and Dorian; variations of these modes were numerous.

7. Mode was relatively important to the Greeks; melody is more important to our musical culture.

8. The Greeks stressed vocal music at the cost of instrumental; they had no clear-cut instrumental scales.

9. The Greeks recognized the transcendent power of music, which they called *ethos.* Music was important in Greek plans for education and government.

10. Modern science has verified that music can relieve pain, lessen fatigue, improve mental health, and increase factory production.

11. Greek music was monophonic, following the rhythm and meter of the text. Melody was guided by inflection. There was neither discord nor concord since there was no harmony.

12. When the cultural center of the world shifted to Rome, Greek music and art was generally adopted.

13. Roman music, as well as the instruments developed to play it, was essentially functional and made little contribution to music as art.

Examples of Music

1. Sophocles, *Oedipus Rex*. Caedmon (TC 2012).
2. *The Theory of Classical Greek Music* (Theory Series A, No. 1). Musurgia. (This record is meaningful only for the advanced student.)
3. *2000 Years of Music,* compiled by Curt Sachs. Folkways (FT 3700).

3 ∿ The Romanesque Period

It must have been discouraging for those citizens of Rome who lived in the provinces of the Empire during the fourth and fifth centuries A.D. All roads still led to Rome, but they were badly deteriorated and there was no one to keep them repaired. The heavy traffic they had once known was no longer there. The fine buildings and amphitheaters which had once housed large and enthusiastic crowds of people were now empty and falling into ruin. The people with each generation were becoming poorer and more insecure. Rome had become weak and unable to defend herself from the barbarians who were coming down from the north and east.

The great historical events which brought about the decline and fall of Rome occupy such an important place in history that we are likely to overlook the few creative forces which were at work. The Christian Church was thriving and experiencing growth and development while the process of general destruction was evident on every hand. The Church was the most stable influence in the Roman culture of that time.

The Romanesque period spans a rather dark and gloomy age in history, but if we examine it closely we find some interesting events. The general practices in music of the early Church were gradually modified by Roman ideas; and since the Roman Empire left its imprint on all of Europe during the Medieval Age, it is quite proper to use this name for the whole period which extends roughly from A.D. 400 to 1100.

The Romanesque concept was that a God-inspired mystery could be expressed in terms of simple and direct art, whether painting, sculpture, or music. The chief characteristic of the Romanesque style is its stark simplicity. The Church said, "Be not concerned with material things," and this doctrine resulted in the down-grading of instrumental music. St. Clement of Alexandria told his followers, "The only sound of music pleasing to God is the clear strong voice of his worshipers." The number of worshipers grew steadily in spite of political turmoil in the world. This was a new kind of religion. It was not reserved for a special group or class of people. Everyone could identify with it—men, women, and children, whether rich or poor, enslaved or free.

There was a need for a universal religion because of the great diversity of the people of the Roman Empire. There was a time, in the later years of the Empire, when half the population were slaves whose masters were far from wealthy. Rome depended upon a few intelligent, aggressive leaders, and when the poor and downtrodden joined with people from outside, they were able to overthrow the political leadership and provide an opportunity for a very strong Roman church to emerge.

The historical transition from early Greek and Roman music to that of the twelfth century is not easy to trace or describe. We have considerable information about the beginning and the end of this period, but it is difficult for us to be certain of things musical during the intervening thousand years. Certain facts are well established, but it is not easy to fill this relatively long period of history with the living interest that music deserved. It is certain there was a good deal of musical life, but vestiges of it are difficult to find and there are very few discernible personalities.

We should keep in mind that there were no national states and that feudalism was the common political system. In the atmosphere of feudalism there was little place for artistic development or for recognition of a talented musician. There was the universal ideal of Christianity, represented by the organized church. It was in this Christian ideal that music found a place for several centuries.

The Roman Empire reached its greatest area and prosperity in the second century. In the third century, symptoms of decay began to appear; and, in the fourth, the repeated attacks of Goths, Vandals, and Huns finally forced the seat of government to move from Rome to Byzantium, the city we know today as Istanbul. The latter part of the sixth century saw the rise of Mohammedanism, which in the seventh swept over Syria, Egypt, and North Africa, and which reached Spain in the eighth. These severe changes destroyed the continuity of civilized life and thought, and interrupted the development of all the fine arts.

When the seat of Roman government was moved to the rebuilt city of Constantinople in 313, the Emperor Constantine accepted the Christian faith and Christianity became the official religion of the Empire. Christianity was then carried into the North and West, highly organized with the usual Roman efficiency, and was eagerly received, especially among the Teutonic peoples. The Christian Church was, at last, ready to become a mighty social institution.

Because of the complex social and political situations of the day, cathedrals and religious houses were the only places where continuous and peaceful intellectual work was possible; these became the repositories of learning and the fountains of education which furnished the one persistent light in the so-called Dark Ages.

Singing in public and in private was taken as a matter of course for the early Christian. For Jewish converts, this was a continuation of the synagogue customs; but the Church grew mostly among the non-Jews, and the technical form employed was more Greek than Hebrew. In addition to Hebrew psalms, usually translated into Greek, the new faith produced many new hymns, especially from the second to the fourth centuries. Most of these early hymns, apparently, took the form of rhapsodies, drawing liberally from sources of folk music and sacred poems. The New Testament mentions the singing of hymns, but the earliest complete hymn extant is by Clement of Alexandria (d. 220). During the next three hundred years, there was such an abundance of original music supplied to the Church that it is evident that music was encouraged and cultivated.

After the year 350, the Church placed greater emphasis on unity of organization; the liturgy and creed became fixed, and the whole ritual of worship tended to become ornate. This focused so much attention on music and encouraged so much interest in it that various monasteries set aside rooms known as *scriptoria* in which monks dedicated their lives to copying, in the crude symbolism of their day, the hundreds and even thousands of plainsongs that were available to them.

Ambrose, Bishop of Milan (340–397), was the first important name to be connected with the music of the early Church. He was responsible for the collection of several hundred songs which were then in use in the Christian Church; after editing these, making changes in the texts as well as in the music, he gave them back to the Church in the form of Ambrosian chants, plainsongs, and hymns. These chants were the first to be written in the distinct style that was later to be called Gregorian. Pope Gregory the Great (d. 604) is often cited as the founder of the Gregorian musical style, but most historians today believe that the system was not completed until the eighth century, probably under Gregory II (d. 731) or Gregory III (d. 741), and that the name Gregorian came either from them or from those who wanted to glorify the earlier Gregory.

It should be remembered that the Gregorian style was the property of the Roman Church. There were analogous developments in each of the other branches of the early Church; but none of these had any significant influence on the development of modern music. Since the Gregorian style originated for liturgical reasons, its home was in the monastic chapels or the cathedrals of the large cities. From these centers it spread to the parish churches; but since this type of music was cultivated only by the ecclesiastics, it was always remote and never well understood by the laity or common people. Its direct influence upon the general progress of music was therefore limited. In the general evolution of music the Gregorian chant has always been a peculiar specialty, representing the persistence of a style which is essentially antique; it remains a remarkable example of melodic beauty.

During this long period—which saw Greek notation used, then misused, and then forgotten—Latin letter notation was developed. The chief worker with this Latin notation was Boethius, a Greek who lived in the sixth century. Throughout the next two hundred years, we find the Latin letters gradually emerging into a system of neumatic notation much like the accent marks of speech and comparable to the symbolism used by the Hebrews two thousand years earlier.

It is evident that the tone system of medieval music came from that which had been used by the Greeks, although the stages of development are not entirely clear. Only after the plainsong had reached a complex stage of development was an effort made to systematically establish the principles on which it was based. The basis chosen was a series of modes resembling those the Greeks used about 500 B.C. These modes were known by their Greek names, but they were transposed from their ancient meaning. The new scales progressed upward from the lowest note rather than downward from the highest, as the ancient Greek scales had done.

This gave the new church modes a sound very different from that of the Greek modes of the same name.

In the first thousand years of the Christian era, the Church was primarily concerned with absorbing the music of the ancients. This means that the monophonic style of song was gradually refined until it reached its highest peak in the Gregorian chant. Singing in octaves was a common practice and the occasional addition of some chord-tones was part of the musical inheritance from the East, but the actual practice of polyphony prospered especially in Western Europe and became the specialty of Western composers. The practice of singing in parts developed with the continued growth of the Church; but whether it evolved out of early musical practices, or established itself as a separate tradition, is hard for us to tell. Evolution is not always the preferred method of development for art. The first mention of part-music appears in a treatise dated in the ninth century and probably the practice was quite new and experimental at that time.

Many of the musical experiments of the day came from the school of St. Martial, located at the Abbey of St. Martial in southern France. The St. Martial style borrowed a part or the whole of the traditional chant and cast it in the tenor voice in long-sustained note-values. Above this tenor sang a second solo voice of freely composed melismatic, or vocally embellished, passages. This style is variously known as St. Martial Organum (or'-gah-noom), Melismatic Organum, or Sustained Organum. In this way, the school of St. Martial closed out the scholarly development of the Romanesque period and ushered in the new styles of writing.

Summary

1. The transition of music from the fall of Rome to the twelfth century is difficult to trace.
2. Severe political and religious changes destroyed the continuity of civilized life and thought and interrupted the development of all the fine arts.
3. In spite of the political turmoil of the world, the Christian movement grew steadily.
4. The Roman Emperor Constantine accepted the Christian faith in

A.D. 313; Christianity became the official religion of and was gradually accepted throughout the Empire.

5. Because of the complex social and political situations of the day, religious houses were the only places where intellectual work was possible.

6. After the fourth century, the ritual or worship became ornate and focused new attention on music.

7. The plainsong of the fourth century had no fixed rhythm or harmony.

8. Ambrose, Bishop of Milan (340–397), collected and edited available church songs, producing Ambrosian hymns and chants in a style later called Gregorian.

9. The Gregorian style of music was the property of the Roman Church. Its style is simple and primitive but still artistic.

10. The tonal system of the Middle Ages was based upon eight modes resembling those the Greeks used about 500 B.C.

11. The positive musical achievements which came after 1200 contrast sharply with the timid experiments before that time.

12. Music did much to mold the service of the Church. Gregorian music furnished a setting for the Mass, the entire church service.

13. In Greek and Gregorian music, the chief desire was for a single melodic line to reinforce and beautify the text.

14. With the polyphonic era came the idea that music might have beauty and meaning apart from the text.

15. The Reformation served as a background for the development of homophonic music.

Examples of Music

1. *Early Medieval Music,* Vol. II of *The History of Music in Sound.* RCA Victor (LM 6015).

2. *The Play of Daniel—Music of the Middle Ages* (Theory Series A, No. 1). Musurgia.

3. *Chant Gregorian.* London (A 4501).

4. *Court Dances of Medieval France.* Turnabout (TV 34008S).

4 ∾ The Gothic Period

During the Romanesque period, it was held that God-inspired mysteries of life and religion could be expressed in terms of simple and direct music. The Renaissance concept of rationalism, which came later, supports the theory that human reason or intellect rather than the senses or divine revelation is the true source of knowledge. Between these two periods came the Gothic (roughly defined by the dates 1150–1400). During these two hundred and fifty years, there was a gradual swing toward humanism, which caused music to be centered upon the human being rather than the divine. This transition toward humanism was quite gradual; so much so that when we view the whole period, we think of Gothic music as an expression of the religion, mysticism, and scholasticism which permeated the age. We can also see the emergence of many factors which eventually broke down the barrier between the "vulgar" and the "higher" music, as they were then called.

Gothic art is more universal than Romanesque, which tended to be monastic or aristocratic, thereby excluding the outside world. Gothic architecture, with its high ceilings and lofty spires, typifies the human aspirations of that time. The remarkable stained-glass windows (created by techniques which are now in part unknown) diffused the light in a way that supported man's concepts of mysticism. The art of making the very deep blue used in the twelfth century was lost in the thirteenth century, but beautiful shades of red were developed and used in larger panes of glass held together with strips of lead.

Music of the Middle Ages seemed to flow along, guided by countless anonymous composers who provided chants and songs for the church and other occasions. They seemed to feel their creative power was God-inspired and not to be associated with themselves as human beings. During the Gothic period, however, this state of affairs began to change rapidly. In the music of this period are found the first expressions of the most characteristic and basic elements of Western European music—the simultaneous sounding together of tones of different pitch. This is the phenomenon which we call *harmony*, and this harmony is the most characteristic element by which we can differentiate European music from other musical systems throughout the world. Harmony may be achieved in either of two ways. One is called *polyphony* or *counterpoint*, in which two or more melodic lines are sounded simultaneously, that is, the music develops in a linear fashion. The second is called *homophony*, where music is dealt with in a vertical or block fashion, that is, where a single prevailing melody is supported by chords. This is the system most widely used in the song style of today.

The groundwork for creating harmony was laid by Phillippe de Vitry, a French priest (1285–1361). He was also a poet, composer, musical theorist, writer, and diplomat, and was secretary to two French kings, Charles IV and Philip VI. His most notable writing in the field of music was a theoretical treatise called *Ars Nova (The New Art)*. This work is concerned with the notations of rhythm and meter. The English word *rhythm* stems from the Greek word *rhythmos*, meaning measured motion. Thus, rhythm means a flow or movement characterized by a regularly recurring beat or accent that is interspersed with periods of relaxation. *Meter* is the organizing force of rhythm. It may be described as regularly recurring accents or beats in given units of time called *measures* or *bars*. The beats within the measure will be in groups of two, three, four, etc., with the first beat of the measure bearing the strongest accent. The meter of a composition is indicated by a fraction-like sign called a meter signature. The upper figure of the signature shows the number of beats or counts in a measure and the lower figure represents the note value to receive a single beat or count. For example: $\frac{2}{4}$ indicates a duple meter with two quarter notes or the equivalent in a measure; $\frac{3}{4}$ indicates a triple meter with three quarter notes in a measure; and $\frac{4}{4}$ indicates a quadruple meter with four quarter notes in a measure. No longer was the symbolism of music to be dependent upon the words, and this seems to be the key to the rapid development of vast resources of polyphonic music in the following decades.

The polyphony of the thirteenth century was developed in three principal forms:

1. *Conductus* (con-dook'-toos), music with one text and with all parts in one meter. *Conductus* is a Latin term to indicate that the themes were taken from secular music or were original with the composer, instead of being selected from the plainsong of the Church. This form is most in keeping with our music today.
2. *Organum* (or'-gah-noom), music with one text but using different meters in the various parts.
3. *Motet,* with different but related texts, using different meters in each of the related parts.

All three of these forms were widely used in both sacred and secular music of the Gothic period.

A great deal of symbolism was attached to music of this time. Music of the Christian Church was to be written in triple meter to signify the Trinity, God the Father, Son, and Holy Spirit. In the year 1324, Pope John XXII denounced notation with its artificial meters, rapid tempi, ornaments, rests, and all polyphony of the modern school. According to him, these provided an alarming distraction. Polyphony, however, was not discredited for long. Under the watchful eye of Pope John and his successors, and with exact notation available, the period of anonymous creativity so characteristic of the Middle Ages came to an end. Now, men were ready to become leaders in a high form of musical art.

Throughout several centuries the Church developed a well-regulated order of service called *liturgy*. The liturgy since 400 had included Gregorian chants and plainsongs; but after the twelfth century, the service known as the *mass* was entirely set to music. It was in this century that the *credo* was finally adopted and included in the mass service. The aggregation of prayers that makes up the mass falls into one of two different patterns:

1. The Proper Mass, which is designed for Holy days and special occasions such as Christmas and Easter.
2. The Ordinary Mass, which can be appropriately repeated each Sunday throughout the year.

Both of these services are made up of five related sections, but we will concern ourselves mainly with the Ordinary Mass. The first section is called the *Kyrie Eleison* (keer'-ee-ay ay-lay'-ee-son), meaning Lord Have Mercy Upon Us. In this opening section the composer attempts to place the worshiper in a receptive and spiritual mood.

The second section is *Gloria in Excelsis Deo,* Glory Be to God on High. All of the great Glorias have captured a feeling of praise and honor. The third, the *Credo,* is a statement of the creed of the Church or a confession of faith. The Credo was added to the Mass after the final adoption of the Nicene Creed in the twelfth century. Its well-known text begins, "I Believe in One God, the Father Almighty and in Jesus Christ his only Son our Lord . . ." The fourth section, the *Sanctus* (sahnk'-tooss), begins "Sanctus, Sanctus, Sanctus . . ." and means Holy, Holy, Holy, Hosanna in the Highest; Blessed is He that Cometh in the Name of the Lord. The final section is *Agnus Dei* (ahn'-yoos day'-ee), O Lamb of God Who Beareth the Sins of the World. This is a threefold petition ending with *Dona Nobis Pacem,* Grant Us Thy Peace. To summarize the Mass: (1) a prayer for mercy; (2) a glorification of God; (3) a statement of Christian belief; (4) praise of God; and (5) a prayer asking for a Divine benediction, or blessing.

Gothic architecture is one of the most remarkable and artistically refined types of building. About the middle of the twelfth century, especially in Paris and its neighborhood, all the inherited forms of building were gradually changed under the influence of great dominating principles. The leading ideas were freedom, energy, and beauty. There was a great outburst of building, especially churches; and although the perfecting of the stone-vaulted cathedral was the great task of Gothic architecture, all other buildings, such as the castle, bridge, town hall, and house were dealt with in the same spirit. The Gothic cathedral was an amazing masterpiece of architectural beauty that towered above the landscape of many European towns. The polyphonic setting of the Mass was a musical masterpiece of artistic beauty which complemented the cathedral in which it was performed.

During the Gothic period, Italy was so concerned with the visual arts that we find no important composers of music there. At this time, the masters of music were imported from the North, mainly from the Burgundian School that flourished in the fourteenth and fifteenth centuries. These composers abandoned the complex Gothic counterpoint in favor of the four-part harmonization in the homophonic style which has been standard ever since.

Secular monophony before 1100 has not been preserved as well as that of sacred music. This was probably due to the fact that adequate notation had not yet been devised and because there was no institution whose duty it was to maintain the traditions of secular music as the Church maintained those of sacred music.

In recent times the term *minstrel* has taken on something of a glamorous nature, with many romantic overtones. In the Gothic period, however, the term was synonymous with that of *juggler*. These people made up a large and motley group; some had descended from the cosmopolitan vagrants of the disintegrating Roman Empire; some from the Celtic *Druids* and Nordic *Scalds*: while the largest percentage were runaway monks. These could be called dropouts from the rigid church-schools of the day. No well-defined line separated the musicians from the skillful acrobats who juggled balls and missile knives or who entertained by rope-walking or dancing.

Though indispensable in their time and received with delight as entertainers, the jugglers and minstrels were in a sense untouchables. Their visits were especially welcome since there was very little communication between communities. However, the rising middle class, proud of its houses and crafts, frowned upon this nondescript class that lived on the highways and wandered from town to town. They were without a permanent home, without the ties of an honest trade, and without the kind of respectability which the burghers were building for themselves. The Church, on the other hand, resented the high percentage of runaway clerics among the minstrels who directed pointed criticism and comedy at the Church.

The minstrels made an attempt to organize themselves after the model of the craftsman's guilds, but their very nature made any means of control extremely difficult, and the organization was soon forgotten.

Although the minstrels were treated warmly as entertainers, they were subjected to continual hardship. The Church refused them the sacraments, including matrimony. They had no rights and were not protected by civil law. As late as 1406, the municipality of Basel forbade minstrels and jugglers to wear trousers—the symbol of respectability. Still, this group of outcasts was one of the most important agents of medieval civilization. Their poetry and music was an essential part of public and private life. They expressed those sentiments of the common people which the Church in its aloofness was not able or willing to express.

Coronations, weddings, church feasts and councils were the great occasions for the migrant player. Poets of the time delighted in descriptions of minstrel gatherings. Four hundred players performed at the Court of Mantua in 1340; four hundred and fifty during the Reichstag at Frankfurt in 1397; and there have been church councils which are said to have attracted more than a thousand musicians. The men usually played individually or in small groups, but writers have noted that they sometimes did perform together and produced a grand melody and a grand noise.

Another class of people who sang the secular songs of the Middle Ages were the *jongleurs* (zhon-gler'), professional musicians who first appeared in the closing years of the tenth century and carried on for more than three hundred years. The jongleurs were neither poets nor composers; they sang and danced to the songs that others had created, but their professional skill and traditions played an important part in the development of secular music in Western Europe. The terms *troubadour* and *trouvere* (troo-vair') have the same meaning—finder, inventor, or composer of songs. Troubadours flourished in the twelfth and thirteenth centuries in Provence, the region which now comprises southern France. *Trouvere* was the term used in the north of France. The troubadours were at first knights, noblemen, and gentlemen amateurs. Most of them were poets and composers but not performers. They wrote songs and hired jongleurs or minstrels to sing them. Later, the troubadours became performers, developing considerable skill in the art of song. The advent of the troubadours marked a decisive change in knightly practices and concepts of chivalry. They turned from the rougher arts of fighting, hunting, and drinking to the less strenuous pursuits of ecstatic worship of the Virgin Mary and of gentlewomen. They developed elaborate codes of chivalrous ethics, stylized manners, and the appreciation of poetry and music.

The songs of the Provençal troubadours were carefully classified. There were the crusader's songs called *sirventes;* the lament for the fellow knight was called the *planh;* the *tenson* was an extemporaneous type of song on a given topic. This was a common basis for the musical contest known as the *puy,* which is described in the second act of Wagner's music drama, *Tannhäuser.* The *pastoreta* was a pastoral or shepherd song; the *serena,* a serenade; and the *alba* was a song for the morning after a night spent with a lover.

The *minnesinger* (*minne* meaning love) was the German counterpart of the *trouvere*. The singer and his art were modeled after the French pattern, like most art and culture of the Middle Ages. The first minnesingers used French melodies and adapted German words; later they used original German melodies as well. The minnesingers developed some features of their own. The texts were inclined to be religious in nature and the melodies—less popular and dance-like than those developed by the trouveres—were much closer to the style of the Church.

The advent of the *meistersinger* (meaning craftsman singer) was an interesting development in German musical life. This group of middle-class Germans formed a musical and poetic guild which flourished during the fourteenth, fifteenth, and sixteenth centuries. The men whose trades had been organized into guilds used the same system for the meistersinger. A youth with a promising voice was accepted as an apprentice in the music guild; by reason of study and practice and the passing of strenuous tests, and ultimately by some creative work he received the coveted title of Meistersinger. This was one of the first examples outside the organized musicians of the Church where a premium was placed upon musicianship. This movement developed under strong leadership and furnished an impetus for secular music in Germany that helped to make that country one of the greatest musical nations of all times. Because of the training required to be a meistersinger, the guild did much to make the study and performance of secular music a profession to be proud of. Young men of good families could devote their time to secular music without a feeling of shame or subservience. The name meistersinger was made familiar because of Richard Wagner's opera, *Die Meistersinger von Nürnberg*. The hero of Wagner's opera, an historical personage who lived from 1494 to 1576, was able to lift the art of the meistersinger to a high level. Any breach of the accepted rules of music was pitilessly recorded against the name of the man who committed it. This highly critical atmosphere in which the meistersinger performed raised the standard of musical performance, but emphasized petty correctness rather than musical development.

The chief difference between the singing groups of the various countries depended upon the location. Those in the warmer climates tended to emphasize the glory of love and romance, those farther north sang more of great adventure and feats of courage and

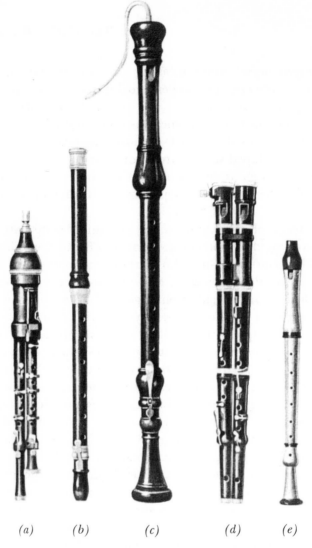

Musical Instruments *by A. J. Hipkins:*
A & C Black, Ltd., London

Fig. 4-1. (a) *Double Flageolet (which might be called a highly refined
Greek Aulos); (b) German or Transverse Flute; (c) Bass Recorder;
(d) Double Flageolet—a second model; and (e) Tenor Recorder*

The principle of these instruments differs from that of the horn and shawm in
that these are bored with reverse cones, that is with the embouchure, or mouthpiece,
at the larger end.

Samuel Pepys writes in his diary on the 20th of January, 1667: "To Drumbleby's
the pipe-maker, there to advise about the making of a flageolet to go low and soft.
He do show me a way and also a fashion of having two pipes of the same note fastened
together so I can play in one and echo it upon the other, which is mighty pretty."

40

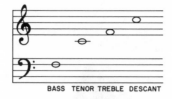

BASS TENOR TREBLE DESCANT

Fig. 4–2. Range of the Recorder From Its Lowest Note

strength. The development of secular music further severed the connections between singing and dancing. Several kinds of music which had been in general use for centuries became purely vocal forms. Most notable of these were the *ballad* (a simple, often sentimental song-story), and the *rondeau* (a musical setting of French poetry with a recurring refrain). The whole concept of the song took on a new importance as an artistic expression since it depended for its success upon the performer's ability to fuse music and text—the music was expected to intensify the emotions in the poetry or text. The vocal forms became unsuitable for dancing as the concern with refinements of textual interpretations increased. Music for festivals and dances was supplied by the instruments of the day.

Instrumental music developed in a remarkable manner after the *Ars Nova,* and many new instruments were created as the possibilities of the new music became evident. The little end-blown, flute-like instrument known as the *recorder* had been used since the Middle Ages by the clerics in the scriptoriums of the monasteries (Fig. 4–1). After 1300, however, it gained popularity and was widely used in the performance of secular music. By the sixteenth century, recorders with a playing range of just over two octaves were being made in sets or consorts called *choirs.* Using German terminology, a consort usually included four recorders—bass, tenor, treble, and descant. The lowest note of each is shown in Figure 4–2.

In addition to recorders, several other kinds of instruments were widely used. The *harp,* which came to the Continent from Ireland and Britain as early as the ninth century, was often a beautifully constructed instrument of twenty-four to fifty strings (Fig. 4–3). The Irish had well-established schools of harp playing which contributed greatly to the artistry of performance upon the instrument. The principal bowed instrument was the *vielle* (vee-ell') or *fiedel* (fee'-del), which had many different names and a variety

Musical Instruments *by A. J. Hipkins:*
A & C Black, Ltd., London

Fig. 4–3. *Irish Harp (Shown Without Strings)*

This venerable Irish harp (known as Queen Mary's Harp), probably built in the thirteenth century, was presented to Mary Stuart when she was crowned Queen of England in 1542. It is small, being only 31 inches high and 18 inches from back to front. It was played resting upon the left knee and against the left shoulder of the performer, whose left hand touched the upper strings. The sound chest, hollowed out of a single piece of wood, is 5 inches wide at the top and 12 inches at the bottom, the depth being 4½ inches. The forearm forms a convenient hand-hold for carrying the harp. The strings were of brass, 29 in number, varying in length from 2½ inches to 24 inches. They were sounded by the player's finger-nails, which were allowed to grow long for the purpose. The exact tuning of the Irish harp is not known, but we are assured that the thirteenth-century Irish had three modes in their music, the "Crying," the "Laughing," and "Sleeping."

of shapes and sizes; it is the prototype of the viol of the Renaissance and of the modern violin. The thirteen-century vielle had five strings, one of them usually a drone. This was the instrument which the jongleurs used most often to accompany their singing and recitations. In addition to the great organs found in the cathedrals and churches, there were two smaller types called the *portative* (portable) and *positive* (in position). The portative organ (Fig. 4–4) was small enough to be carried suspended by a strap over the shoulder of the player. It was a single rank of pipes with keys which were played with the right hand while the left hand worked the bellows. This was obviously a prototype of the modern piano accordion. The positive

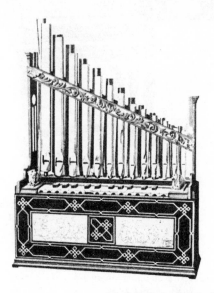

Musical Instruments *by A. J. Hipkins:*
A & C Black, Ltd., London

Fig. 4–4. Portative Organ

 The Portative or Portable Organ was a processional instrument slung by a strap over the player's shoulder, so as to allow the bellows at the back of the instrument to be worked by the player's left hand, while the keys were touched with the fingers of the right hand. From the high pitch of the pipes, the limited number of keys, and one hand only being used for touching them, it is concluded that only one voice, or part, was played. It has twenty-six metal pipes arranged in two rows and has one key for each pipe. The range extends from the first E to the third F above middle C. The height is 2 feet 6 inches; width, 2 feet; and depth, 8 inches.

Musical Instruments *by A. J. Hipkins:*
A & C Black, Ltd., London

Fig. 4–5. Positive Organ

This instrument is a chamber organ from the period of the French King
Louis XIII—about 1630. The Positive Organ, as the name implies, was intended to remain in a fixed place. It is not intended for choir use, although
it has three registers controlled by draw stops. The principal register, that
of the visible pipes, is of gilt tin, and is called the Montre; and its range
is from the E below to the third C above middle C. The second register,
also of tin pipes, is an octave higher in pitch. The third register is the
Bourdon, which uses wooden pipes stopped at the upper end, and is an
octave lower in pitch than the Montre. The dimensions of this Positive
Organ, including the stand, are: height, 6 feet 4 inches;   width, 2 feet 6
inches; and depth, 1 foot 4 inches. The paintings inside the doors are, to
the left, St. Cecilia playing upon a positive organ, while three angels sing
and a fourth blows the bellows; to the right, a warrior crowned with laurel
is in the attitude of listening; outside the doors there are panels with
paintings of a woman playing on a viol, and another playing a flute. There
is a crowing cock upon the apex of the cornice. This Positive Organ is the
property of the Conservatoire Royal, Brussels.

44

organ (Fig. 4–5) could also be carried but had to be placed on a table to be played and required an assistant to work the bellows. The *Bible Regal* (Fig. 4–6) was the earliest form of the reed organ, which became a common household instrument in the nineteenth century. The instrument is so constructed that it can be folded up and, when closed, it looks like a large book. Its name is derived from this arrangement. The bellows for the instrument is under the covers of the book. The *lute* (Fig. 4–7) was a stringed instrument belonging to the guitar family and was of extremely ancient origin, having been introduced into Europe by the Moors. It resembles the mandolin shape and is strung with from six to twenty gut strings; the bass strings were wire and did not pass over the fretted fingerboard. The music for the lute, which became the most fashionable of instruments for several centuries in Europe and England, was written in a system of symbolism called *tablature*.

Wind instruments were plentiful, but they had yet to be improved and developed. There were *shawms* and *flageolets* (flah-zho-lay′) of various sizes, double-reed instruments of the oboe and bassoon variety (see Fig. 4–1). The double-reeds were made by tightly binding the ends of two small pieces of bamboo around a metal

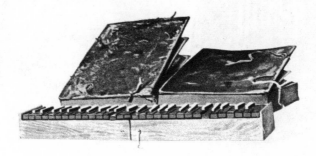

Musical Instruments *by A. J. Hipkins:*
A & C Black, Ltd., London

Fig. 4–6.   Bible Regal

The Bible Regal was the earliest form of the reed organ which became a common household instrument in the nineteenth century. The instrument is so constructed that it can be folded up and, when closed, it looks like a large book. Its name is derived from this arrangement. The bellows for the instrument is under the covers of the book.

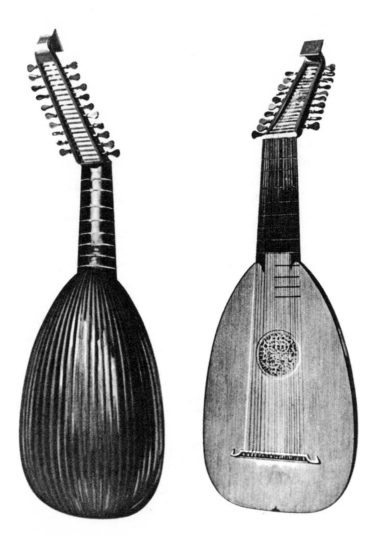

Musical Instruments *by A. J. Hipkins:*
A & C Black, Ltd., London

Fig. 4–7. Lute

The Lute pictured here bears the label "1600, In Padova Vvendelio Venere." It is 42 inches in length. The greatest width is 14 inches and the greatest depth is 8 inches. The mean width of the finger board is 4 inches. The instrument is fitted with 20 strings, which are divided into six pairs of unisons; and eight single strings for basses. Notice in the picture that the higher frets do not extend under the bass strings.

Fig. 4–8. Bagpipe Player (Artist Drawing)

Renaissance instruments were considered either noble or plebe-
ian according to their social acceptance. The bagpipe and other reed
instruments were considered unsuitable for noblemen. Refined
people were expected to play stringed instruments.

tube. This was done in such a way that they would vibrate freely
and together when placed in the mouth and air pressure was exerted.
The tube was inserted into the end of the instrument. There were
flutes, both the recorder-type, blown at the end, and the transverse-
type, blown through a tone hole in the side of the head joint. The
universal folk instrument was the *bagpipe* (Fig. 4–8), which also used
the double-reed principle. It is said that Romulus, the founder of
Rome, used a hunting horn to call the people together. From
ancient times through the medieval period, the hunting horn played
an important role in the lives of people in all classes of society. In
the last centuries of its general use, it was usually made from an
elephant tusk, from which it derived the name *oliphant* (Fig. 4–9).
During the fifteenth and sixteenth centuries, these horns were

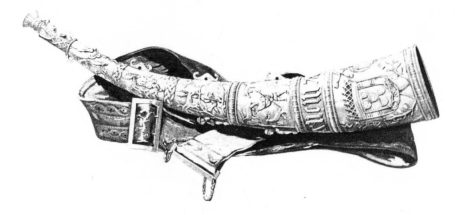

Fig. 4–9. Oliphant

The Oliphant pictured here bears the arms and badges of Ferdinand and Isabella of Portugal. The expert carving was done in 1543 by Negroes of the West Coast of Africa, who carved ivory for the Portuguese. The extreme length of the instrument, measuring along the outside of the curve, is 28¼ inches. The greatest circumference is 11½ and the least is 2¾ inches.

often elaborately carved and became more of a trophy than a musical instrument.

The *sackbut* was a forerunner of the slide trombone, but it was considered too blatant for most orchestral use. *Trumpets* and *horns* were skillfully played, but their use was strictly reserved for the nobility. *Drums* came into use by the twelfth century, mainly to beat time for singing and dancing, and other percussion instruments, such as small bells and cymbals, were common in music ensembles of all kinds. It is interesting to note that the thirteenth-century concept of "high" (*haut*) and "low" (*bas*) instruments referred not to pitch but to loudness.

There is some degree of illusion in what we see of the rapid rise of fifteenth-century instrumental music. Since much of it was written down during this period, we know something definite about it, but this should not entirely hide the evidence we have of dances, fanfares, and independent instrumental forms of music which were traditional and which, apparently, were played from memory or improvised. The fact that music was written down at all indicates an improvement in the status of instrumental musicians who were formerly regarded with contempt or condescension.

Summary

1. The Gothic period is roughly defined by the dates 1150–1400.
2. These two hundred and fifty years saw a gradual swing toward humanism, which caused music to become centered upon man rather than God.
3. In this movement, the composer at last received recognition for his work.
4. Two types of harmony were developed: *polyphony* and *homophony*.
5. Phillippe de Vitry, a French priest, wrote the *Ars Nova*.
6. The *lute* was widely used to accompany secular songs of that age.
7. Polyphony of the thirteenth century developed in the forms of *conductus, organum,* and *motet.*
8. The service known as the Mass developed when the entire Order of Service was set to music.
9. The Mass developed in two patterns, known as *proper* and *ordinary.*
10. Secular music before 1150 has not been as well preserved as the sacred music.
11. The *minstrel* held an important position in society, although his status was very low.
12. The *jongleurs* were professional musicians who performed the music others had created.
13. The advent of *troubadours* marked a decisive change in knightly practices and concepts of chivalry.
14. The *meistersinger* symbolized a rapid shift of spiritual life from the degenerated chivalry to the working man in the cities and towns.
15. The movement created a distinction between music for singing and music for dancing.

Examples of Music

1. *The English Country Dancing Master, Riggs O'Marlowe.* Vox (DL 470). (This bit of music, typical of Old England, was written for soprano recorder and harpsichord.)
2. *Masterpieces of Music Before 1750, Lute Dances: Der Prinzen-Tanz; Proportz* (c. 1550). Haydn Society (HS 9038); recorded in conjunction with W. W. Norton & Company, Inc. (These dances show another Renaissance instrumental form. The first is a slow dance in duple

meter; the second is a transformation of the first, in a fast tempo and in triple meter. The lute soloist is Tage Nielsen.)

3. *Music of the Middle Ages,* Vol. I of *A Treasury of Early Music.* Haydn Society (HSE 9100); recorded in conjunction with W. W. Norton & Company, Inc. (*Organum Duplum:* Below the melody is a drone sound, which creates the *Organum;* the *Duplum* is brought about when there is a parallel part above the melody or *Cantus Firmus. Motet: Ave gloriosa mater.* Each of the three voices carries on its own, but related, rhythmic pattern. There is a simple repeated movement in the tenor or melody. The middle voice is more varied and the movement becomes still livelier in the top voice. The use of related, but different, texts in the two upper voices is characteristic.)

4. *2000 Years of Music: The Troubadours—The Minnesingers,* compiled by Curt Sachs. Folkways (FT 3700).

Part Two ∿ *1400 = 1800*

5 ～ The Early Renaissance

Renaissance is a beautiful but also a misleading term in the history of culture. It is beautiful because it defines an awakening of intellectual awareness patterned after classical models; it is misleading because it suggests a sudden rebirth of learning and art after the presumed stagnation of the Middle Ages. History moves continuously, and the Renaissance was merely the next phase in a cultural process that had been developing in the universities and royal courts for many years. A remarkable number of historical events took place during the fifteenth century; these events combined to end the Middle Ages and to begin modern times. Medieval man merely existed; Renaissance man became excited about the possibilities of his present life and curious about what the future might hold.

Some of the most significant contributing factors to the Renaissance in this widening of human horizons were:

1. The fall of Constantinople to the Turks in 1453, and the subsequent emigration of Greek scholars to the West.
2. The invention of paper and printing, around 1440, which made books and music available on a wide scale.
3. The invention of gunpowder, bringing the age of chivalry and knighthood, minnesinger and wandering minstrel, to an end.
4. The development of the compass, making possible long voyages of discovery which incidentally carried Western music around the world.
5. The overthrow of feudalism and a rising spirit of nationalism, which found expression in national music, art, and literature.

The Renaissance is first discernible in the artistic and cultural life of fifteenth-century Italy. At that time most Italian creative effort was directed toward sculpture and painting; the peak of musical perfection, developed in Venice and Rome, was to come later. We find the best expression of Early Renaissance music coming from the efforts of the Burgundian School, which included the creative artists of England and Burgundy.

Although English music had shown considerable development during the Gothic period, it was not until the fifteenth century that an Englishman by the name of John Dunstable (1370–1453), composer, astronomer, mathematician, and canon of Hereford Cathedral (1419–1440), exerted great influence in European music as founder of the "Continental School of English Music." It is probable that Dunstable spent considerable time in Europe while in the service of the Duke of Bedford, who represented King Henry V as Regent of France. The Hundred Years' War was just beginning and the English had large holdings on the Continent, especially in France and Burgundy, where English music became quite influential. The Continental School was the first to drop the modal type of writing and develop the trend toward tonality, or what we know as the development of a key feeling. Dunstable's works rise above the strict and antiquated techniques of the French motet and display an original creative style of simple beauty.

Apart from the general style of English music, Dunstable's art also reflects his liking for a flowing line, often expressed by a free treatment of borrowed melodies. It is also notable that about half of his considerable output of masses and motets were based upon original compositions which borrowed little or nothing from the melodies of the Gregorian chant. He was also among the first—along with another English composer, Lionel Power—to link together sections of the mass by using the same chant melody in each. After the death of Dunstable in 1453, English music declined on the Continent, although Dunstable's influence continued in England for several decades.

The Burgundian School of music derived its name from the flourishing cultural activities of the Kingdom of Burgundy, activities that set the pace for all of Europe. This kingdom grew during the fifteenth century through intermarriages, purchases, and conquests under the reigns of two Dukes, Philip the Good (1419–1467) and Charles the Bold (1467–1477). Burgundy at its height included what is today Belgium, the Netherlands, and parts of eastern France. Its capital was the city of Dijon. Many of our fairy-tale concepts of court life, dress, and manners come from this time and place.

The name "Burgundian" has been given to both the style of

music and the school of composers which flourished at this time. The term does not point to any particular region or even nationality, since the Dukes of Burgundy had no fixed residence and moved from place to place within their dominions. Their chapel usually numbered from fifteen to twenty-seven musicians; in the early years these were recruited largely from Paris. Later, however, musicians from the Netherlands achieved a more important place. In addition to his chapel, Philip the Good maintained a band of minstrels who were excellent performers on the trumpet, vielle, lute, harp, and organ. This cosmopolitan group included men from France, Germany, Italy, and Portugal as well as local musicians, and it is not surprising that they had developed a musical style which was truly international for that time. The English influence on the Burgundian School was noted by the French poet, Martin le Franc, when he wrote in a poem of the early 1440's how the great Burgundian composers, Dufay and Binchois, followed Dunstable in the English manner.

Guillaume Dufay (1400–1474) was the leader and most outstanding composer of the Burgundian School. His harmony is based upon musical intervals of thirds and sixths, comparable to our modern chord structure, and has, for the first time, a well-defined bass part. His masses are sung without instrumental accompaniment, or *a cappella* ("of the chapel"). This type of religious music is representative of the entire Burgundian School. Dufay himself was a cosmopolitan gentleman who traveled widely, spending several years in Italy after 1436, and it was quite natural that he create music in forms other than the mass and motet. One of his very interesting compositions has to do with that occasion in 1453 when Constantinople, the capital of Christendom, fell to the Turks. Under the title of *Lamentations for the Church at Constantinople,* he wrote a two-part song accompanied with "sacqueboutes," the primitive trombone of the period, and used a text from the *Lamentations of Jeremiah,* which says in part: "all her friends have dealt treacherously with her; among all her lovers she hath none to comfort her." The message likened Constantinople to Jerusalem, and to the listeners of that time it had a chilling effect.

Gilles Binchois (zheel been-shwah') (1400–1460) was a soldier in his early years; later he became a priest and a singer in the famous chapel of Duke Philip the Good of Burgundy. Although he wrote works for the church, his chief contribution to Burgundian musical art was the development of short secular forms: the traditional *rondeau,* the *ballade,* and especially the *chanson.* Binchois showed a rare gift for creating melody which he used effectively in the soprano voice of the chanson. The lower voice parts were often performed on various instruments. This arrangement of instruments and voices proved to be the most popular type of entertainment in the Burgundian courts. So strong was the charm of the Burgundian musical style that the tradition of it lingered on in Europe long after the downfall of Burgundy as an independent political power.

Burgundy, so prominent in the Early Renaissance, allied herself with England in the war against France. After the year 1477, most of the territory of Burgundy lost its independence, and Burgundy as such lost its identity after 1506. At that time Charles I, young king of Spain (also known as the Holy Roman Emperor Charles V), inherited the entire Duchy. Under the influence of the Spanish King, what had been known as Burgundian art now became known as Flemish. In modern times we would call some of the composers French, some Belgian, and some Dutch; in the sixteenth century, these terms indicated a general geographic area also known as the Low Countries.

The wealth of Flemish and Dutch cities, achieved through trade and commerce, made it possible for them to maintain their positions as splendid centers of Renaissance culture somewhat beyond the close of the sixteenth century. After 1477, however, the creative art of these cities became more Germanic in style and thought, resulting in the Flemish or Netherlands School of art. With this shift in emphasis, the second period of the Renaissance began.

The Flemish School

During the Hundred Years' War, most of the important musical positions in Europe were held by musicians from the Low Countries, and the profound, scholarly art of these Flemings dominated the music of all Europe. These men were great teachers, and the fact that they chose to travel to all of the cultural centers of Europe made possible one of the most uniform styles of music that the world has ever known. Flemish musicians even played a large part in the development of such national forms as the French *chanson,* the English and Italian *madrigal,* and the German *lied.* In this way they did much to establish music as a universal art.

Flemish composers were the first to have music printed from movable type. No single event in the evolution of music in its social applications is more important than the invention of a practical method of music printing. Throughout the Middle Ages most music had been copied by hand or printed by using elaborately carved blocks which were often marvels of laborious patience. In this way, cathedrals and large churches managed to supply their priests and choirs with all needed service books, but the time, effort, and expense required to produce them was so excessive that they were considered priceless and no effort was made to circulate them.

The people who conceived the idea of movable type for letters advanced almost at once to movable type for notes, which led to the business of music publishing and music selling. Although early editions were small and copies were relatively expensive, the masterworks began to circulate in authentic form and to be studied as never before. The earliest known printing of music from movable type was in 1476 by Ulrich Hahn of Rome; in 1481, by Jörg Reyser of Würzburg; and in the same year, Ottavio Scatto of Venice. By the beginning of the sixteenth century, highly skilled workmen had established the music publishing trade in most of the music centers of Europe.

In the late fifteenth century, several changes occurred in the texture of music which formed a basis for the style of the Late Renaissance. Voice parts were equalized by retaining the same text in all parts and by having each part imitate the other; a desire for greater sonority led to the use of four and occasionally more voices rather than the traditional three; the style in which the voices proceed together in the form of chords was widely adopted. Leaders who were most responsible for bringing about these innovations were Johannes Ockeghem, Jacob Obrecht, and Josquin des Prez, three masters of the Flemish School who seemed to be most responsible for the high degree of musical artistry attained in the fifteenth century.

Johannes Ockeghem (yo-han'-ness ock'-eh-gum) (1425–1495) stands as the leader and the head of the Flemish School. Born probably in Flanders, he studied music with both Binchois and Dufay and developed devices of imitation which served as models for those who later perfected the *a cappella,* or unaccompanied, singing style. His influence was tremendous and practically the whole succeeding musical generation studied with him. The title "Prince of Music" was affectionately conferred on him by admiring colleagues while he was still a relatively young man. Ockeghem continued the art of the Burgundians but converted the simplified style of Dufay into a freely unfolding polyphony. His short, secular works are delightful but his greatest achievements are in the larger liturgical forms. He went to France in 1453 and spent the rest of his life there as the King's conductor. His death in 1495 was mourned by the entire artistic world.

Jacob Obrecht (1452–1505) was one of the first composers to have his works published during his lifetime. He carried out the innovations of Ockeghem but added an expressive quality to his music that showed an artistic use of phrase and cadence following the meaning of the text. He commonly used four voices with the lower one becoming a true bass line. Obrecht was born in the Netherlands. He lived the typical life of a musician in the Renaissance Netherlands, singing and conducting in the large cathedrals of his country, joining one of the brilliant court-chapels of Italy for a time, and then returning North. He held leading positions in Antwerp, Burges, and Cambri. In 1504, he returned to Italy where he met his death in the plague the following year.

Obrecht's works include a large number of masses, motets, hymns, and French chansons. Like Ockeghem, his melodies were intense and often passionate, stretched in powerful arcs with the voices required to sing pitches high and low, which made new demands upon the performers. In his later works he broke with the polyphonic traditions of Ockeghem's school and used clear and balanced harmonies, bringing his music close to the Renaissance ideal.

Josquin des Prez (zhos-can' day pray) (1450–1521) is ranked as one of the great composers of all time. The elements of modern Western European music may be found in his writing. He was fortunate enough to have the majority of his music published during his lifetime and because of this fact coupled with his musical genius, he was well known and had considerable influence upon other composers of his time. Like most of the Flemish musicians he traveled to Italy where he spent some time in the ducal courts of Florence,

Milan, and Ferrara. He entered the Papal Chapel in 1486 and re-mained there for eight years. After leaving Italy, he entered the service of King Louis XII of France, where his music was the admiration of the musical world, unrivaled until the advent of Palestrina and di Lasso.

The works of des Prez may be divided into two classes: those in which elaboration is the chief feature and those in which the sentiment of the words is given musical expression. It was in the com-position of his seventeen masses that he lavished his full genius and ingenuity; these are truly works of art.

As we look back upon the remarkable musical activity of the Early Renaissance period, we must credit the Burgundian masters with three major contributions which greatly assisted the develop-ment of the Flemish School. These contributions, later adopted by the Italians, were: (1) the four-part harmony that has been standard since that time; (2) the basing of all movements of the mass on the same melody, thereby achieving a large-scale musical form; (3) the use of voices in the higher register, along with an accompaniment of contrasting instruments, such as double-reeds, recorders, violas, or trombones, to achieve an interesting musical sound. During this period the *cantus firmus*—the melody on which the mass was based —was often drawn from a popular song, and at times gave its name to a particular mass. The mingling of sacred and secular music and ideas would prove disturbing to the churchmen of today, but it was completely in keeping with the innovative spirit found in all aspects of Renaissance life.

Summary

1. The Renaissance was the next phase in a cultural process which had been developing in the universities and royal courts.
2. Significant events in the development of the Renaissance:
   a. The fall of Constantinople to the Turks in 1453; emigration of Greek scholars to the West.
   b. The invention of paper and printing; the consequent availability of books and music.
   c. The invention of gunpowder; the end of the age of chivalry.
   d. The development of the compass; great voyages of discovery inci-

dentally spreading Western music to other countries around the world.

e. The overthrow of feudalism; the rise of nationalism, which found expression in national forms of music, art, and literature.

3. We find the best expression of Early Renaissance music coming from the creative artists of England and Burgundy.

4. John Dunstable was the founder of the Continental School of English Music.

5. Leaders of the Burgundian School were Guillaume Dufay and Gilles Binchois.

6. During the Hundred Years' War, the scholarly art of the Flemings dominated the music of all Europe.

7. The best-known leaders of the Flemish School were Ockeghem, des Prez, and Obrecht.

8. The major contributions of the early Renaissance composers were:
   a. The four-part harmony that has been standard since that time;
   b. The basing of all movements of the mass on the same melody, achieving a large-scale form;
   c. The use of voices in the higher register, along with an accompaniment of contrasting instruments.

9. The mingling of sacred and secular music was a common practice, in keeping with the spirit of Renaissance life.

Examples of Music

1. *Masterpieces of Music Before 1750.* Haydn Society (HS L2071).
2. *Medieval and Renaissance Music for Harps, Vielle, Recorders, and Tambourin.* Turnabout (TV 34019S).
3. *Anthology of Renaissance Music.* Period (SPL 597A).
4. *Music From the Courts of Burgundy.* Nonesuch (H 71058B).
5. *Masterpieces of Early French and Italian Renaissance.* Nonesuch (H 71010).
6. *History of Music in Sound*, Vol. II. RCA Victor (LM 6015).
7. Josquin des Prez, *Missa de "Beata Virgine."* Vox (SL-600).
8. Guillaume Dufay, *Vergine Bella* from *Music from the Court of Burgundy.* Nonesuch (H 71058, stereo).

6 ～ The High Renaissance

The Renaissance spirit, like the spirit of early Greek culture, was of this world. It was quite different, however, from that of Greek culture in its emphasis on individuality and the worth of the human personality as motivating forces. The Greeks were interested in the various facets of the ideal human being; the men of the Renaissance were concerned with the real human being as he lives in the world. Renaissance culture was interested in man's personality, his mind, his body, his social relationships, his personal religion, his economic condition, and his place in the political scheme of things. The Renaissance designates a period of time, but we should remember that it was characterized by a spirit, a philosophy, and a way of life that changed man's entire outlook and attitude toward himself, his fellow men, and his God.

The Renaissance in Europe makes the change from an exclusively religious society to a more secular one; from an age of unquestioning religious faith to a belief in reason and scientific inquiry. Because of the complexity of the Renaissance, there have been different interpretations of its cultural impact. But there is no doubt that music was involved in the movement in an important way. New instruments were invented, new musical forms were perfected, and a new appreciation of music was developed along with a better understanding of its principles.

Since all music of this period was based upon similar polyphonic practices, a remarkable unity of style in both secular and religious music was achieved. The primary purpose of Renaissance music was still liturgical, and it served both the traditional Roman Catholic Church and the newly founded Protestant Church. The demand for secular music of good quality grew rapidly as well because of the many highly cultivated groups of amateur performers, both among the aristocracy and from the upper middle class, who needed appropriate music for their singing and playing. One of the marks of the cultivated lady or gentleman of the Renaissance was familiarity with music; he was expected to have some competence either in singing or in playing an instrument. The lute, as the most popular instrument of the time, was widely used for solo playing and to accompany the songs of the day. It achieved a place in society similar to that of the piano today.

Popular songs and dances of folk-like character supplied the great mass of people with music for festivals and other social occasions, while serious composers wrote in a variety of dance forms to meet the demand for formal court functions. Yet, with all the emphasis upon instrumental music, the human voice in solo and ensemble was generally accepted as the finest performing medium.

The musical forms most widely used during the Renaissance period were vocal forms; they were the mass, the motet, and the madrigal.

The Mass

The mass was the musical service of the Catholic Church, and was carefully nourished and sponsored by it. The great composers of the Renaissance period, without exception, felt called upon to contribute something in this religious form. (See Chapter 7.)

The Renaissance Motet

During the Gothic period, the motet was a religious composition based upon a line of Gregorian chant to which other melodies, containing other words, often in different languages, were added. The motet of the Renaissance was quite different; it was a unified composition with all voices singing the same text. Its theme was often, not always, drawn from the Gregorian chant. Its spirit was deeply religious, and certainly suitable for use in worship. The Renaissance motet was serious, restrained, and entirely appropriate to the liturgy. Any show of emotionalism or technical display was considered insincere, out of keeping with the attitude of respect and awe that should prevail in the worship of God.

The Madrigal

The Renaissance period was one of religious idealism, but it also had a distinctly earthy side. There were many kinds of secular compositions, some of them national in character. The main type, which was popular in most countries of Western Europe, was the madrigal. It has sometimes been described as a secular variation of the motet, but there are differences between the two forms. The madrigal was in the vernacular rather than in ecclesiastical Latin. Its text dealt with sentimental and sometimes erotic love. The text used for madrigals in the early Renaissance had little literary merit, but later texts, especially the poems of Petrarch, were often of exceptionally high quality. Instead of being sung in church, madrigals were performed in courtly social gatherings and at meetings of learned and artistic societies. Madrigals were very popular and an enormous number were composed. In England, madrigal-singing ability, which required a knowledge of music reading, was expected of an educated person. Because madrigals were prominent in circles not bound by religious custom, they developed great freedom of expression and offered the composer an opportunity for experimentation. Instruments were often used to accompany the singing of secular music. It was common practice to accompany the madrigal with either the lute or the harpsichord.

The madrigal was largely an Italian development, but by the middle of the sixteenth century, it had become popular in other countries. The first madrigals with English translation, printed in 1588, ushered in a brilliant period of original English secular music. The English madrigal is still a popular musical form; it is enjoyable for three reasons: (1) its text is English—no translation is necessary for English-speaking audiences; (2) English composers had the rare ability to make their music simple and tuneful; and (3) the English had a delightful trait of not taking themselves seriously, no matter how sad the song might be.

About midway through the sixteenth century, musical leadership and accomplishment shifted to Italy. The Italians had become educated in the styles of the period by a long influx of Burgundian and Flemish composers, whose combined musical forces brought about the beginning of instrumental music as an independent art.

The two main centers of Italian musical development were Venice and Rome; in Rome *a cappella* choral music, both religious and secular, was characteristic of the time. Venetian music was centered in the Cathedral of St. Mark; instrumental music began to be prominent there. St. Mark's, like many other Renaissance churches, was built in the form of a cross; music performed in the arms of the cross could achieve a stereophonic effect. This was called *antiphonal music* when it was coordinated and performed with some distance between the choirs. Organs and a variety of other instruments were gradually brought into this type of church music and accepted as part of the total musical effort. When instrumental music was accepted in the Church, it brought with it music characteristic of the instrument. Claudio Merulo (1533–1604), who was organist at St. Mark's Cathedral for thirty years at the height of the Renais-

Fig. 6–1. Examples of Final Cadences,
(a) "Old Black Joe," and (b) "America"

instr. style
?

sance, did much to further organ playing and developed an instrumental form for organ called *toccata*, literally "touch piece." This music could not be sung, since it included many special effects such as runs, trills, and other musical devices made possible by the technical capabilities of the organ. This form has remained popular even with twentieth-century organists.

Andrea Gabrieli (1515–1586), and later his nephew, Giovanni Gabrieli (1555–1612), were highly successful in composing antiphonal music for brass instruments. Instruments were often combined with one or more choirs and an organ to furnish a lavish and exciting

Fig. 6–2. (a) Authentic Cadence; (b) Plagal Cadence

setting for chapel music. The highest musical point of the Venetian School was probably attained when Giovanni Gabrieli composed his *Sacrae Symphoniae* (Sacred Symphony), which employed several organs, four vocal choirs, a large group of recorders, and a complete choir of brass instruments.

The music masters who were working in the school at Rome concentrated on the development of vocal music. They were able to achieve an ethereal quality and a high degree of technical perfection, but their music remained somewhat colorless and not nearly as interesting or exciting as the Venetian music.

Giovanni Pierluigi da Palestrina (c. 1525–1594) was the most esteemed Italian composer of the sixteenth century. He is generally known simply as Palestrina, which is the name of the small Italian town where he was born. Many of the practices of Josquin des Prez reached their highest development in Palestrina's music. Unlike the Flemish composers, most of whom traveled and changed jobs rather frequently, Palestrina confined his career largely to Rome where he held several important positions, the most notable being choirmaster at St. Peter's.

Historical circumstances encouraged Palestrina to be a conservative reformer rather than a musical innovator. The impact of the Reformation brought complaints regarding the music of the established Church. People were especially critical of complicated polyphony that made words unintelligible, the use of noisy instruments, and the irreverent attitude of church singers. The result of this criticism was an order from the Council of Trent to "purge the music of its barbarisms, so that the House of God might rightly be called the house of prayer." Palestrina composed for a church that wanted to return to the purity and simplicity of its earlier music. His genius is clearly shown in the way he was able to achieve this ideal while composing within the framework of the highly developed styles of his predecessors. It is against this background that the worshipful spirit of his music can be best understood. Palestrina led in the development of music toward a new stage in its growth—the *Baroque*.

Claudio Monteverde (1567–1643) was the man most responsible for shifting the spotlight from vocal to instrumental music and for bridging the gap between the styles of the Renaissance and the Baroque. The madrigals of the Renaissance were often performed by instruments, but they were considered a substitute for the human voice. This practice, however, became so common by the end of the sixteenth century that many madrigals were inscribed "apt for voyces or viols." Monteverde's madrigals were among the finest of the Italian school. He is best known as the composer of *Orfeo*, the first great operatic masterpiece in a modern style. In *Orfeo*, he adapts the Florentine recitative style to the use of closed forms such as the aria and dance song. He also wrote for an enlarged orchestra and used a selection of the instruments in his dramatic scenes. Among his most important works are eight books of madrigals, a number of operas in addition to *Orfeo,* as well as dramatic scenes and religious music. With the development of the opera, Monteverde began to exploit the dramatic possibilities of the instruments and their individual tone color. As a result, instrumental interludes began to play an increasingly important role in the opera and it became fashionable to open the performance with an overture for instruments alone. These compositional devices led to what was called the *Modern* style of the *Baroque*.

1607 (handwritten in margin)

Summary

1. The term *Renaissance* designates a philosophy and a way of life as well as a period of time.
2. Christian music served both the highly organized Roman Catholic service and the newly formed Protestant Church.
3. The Renaissance marks the change in Europe from an exclusively religious society to a more secular one.
4. The rise of wealthy aristocratic patrons in fifteenth-century courts exerted a powerful influence on music.
5. The demand for secular music grew rapidly.
6. Secular music was widely practiced among the aristocracy and upper middle-class people.
7. The lute was the most popular instrument of the time.
8. The human voice in solo and ensemble was considered to be the finest medium for musical performance.
9. Instruments (sometimes strings, brass, and woodwinds together) were used mainly to reinforce the voice.
10. Instruments began to be used independently in the sixteenth century, particularly organ and clavier instruments.

11. The musical forms most widely used during the Renaissance were the mass, the motet, and the madrigal.
12. In mid-sixteenth century, musical leadership shifted to Venice and Rome.
13. The Church maintained leadership in musical production throughout the world.
14. St. Mark's Cathedral in Venice sponsored the early rise of instrumental music under Andrea and Giovanni Gabrieli.
15. Palestrina and the other masters who worked in Rome concentrated on vocal music.
16. As polyphonic music reached perfection in Italy, reaction set in, and Palestrina led the way to a new musical concept called *Baroque*.
17. Monteverde was responsible for shifting the emphasis from vocal to instrumental music and bridging the gap between the Renaissance and Baroque periods.

Examples of Music

1. *Renaissance Music for Brass.* Nonesuch (H 71111).
2. *The Pleasures of Cervantes* from *Vocal and Instrumental Music of Spain: 15th, 16th, and 17th Centuries.* Nonesuch (H 71116).
3. *Renaissance Vocal Music.* Nonesuch (H 71097).
4. *Masterpieces of Early French and Italian Renaissance.* Nonesuch (H 71010).
5. *Music of the High Renaissance in England.* Turnabout (TV 34017S).
6. Palestrina, *Missa Brevis and Missa ad Fugam.* Epic (L C3359).

7 ∿ The Reformation

The most obvious result of the Protestant Reformation was the division of Western European Christendom into a multitude of hostile sects. No longer was there one Church and one Pope for the whole of Latin and Teutonic Europe as had been true in the Middle Ages. Northern Germany and the Scandinavian countries had become Lutheran; England adopted a compromise Protestantism of her own; Calvinism had triumphed in Scotland, Holland, and French Switzerland. In all of the vast domain once owing allegiance to the Vicar of Christ, only Italy, Austria, France, Spain, and Portugal, southern Germany, Poland, and Ireland were left; and even in several of these countries, Protestant minorities were active.

Historians have discussed the economic and political benefits which came by way of the Reformation. We will examine here the place of music in the various new Christian churches. In one sense, the Reformation had an adverse effect upon art. Although Martin Luther had some gifts of aesthetic appreciation, his followers were too deeply absorbed in theological controversy to care whether any form of art survived or perished. Calvin took a strong negative stand, saying that everything that appeals to the senses is to be deplored as godless and immoral. The Catholic Church, influenced by the reformers, called together the Council of Trent, in session periodically between 1545 and 1563, and adopted severe restrictions against representation of the human form, and employed a second-rate artist to paint breeches and skirts on the naked figures in Michelangelo's *Last Judgment.*

Lutheran church music demonstrates the essential differences between Catholic and Protestant music. It recognizes the direct appeal of the worshiper to the throne of grace and its basis is the communal singing of the congregation. The Lutheran priest is not a mediator between the laity and God, but a leader of the congregation in seeking the mediation of Jesus Christ. Equally important,

Luther considered the use of the national tongue of the worshiper necessary to the propagation of his religious ideas. The propagation of his beliefs was greatly aided by the Lutheran chorale, which was to the Reformation what Gregorian music was to Catholicism—sure, confident, and solid.

After the tenth century, the religious lyric played an important part in German popular song. The fourteenth century saw the introduction of hymns that were highly introspective in character adapted to secular melody. The forms of worship were still in the hands of the clergy but there were undercurrents of restlessness. These pre-Reformation hymns did not reach the high level of the Latin hymns, but they disclosed many of the secular traits and characteristics of the popular songs of the day. German religious poetry of the Middle Ages was full of crudity and superstition, but it also contained many lofty ideals common to the hymns of all ages. A wide range of topics covered an enormous quantity of material and it was from these songs that Luther organized his religious music. In this way the sources of Lutheran church music differed widely from those that supplied the Catholic Church. However, freedom in the individual's approach to God was bought at the price of artistic musical expression.

Through his intellect and personal prestige, Luther was able to give dignity to the German folk-hymn. His hymns were credited with the conversion of more people than all of his sermons and writings combined. At the close of the Thirty Years' War, about 1650, the sources of Lutheran inspiration seemed to dry up, and the church came upon difficult times.

In England the revolt against Rome affected religious affairs quite differently. Political upheaval preceded rather than followed religious changes. This was illustrated in a dramatic way when Henry VIII enforced the Act of Supremacy in 1534, in which he repudiated papal authority and declared himself the supreme head of the Church of England. This involved at first no change of doctrine since Henry's main purpose was to clear his way to marry Anne Boleyn; as a member of the Roman Church, he could not get a divorce from his wife Catherine.

Under Henry VIII the unbroken succession of priesthood was maintained. The Book of Common Prayer was adopted in its modern form and the essential parts of the Latin Mass were kept. It is in

not clear
?? ' '

this service that the anthem makes its appearance, having a separate liturgical office from the service proper. Its words are not found in the Book of Common Prayer, so it is employed as a commentary upon the scripture or the sermon of the day. Fortunately, for the anthem, the best resources of English musicianship have been lavished upon it.

George Frederick Handel was the first composer to bring the anthem into recognition on the Continent. This form seems to have combined the style of the German cantata and the older motet, the cantata influence being seen in the solo passages and the motet influence in the well-constructed choruses. The great freedom of the anthem made possible the use of the organ as well as other instruments for solo purposes. Under the leadership of Henry Purcell (1658–1695), the orchestra assumed an important part in accompanying the anthem and adding incidental music at suitable times during the service.

Calvin was unique in leaving music completely out of the church service. He recognized man's delight in music but wanted to destroy all vestiges of the Roman Church. However, with the Restoration of the Monarchy in England in 1660, there was a gradual return to the liturgy of the church and to the musical service. The Wesley brothers, John, Charles, and Samuel, were responsible for reviving the spiritual life of the church through both poetry and song. Isaac Watts was also active in the movement to bring spiritual songs into a vital place in the church service. One of his better-known songs of this type, "When I Survey the Wondrous Cross," is still widely used in Protestant churches. These men were followed by a large number of poets and musicians who greatly enriched Protestant hymnody after the turn of the eighteenth century.

Council of Trent

We usually think of the Reformation as being a Protestant Revolution, but that was only one phase of the total movement. When it was apparent that the whole of Germany would become Lutheran, Pope Paul III became concerned about the need for a Catholic Reformation and called a great Church Council, which met in the city of Trent on several occasions between 1545 and 1563. This Council was summoned for the purpose of redefining the doctrines of the Catholic faith and several of the steps taken were highly significant, although very little was done to bridge the differences between Protestants and Catholics.

The important effect of the Council's decrees concerning music was to recognize and sanction stylistic tendencies in church music which were already established. This was particularly true in Rome, where the great Palestrina was at work on the new music of the Church. Palestrina's style was the first in the history of music to be consciously preserved, isolated, and imitated. In later ages, when composers quite naturally were writing altogether different kinds of music, this kind of stylistic study was used as a model. His work has come to be regarded as embodying the musical ideal of certain aspects of Catholicism. Partly because of this fact and partly because of the legends that have clustered around his name, Palestrina's reputation is probably higher than either his excellent music or his historical position actually warrant. However, there is no doubt that his art fulfills two of St. Thomas Aquinas's three requirements for music of the church—harmony, radiance, and wholeness. It possesses to a supreme degree harmony and radiance, but there may be some question as to its wholeness. An excellent example of Palestrina's art may be found in the Agnus Dei from the famous *Mass of Pope Marcellus.*

Two of Palestrina's contemporaries who also contributed much to the music of their day were Tomás Luis de Victoria (c. 1549–1611) and Orlando di Lasso (1532–1594). Victoria was a leading representative of the Roman School in Spain. He studied in Rome, probably with Palestrina, but his music has a dramatic intensity and spiritual fervor that is thoroughly Spanish. He is best known for his *Requiem Mass,* but he also wrote a large number of other works, including a book of hymns for four voices. Orlando di Lasso was a product of the Flemish School, but was international in the scope of his music; born in Belgium, he spent his formative years in Italy and his last thirty-eight years in Bavaria. His fame rests mainly on his religious music; he was equally effective, however, with Italian and German madrigals and with French chansons. He wrote over two thousand compositions and is generally considered the greatest of the Flemish composers. Along with Palestrina, he is one of the most important figures in Renaissance music.

The Reformation did not prove to be a musically creative force even in Germany, where the movement started. The ravages of the Thirty Years' War pretty well extinguished the small amount of original activity that had been going on there. Almost the whole of German music of the sixteenth century was dominated by foreign art and music: the Italian in the south and the French and Dutch in the north. The music of the Protestant Reformation actually prevailed only as long as Luther's fervor flamed behind it.

The last decades of the sixteenth century were full of bewildering contradictions. Both the religious and political institutions had been shaken to their foundations. New forces making themselves felt in religion, politics, and music were bitterly opposed. The catastrophic conflicts, the reform movements and religious wars, changed the face of Europe.

In Italy and France, musical life was mainly centered on opera, but in Germany, most of the people had been so distressed by the religious wars that they turned to religious forms in music. The Lutheran chorales composed for one voice and accompaniment instilled in Protestant Germany a love for simple, forceful music. The character of Protestant Christianity strongly influenced the form, style, and force of its music; Lutheran chorales were to remain the basis of Protestant church music. Austria and the Catholic South were so thoroughly dominated by the magnificent Italian Baroque concepts that they did not take up song-writing until very late in the seventeenth century. Even then the Northern composers were the true masters of song—never entirely abandoning a touch of Gothic polyphony until the time of Johann Sebastian Bach.

Summary

1. The most obvious result of the Protestant Reformation was the division of the Catholic Church into a multitude of hostile sects.
2. The Reformation had a very depressing effect upon the development of art.
3. The hymns were often adapted to secular melodies.
4. Through his intellect and personal prestige, Luther was able to give dignity to the crude German folk-hymn.   *Morley*
5. The Reformation in England saw the development of the anthem under the leadership of Henry Purcell and George Frederick Handel.
6. Calvin's religious doctrine was antisensual, and left music completely out of the church service.
7. John, Charles, and Samuel Wesley were responsible for reviving the spiritual life of the church through poetry and song.

8. The Counter-Reformation, the Catholic Church's response to the Reformation, served to stimulate creativity in music and art.
9. Musical leaders of the time were Palestrina, Victoria, and di Lasso.
10. The Reformation did not prove to be a musically creative force.
11. In Italy and France, musical life was mainly centered on opera. In Germany, people turned toward religious forms of music.
12. Lutheran chorales, often using a touch of Gothic polyphony, maintained a strong position until the time of Bach.

Examples of Music

1. Luther, *A Mighty Fortress* (collection of 15 hymns). RCA Victor (Red Seal LM 2199).
2. *Court and Ceremonial Music of the Sixteenth Century.* Nonesuch (H 71012).
3. *Johann Hermann Schein* (1586–1630). Lyrichord Discs (LLST 7146).
4. *Baroque Trumpet Music.* London (OL 50137).
5. *Masters of Early English Keyboard Music.* London (OL 50131).
6. Palestrina, *Stabat Mater.* Vox (PL 9740).
7. Orlando di Lasso, *Adoramus Te Christe.* Epic (LC 3359).

8 ᥲ The Baroque Period

The Baroque period was ushered in by a wave of intellectual, spiritual and physical activity. In that age we find the activities that are the practical basis of our systematic civilization of today. The Renaissance had failed to fulfill the hopes and ideals that had produced it. From the final decades of the Renaissance, characterized by doubt and contradiction, arose the positive style of Baroque art, which was full of vigor, strong emotion, symbolism, and subtlety. Renaissance music was not made for the concert stage; its charm and delicate nuances are lost in a big auditorium, and the few forms in which it was composed were insufficient to meet the needs of a changing society.

One of the most striking features of the Baroque was its fondness for the grandiose. This was evidenced by the prominent role assigned to the pipe organ and to music which required large choruses and massive effects.

In 1619 the pipe organ was on the threshold of its greatest era. Michael Praetorius described it in this way:

> . . . the organ possesses and encompasses all other instruments of music—large and small, however named—in itself alone. If you want to hear a drum, a trumpet, a trombone, cornetts, a recorder, flutes, pommers, a shawm, a dulcian, racketts, sorduns, krummhorns, violins, lyres, etc., you can have all these and still many more unusual and charming things in this artful creation; so that when you have and hear this instrument, you think nought but that you have all the other instruments one amongst another. (*Syntagma musicum II. De organographia,* 1619.)

Organs of some sort have been used by man since well before the time of Christ. The Greeks and Romans employed their water-driven organ, known as a *hydraulis,* at circuses and festal gatherings. The Hebrews refer to a form of organ in the early synagogue services.

In the Middle Ages, the Byzantines had similar large instruments that were admired by visiting Westerners. By the end of the ninth century, the organ made its way into most of the European churches, which have remained its principal home since that time. The organs of the medieval churches must have been cumbersome and over-powering monsters. The keyboard had not yet been developed; to select a tone, one pulled out a long slat which covered the end of one or more pipes. Compressed air was then free to rush in and produce a sound. The separate or combined use of various ranks of pipes, which we call registration, did not appear until the fourteenth century. Keys also began to replace slats at about this same time, but the keys were much wider than those used today and separated from one another by some distance. Around 1400 organ builders began to eliminate spaces between the keys, but it took almost another century to bring the keys down to the comfortable size of today. When this was accomplished, there was a rapid development, which led to the great organ described by Praetorius.

When we speak of a Baroque organ as such, we usually refer to a small instrument of great clarity and mellowness of tone, but lacking in ability to execute dynamics. All constrasts in dynamics followed the Baroque idea of contrasting sonorities and tone qualities which could be achieved on the organ by changes in registration. Although the small Baroque organs were widely used, the great organ experienced the most remarkable development and popularity.

Closely paralleling the development of the organ in France and northern Germany was the cultivation of its music. Probably the greatest center of organ music development was Lübeck, in northern Germany, which was known as the "Organ City." Three of Lübeck's five Gothic cathedrals had two organs each and the largest of these cathedrals, the Marienkirche, had three. The outstanding organists of the time were those who played at the Marienkirche: Franz Tunder (1614–1667), who is often credited with being the founder of the North German School of organ music, and his son-in-law, Dietrich Buxtehude (1637–1707). These men, along with Johann Sebastian Bach (1685–1750), are ranked with the greatest organists of all time.

Most of our modern orchestral instruments were in use or were developed during the Baroque period. Brass and woodwind instruments were effectively used, although modern types of valve mechanisms were not patented until the early nineteenth century. It was customary for instrumental music of the sixteenth and early seventeenth centuries to be composed for organ, harpsichord, or lute, but since there was no traditional instrumentation for brass and woodwind ensembles, composers experimented with all sorts of instruments in a wide variety of groupings. Some of the best ensemble and multiple choir music of the early Baroque was produced by the Gabrielis, Andrea and Giovanni, in Venice (see Chapter 6). A generation later, however, Girolamo Frescobaldi (1583–1643) and Heinrich Schütz (1585–1672) were also composing effectively in this new medium.

To better understand how Baroque society used the music of its day, a reference to the music of the French court of Louis XIV is enlightening. The music of the court was literally a part of its magnificent décor. It was as necessary to the proper succession of events as were the elaborate costumes of those in attendance; music served the ear much as the presence of the musicians served the eye and added color, dignity, and beauty to the most routine functions. The entire day was carried out with carefully wrought background music, and this background was the most magnificent the world had ever seen.

Musicians in Louis XIV's court were artisans in the same manner as the architect, the jeweler, the hairdresser, and the sword maker; but all of these artisans shared an exalted equality, and each maintained a goal of excellence which would admit nothing but the best. Life itself was a cheaper commodity and more readily expendable than was superior craftsmanship. Within the court, there was music to rise by, to eat breakfast by, to set the mood for making one's toilet, music for dalliance, music for worship, and music for dancing. The King had his twenty-four violins in constant attendance. Lesser dignitaries in the court had their own music at hand in proportion to their position. The King had outdoor music for his stable, for the hunt, for processions, and for spectacles of every sort. All of this vast quantity of musical production served first a decorative and pleasing purpose, but it also carried on the important function of creating an air of magnificence.

Much of this decorative music was preserved and put into print for further usefulness in successive events, but little thought was given to preserving it for posterity; it was simply filed away. In 1680 André Philidor was appointed "Keeper of the Library of the King's

Music." He began the gigantic task of bringing together all of the music ever produced in France, but never accomplished it. A century later the French Revolution disrupted the still uncompleted project. However, much of the military music of the day, and that composed by Philidor and by Jean-Baptiste Lully, was preserved.

Jean-Baptiste Lully (lew-lee') (1633–1687) was the most successful composer of his time. His success was due not only to his high degree of musical talent but also to his political talent, his opportunism, and his driving ambition. Born in Florence, Italy, Lully came to France as a boy. In 1652 he entered the service of the young King, Louis XIV, who was the same age as Lully. Under the protection of Louis, he engaged in a series of shrewd maneuvers that made him successively composer of the royal chamber music, superintendent of the King's music, and finally holder of the royal patent. The latter position gave him a virtual monopoly on French operatic composition and production, and, at his death, he had accumulated a large fortune from his operatic ventures as well as from his real estate speculations.

Lully's operas differ basically from those by Italian composers. His works emphasize choruses, huge ballets, and spectacular stage scenes. The Lully type of overture, usually called the French overture, has imposing dotted rhythms in the slow first part and fugal passages in the fast second section. The French overture form was widely used by Baroque composers for half a century after Lully's death, and it is still occasionally heard today. The opening *sinfonia* or overture of Handel's *Messiah* is an excellent example of the French overture. In composing his operas, Lully used varied and interesting orchestral accompaniment and completely disregarded expense in the cost of staging and costuming his work. These factors, combined with the musical genius of his composition, made his productions suitable for the exacting taste of Louis XIV, who was Lully's principal auditor.

Lully had achieved such status by 1655 that he petitioned King Louis XIV for an orchestra of his own and was granted an organization of seventeen players. This was later expanded to twenty-one and, without doubt, this orchestra and the twenty-four violins of the King were the two finest string orchestras in all of Europe.

After the death of Lully in 1687, French music began to turn away from the expressive grandeur generally associated with the

Baroque age to seek a more delicate, highly ornamented, and entertaining style which was known as the *Rococo*. This name, derived from the French word *rocaille* (ro-kie') (a kind of artificial rock work), denotes in the visual arts, a style rich in curving forms of rocks, shells, and plants, and in other graceful motifs imitating natural forms. Rococo was also called a "gallant" style, this word reflecting its origins in the aristocratic manner of the times. Rococo music appeared in the late years of court life under Louis XIV and reached its height under Louis XV, who reigned from 1715 to 1774. The style was almost entirely French but its influence was felt in Germany and Italy, where it can be detected in some of the works of Georg Philipp Telemann (1681–1767) and Domenico Scarlatti (1685–1757).

The outstanding figure of eighteenth-century French instrumental music was François Couperin (fran-swah' coo-pe-ran') (1668–1733), also known as Couperin le Grand because of his superior skill as an organist. In 1693 he became "Master of the Organ and Harpsichord" at the court of King Louis XIV at Versailles. He also taught several children of the royal family. He excelled as a composer of keyboard music, works for instrumental ensemble, and secular songs. In 1724 he demonstrated his versatility by composing "A Concert for Corelli" with the music written in the style of the Italian master. The following year he composed "A Concert for Lully," written in Lully's distinctive style. Couperin was a master composer in many forms of music, but his most important works were those which he wrote for harpsichord during the last years of his life. In these he shows a delicacy and creativeness which has never been surpassed. His works are generally characterized by a well-defined bass and melodic lines decorated with the ornamentation typical of the rococo style of his time.

Musical culture during the last part of the seventeenth century was dominated by French, Italian, and English musicians. The French exported orchestra players; the Italians exported composers, conductors, and singers to most of the courts of Europe; and the English followed the lead of the Italians with Henry Purcell, composer to the Royal court, as their greatest master. This period in history produced a bewildering array of musical forms. Those of choral music were only slightly less complex than those of the instrumental (see Figs. 9–2 and 9–3, pp. 90 and 91). Further confusion arose when only a few of these forms were standardized or accepted on an international scale.

The development of eighteenth-century opera and its sacred counterpart, the oratorio, served a useful purpose in directing the full resources of music into orderly forms acceptable to various classes of people. The polyphonic style of the Renaissance lingered on for some time, practiced by conservative composers throughout Europe. Sacred works continued to be written in the style of Palestrina, but the strength and spirit of the Protestant movement required a new and more vigorous kind of religious music. These demands were met by the oratorio, the church cantata and the Lutheran chorale as they were developed by George Frederick Handel and his contemporary, Johann Sebastian Bach.

Summary

1. Renaissance music was not composed for the concert stage and did not meet the needs of a changing society.
2. In 1619, the pipe organ was on the threshold of its greatest era.
3. The Baroque organ is a small, specialized instrument.
4. Lübeck, Germany, was known as the "Organ City."
5. Franz Tunder, Dietrich Buxtehude, and Johann Sebastian Bach are Baroque organists who are ranked with the greatest organists of all time.
6. Music was played constantly in the court of King Louis XIV.
7. Lully was the most successful composer of his time, receiving many advantages from King Louis XIV.
8. Lully initiated the form of the French overture. Handel used it as an introduction to his *Messiah*.
9. The Rococo period was largely a French movement which stressed a delicate, highly-ornamented musical style.
10. François Couperin was an important organist, composer, and musician of the French royal court.
11. The early and middle Baroque periods presented a large number of little-known or little-used musical forms.
12. In the late Baroque period, the oratorio attained great prominence through the works of Handel and Bach.

Examples of Music

1. *Ars Nova,* Vol. III of *The History of Music in Sound.* RCA Victor (LM 6015).
2. *Baroque Masters of Venice, Naples and Tuscany.* Nonesuch (HC 73008).
3. *Dietrich Buxtehude.* Music Guild (M 57).
4. *Xerxes* (Ballet excerpts, Lully). Vanguard (BG 59).
5. Couperin, *Mass for the Convents.* Westminster (XWN 18674).
6. The North German School, *Master Works for Organ.* Nonesuch (H 71105).

9 ～ Bach and Handel

What is known as the Baroque era is not a fixed or well-defined segment of history; rather, it is a kind of style and culture. It represents a line added to architecture, a sound of music, a light in painting. In music it covers roughly the years from the start of the seventeenth century to the middle of the eighteenth century. It had its greatest triumphs in the years following 1650, when music was a vital part of life—whether religious or secular, military or civilian.

A career in music was so important at that time that it attracted the greatest men of the day. Many of these were musicians and composers whose craftsmanship and creativity is still considered superb. The essential spirit of the Baroque arose out of a world given over to self-indulgence and extremes: religious asceticism and extravagant, ritualistic ceremonies; deep scientific and philosophical thought and silly superstitions; wholesale crime, dire misery, and elaborate displays of wealth. Naturally, the art expression of the time reflected these influences.

At its best, Baroque art was a vigorous art combining imagination and elaborate detail with great emotional fervor. At its worst, Baroque was likely to be bombastic, sentimental, vulgar, often degenerate, overly ornate, and confused in its contrasts and divergencies. One should consider both the virtues and vices of the style, for the presence of both extremes is a significant characteristic in itself. It is in light of this that our attention is focused on Johann Sebastian Bach and George Frederick Handel, musical giants of the Baroque, who probably contributed more to posterity than did their most creative colleagues.

Johann Sebastian Bach

The life of Johann Sebastian Bach (1685–1750) offers less material for romantic legend than does that of almost any other composer.

His total experience was identified with his art in a most immediate way. He taught his students, he played the organ, the harpsichord, and the violin, and wrote his emotional and spiritual life into his many compositions. The routine of his life was seldom broken except by occasional professional journeys, when‧ he was asked to test and inaugurate new organs. His last and probably his most interesting expedition was in 1747 when he visited the court of Frederick the Great at Potsdam. His son, Karl Philipp Emanuel, was employed as harpsichordist and accompanist of the flute-playing monarch. On this occasion, Frederick announced to his courtiers, "Gentlemen, old Bach has arrived." He personally escorted the aging composer through the palace showing him the new pianos which were beginning to replace harpsichords. At Bach's invitation, the King gave him a melody upon which he improvised at length. Later, when he had returned to Leipzig, he elaborated further upon the royal theme, and—along with a sonata for flute, violin, and clavier—sent to the King what he called *The Musical Offering*, dedicated to "A Monarch whose greatness and power, as in all the sciences of war and peace, so especially in music everyone must admire and revere."

Bach's music is the earliest that is heard regularly on the concert stage today. That fact has probably contributed to the common belief that Bach is the first of the modern composers, standing at the head of a line which includes Haydn, Mozart, Beethoven, and other great masters of music; but history tells us that the family name of Bach had been synonymous with the best in music for several generations, and that Johann Sebastian represents the culmination of musical developments which began in the early sixteen hundreds.

Johann Sebastian Bach was born in Eisenach, central Germany, not far from where George Frederick Handel was born in the same year—yet these two great musicians never met each other. On the outskirts of Eisenach is the famous eleventh-century Wartburg Castle, where Martin Luther found refuge from his enemies in the sixteenth century and where he completed his translation of the Bible. In all of his music, Bach remained faithful to the spirit of Luther and to the Lutheran liturgy.

As a composer, Bach's position was not that of a revolutionary or an experimentalist; he worked almost entirely with musical forms that had been in use before his time. However, every form he touched —fugue, concerto, mass, cantata—rose so far above his models in technical detail and expressive content that it became in effect a new form.

In 1723 Bach was appointed cantor at the Church of St. Thomas in Leipzig, a position he held until his death in 1750. His responsibilities as cantor were many and varied. At the choir school attached to the church, he trained singers for the choirs of two other churches; he instructed the boys of the school in Latin. He supervised the music at the Church of St. Nicholas. At the Church of St. Thomas he served as organist, choirmaster, and resident composer. One of his duties was to compose a cantata for each Sunday and each feast-day of the year, sixty cantatas a year in all. At his death in 1750, he had completed five such sets, about three hundred cantatas, of which almost two hundred have been preserved.

The six concertos Bach wrote for the Margrave of Brandenburg in 1721 are probably his finest accomplishments in the field of orchestration. Among Bach's organ compositions, two forms were most frequently used, the fugue and the chorale prelude. The form of a typical fugue begins with a theme presented without accompaniment; the theme is likely to be two, four, or six bars in length. When the theme has been presented once, it is imitated by each of the voices in turn but each time at a different pitch-level. This section is called the *exposition*. Several of these expositions are usual in a fugue, each separated from the other by a section called an *episode*. The series of expositions and episodes increase in expressive power and tension during the course of the work and culminate in a *climax* or *stretto*. The fugue is one of the most difficult and demanding of all musical forms. It may be better understood by studying Figure 9–1, which shows the structure of the first movement of Bach's *Art of the Fugue*.

In order to understand the significance of the chorale prelude, we must go back to the Protestant Reformation period, approximately two hundred years before the time of Bach. At that time the organ was a clumsy, loud instrument, used only to play during interludes in the service and to give the pitch for the choir or priest who might be singing in the service. As congregational singing grew in importance and the organ improved in quality, it was customary to have the organ play the chorale entirely through and then rest while the congregation sang it, alternating this way during the performance of as many as ten or twelve verses. It is natural that organists with some imagination might wander after playing the same melody

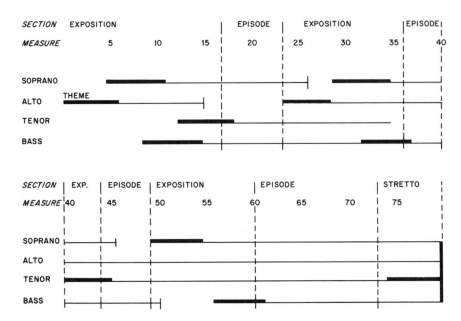

Fig. 9–1. Structure of the First Movement of Bach's Art of the Fugue

so many times in succession. And it does, in fact, seem that one of the problems of the early Protestant churches was to keep organists from "mingling strange notes and variations in the melody of the chorale."

This was the heritage that Bach received, and nothing could have served him better. Countless numbers of these preludes were improvised by Bach and are not available to us, but we do have a series of ninety which were written down during his stay at Wiemar and these brought the form of the chorale prelude to its ultimate height.

We often hesitate to attempt an analysis of Bach's method and an examination of his tools for fear we will lose sight of his genius, but we must understand some of the musical language which he used and which his listeners learned to understand if we are to appreciate his music. His more common devices for translating words into sound were used with artistic care: when "far" occurred in the text, it was assigned a minor ninth chord. "Firm" or "steadfast" was a repeated note. "Anguish" was expressed by narrow chromatic intervals. "Hell" or "Satan" was expressed by intervals of diminished sevenths. "Peace" was a diatonic passage moving upward. The vividness and consistency with which he employed identical intervals for identical concepts is striking.

During his lifetime Bach was known primarily as a virtuoso organist; only Handel was placed in his class. When he was asked about the extent of his talent, Bach's modest reply would usually be, "I was always very diligent. Another equally diligent could do the same."

The last years of Bach's life contained many elements of tragedy. He became blind and completed his last works with difficulty. Financial problems were pressing so that his wife and two youngest daughters were left penniless at his death. The younger musicians, including his own sons, became tired of Bach's polyphonic style and turned toward new leaders that were moving toward classical ideals. Although Bach's music was played by musicians such as Samuel Wesley in England, it was more than half a century after his death before his great contribution to the history of music was realized. Felix Mendelssohn focused the attention of the musical world upon Bach, with a performance of the *Saint Matthew Passion* in Leipzig in 1829.

Bach's style evolved out of his ability as an organist. His early training as a singer and his experience on violin and harpsichord gave him a thorough knowledge of the possibilities of these media as well. He discovered little that was new, but he liberally applied his genius to the musical resources he had at hand.

George Frederick Handel

Of the numerous significant contemporaries of Bach, the most outstanding was George Frederick Handel, born only a few weeks before Bach, on February 23, 1685, in the town of Halle, not far from Eisenach. We think of these men as the dominant musical figures of the Baroque, but their careers and creative accomplishments stand in sharp contrast to each other. Handel seems not to have known of Bach's accomplishments, but this is probably due to the fact that Bach was an obscure cantor in a provincial city. On the other hand, Bach was always a zealous student of the works of other composers; and we know that he studied some of Handel's compositions, since some of them are copied in his own hand.

Unlike Bach, Handel could claim no musical heritage. His

father was a barber-surgeon, the stern head of a German, middle-class family, who decided that his son should embark upon a respectable professional career. When the young Handel showed evidence of marked musical talent, he was permitted to receive systematic musical instruction under the tutelage of Zachow, the organist of the Liebfrauenkirche in Halle. He received excellent training in the technique of composition, and instruction in playing the violin, the oboe, and the organ. Inasmuch as his father had planned a legal career for him, his musical activities were not allowed to interfere with an academic training. After graduating from the local gymnasium in 1702, he enrolled as a student at the University of Halle. He was also given the post of organist at Halle Cathedral. His father's early death made it possible for George to resign from the University after only one year and to pursue his interest in music. He soon moved to Hamburg, where he took a position playing second violin in the orchestra. Italian opera was in vogue, as it was throughout much of Europe, and Handel became so absorbed in the operatic style that by the age of twenty he had written his first opera. Since Italy was the musical center during the Baroque period, it was the logical place for Handel to go.

For three years he studied with leading Italian composers and profited greatly by the experience. He came into close contact with the oratorios of Carissimi (1604–1674) and became personally acquainted with the great opera composer, Alessandro Scarlatti (1659–1725), and his son, the harpsichordist, Domenico Scarlatti (1685–1757). The talented Handel was well received in Italy, and he was becoming known in other countries. During the time he was in Italy, one of his operas was performed successfully in Vienna.

In 1710 he returned to Germany to be musical director of the Electoral Court at Hanover. In his two years at Hanover, he managed to take two leaves of absence to go to London, where his Italian operas were a sensation. His second visit was made on the condition that he return to Hanover within a reasonable time; but he was still in London two years later when his master, the Elector of Hanover, was proclaimed King George the First of England. This was at first embarrassing for Handel, but it was not long before good relations were again established and a King's Pension was conferred upon him when he was appointed music-master for the two princesses.

In 1719 the Royal Academy of Music was founded in London, with Handel as one of its directors. He turned out a steady stream of operas which were performed at the Academy with moderate success until its bankruptcy in 1728. He continued to produce works in this form although he too was forced into bankruptcy in 1737. After his expensive operatic failures, he finally decided to turn from opera to oratorio, and in this form he insured his immortality.

The oratorio is one of the most significant contributions of the Baroque period. It is not an outgrowth of the Renaissance forms, but rather a new entity in the world of music. The roots of the oratorio are in the opera. In fact, the first oratorios were called religious operas and were complete with costumes and staging. By Handel's time the scenery, costumes, and actions were no longer present; but the idea of drama, the fundamental characteristic of Baroque opera, was retained. Each soloist represented a specific character; like opera, an oratorio was a work of considerable scope, requiring two or more hours to perform; it featured an accompanying orchestra and a chorus in addition to the soloists. Most of Handel's oratorios were drawn directly from Bible sources, Old Testament subjects being especially favored.

Handel's best known oratorio is the *Messiah*, which contains fifty-three musical numbers, each being one of three types: recitative, aria, or chorus. He wrote the *Messiah*'s three hours of music in the unbelievably short time of twenty-four days. As he wrote he was aware that he was creating a great work, and afraid that if he stopped he might lose his inspiration. He hardly slept, ate, or left his house for three weeks. At the end of his labor he is reported to have said, "I did think I did see all heaven before me, and the Great God Himself." * The work had its first performance in Dublin, Ireland, in 1742 and since that date it has probably been performed more often than any other large choral work.

Handel has often been referred to as the people's composer since he took a deep and intense interest in his surroundings. It was no coincidence that he wrote nearly fifty operas and musical dramas depicting the problems and situations of human beings. Most of his

---

* Machlis, Joseph, *The Enjoyment of Music* (New York, Norton, 1955), p. 443.

more than thirty oratorios were also based upon the experiences of biblical heroes such as Samson, Saul, Solomon, and Joshua.

The last nine years of Handel's life were spent in blindness, although he maintained a vigorous schedule of conducting and performing. On such programs he sometimes improvised at the organ between sections of the concert. In 1759 Handel collapsed following a performance that he had conducted. A few days later, he died and was buried with state honors in Westminster Abbey; the German who was an English citizen for the last forty years of his life had earned a rightful place among England's national heroes.

In a general way, the objectives of the Bach and Handel period were to simplify, clarify, and further organize the musical forms of their day. This was especially true of the song style which had developed within the opera. At this time also the orchestra was established as an independent musical unit.

The technical discoveries of the eighteenth century led to the scientific explanation of what was called *equal temperament*. This is a system of tuning based upon the arbitrary division of the octave into twelve equal semitones. The octave is the only acoustically corrected interval, therefore the tones within that interval must be tempered or adjusted slightly so that on a musical instrument a single key can represent two tones—for example, both F-sharp and G-flat. As long as music remained largely vocal and in a narrow range, the performer could easily make desirable pitch adjustments. However, with the development of keyboard and wind instruments of fixed pitch, as well as new forms of music which required the techniques of modulating from one key to another, the situation became complicated and a solution such as *equal temperament* was urgently needed. The scale derived from this system is called the *tempered scale* and is the pattern which serves as the basis for our modern harmonic system. Bach made a substantial contribution to the cause of *equal temperament* with his group of compositions called the *Well-Tempered Clavier*. These were published in two volumes and proved that *equal temperament* was practical, since this monumental work included compositions in all twenty-four of the major and minor keys.

The works of Bach and Handel represent and express two different worlds of music. Bach, the master of German Lutheran liturgy and tradition, wrote, above all, Christian music, based on the Christian ideas of Christ, of death and of life after death. His *Passions of St. John* and of *St. Matthew,* as well as his more than two hundred cantatas, deal largely with these themes, which are neither historical nor visible but contemplative. Handel, on the other hand, was not primarily a composer of religious music. His oratorio, *The Messiah,* is a masterpiece, but he treats his subject more historically, basing it on the words of Old Testament prophets. He avoids using Christ as a subject or as a character. He followed no tradition in his English oratorio; it was his development and crowning achievement. These two men can neither be compared, nor joined, nor opposed; they complement each other and thus provide the Baroque with two towers of musical strength.

With the mastery of the new harmonic system came the development of new forms in both vocal and instrumental music (Fig. 9–2 and Fig. 9–3). Those most widely used during the time of Bach and Handel are listed below.

Vocal

1. *Opera,* a dramatic work in which the text is sung with instrumental accompaniment.
2. *Oratorio,* a setting of a text on a sacred or epic theme for chorus, soloists, and orchestra, for performance in church or concert hall.
3. *Passion,* a musical representation of the agony and sufferings of Jesus during his crucifixion or during the period following the Last Supper.
4. *Mass,* in a musical sense, is a setting of the ordinary or invariable parts of the worship service. The Latin names for these parts are: Kyrie, Gloria, Credo, Sanctus, Agnus Dei.
5. *Cantata,* a musical setting of a story, either religious or secular, done without costumes or scenery and intended for concert performance.
6. *Chorale* (coh-rahl'), a hymn-tune of the Lutheran church. From the seventeenth century onward, the chorale was used as the basis of two main types of extended music, the church cantata and the chorale prelude for organ.
7. *Anthem* (an English corruption of antiphon), a musical setting of nonliturgical English words used in the Protestant church service. The words are generally a commentary upon the sermon.
8. *Aria,* a vocal solo as it is used in opera, oratorio, or cantata, contrasting with the declamatory style of *recitative.*
9. *Motet,* of the thirteenth century, was usually in three parts; the

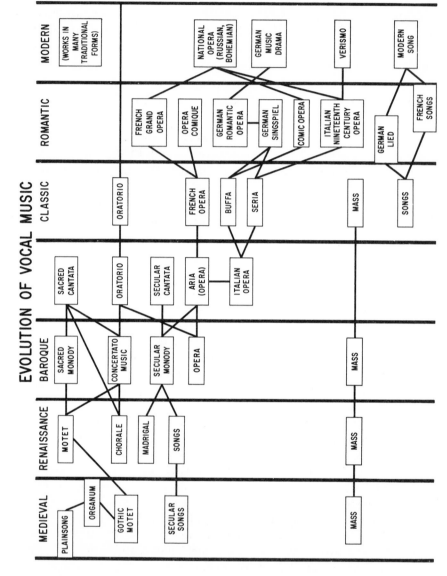

EVOLUTION OF VOCAL MUSIC

| MEDIEVAL | RENAISSANCE | BAROQUE | CLASSIC | ROMANTIC | MODERN |

PLAINSONG

ORGANUM

GOTHIC MOTET

MOTET

SACRED MONODY

CHORALE

CONCERTATO MUSIC

SACRED CANTATA

ORATORIO

ORATORIO

MADRIGAL

SECULAR MONODY

SECULAR CANTATA

ARIA (OPERA)

OPERA

ITALIAN OPERA

FRENCH OPERA

BUFFA

SERIA

FRENCH GRAND OPERA

OPERA COMIQUE

GERMAN ROMANTIC OPERA

GERMAN SINGSPIEL

COMIC OPERA

ITALIAN NINETEENTH CENTURY OPERA

NATIONAL OPERA (RUSSIAN, BOHEMIAN)

GERMAN MUSIC DRAMA

VERISMO

(WORKS IN MANY TRADITIONAL FORMS)

SECULAR SONGS

SONGS

MASS

MASS

MASS

MASS

MASS

SONGS

GERMAN LIED

FRENCH SONGS

MODERN SONG

Fig. 9-2

EVOLUTION OF INSTRUMENTAL MUSIC

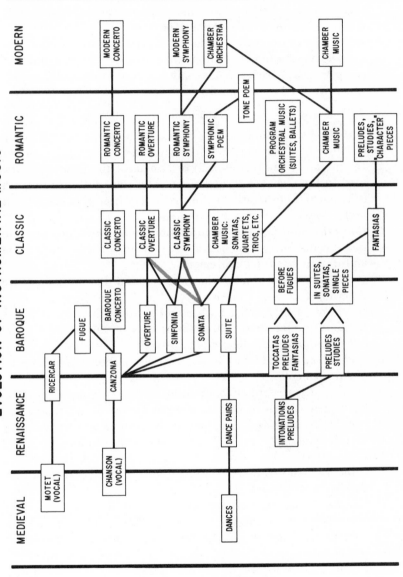

Fig. 9-3

91

lowest was called tenor and was taken from a plainsong. The two higher parts called *duplum* and *triplum* had different words, either sacred or secular. After 1600 a motet was a setting of a sacred text in the current style of the period. It was usually done for solo voices and/or choir with or without instrumental accompaniment. Bach's motets are for unaccompanied double chorus in four or five parts.

Instrumental

1. *Suite* (as used before 1750), a composition consisting of a group of dance-type movements in the same key.
2. *Sonata da Chiesa* (kee-ay'-zah) or Sonata of the Church, a title used in the seventeenth and eighteenth centuries to distinguish instrumental music suitable for the church from that suitable for performance in secular surroundings.
3. *Concerto* (kon-cher'-to), a composition for one, two, or three solo instruments and an orchestra. It is based on the sonata form and usually has three movements.
4. *Canon,* a form of composition like a round, in which there are exact repetitions of a preceding part in the same or related keys.
5. *Invention,* a title which Bach used often for his two-part pieces in contrapuntal style. Three-part pieces in this same style he called *sinfonie* (seen-foh-nee'-ay).
6. *Prelude,* an introductory movement; also a short piano piece in one movement.
7. *Toccata* (to-cah'-tah), a composition in free style for a keyboard instrument, generally characterized by the use of full chords and running passages and often used as the prelude of a fugue. It was originally designed to display a performer's technique.
8. *Variation,* the process of modifying a theme with changes and embellishments while leaving the resulting product recognizably derived from the original.
9. *Rondo,* a form of instrumental music with a recurring section. The opening section may alternate with a number of different sections or episodes in the form represented by the letters ABACADA.
10. *Fugue,* a musical form or composition in which a theme (called a subject) is taken up and developed by the various voices or instruments in succession, according to the strict laws of counterpoint.

Summary

1. The term Baroque designates a style and culture rather than a well-defined period of history.
2. Baroque music reached its height in the years following 1650.
3. There was great variation in the quality and forms of Baroque music.
4. Johann Sebastian Bach and George Frederick Handel were the greatest masters of music to emerge from this period.
5. These men were not revolutionary in their work but were masters of the forms they inherited.
6. The chorale prelude was important in the development of the Lutheran church service.
7. Much of Bach's music has been lost, but we do have ninety chorale preludes, more than two hundred cantatas and many major works in most forms of the period.
8. Handel was born not far from Bach's birthplace in Germany, but the two were not acquainted.
9. Handel was well educated. He mastered the style of Italian opera before going to England.
10. He achieved fame and fortune in England.
11. The general objectives of the late Baroque were to clarify musical forms.
12. It is difficult to compare the works of Bach and Handel, since they represent different concepts. They complement each other to provide towers of musical strength.

Examples of Music

1. J. S. Bach, *St. Matthew Passion.* Archive (ARC 3125) (3 records).
2. *A Treasury of Immortal Performances:* Arias of Bach, Handel and Mendelssohn. RCA Victor (Red Seal LCT 1111).
3. J. S. Bach, *Jesu Joy of Man's Desiring,* Cantata 147. London (5277).
4. J. S. Bach, *Anna Magdalena Book.* Vanguard (BG 510).
5. J. S. Bach, *Great Arias from the Cantatas.* Vanguard (BG 526).
6. Handel, *Apollo & Dafne,* Cantata for two voices. London (OL 50038).
7. Handel, *Concerto No. 3 for Oboe and Strings.* Columbia (ML 4629).
8. Handel, *Messiah, Oratorio,* Mormon Tabernacle Choir. Columbia (Masterworks 5405).

10 ∿ Classicism

The term *classical* is generally used to describe a style of expression that is concerned mainly with form, logic, and a balance characterized by restraint. "Classical" usually points to the way in which the arts are based on models of Greek and Roman art, but there are virtually no such models for classical music to emulate. The term as applied to music refers to the works of those eighteenth-century composers whose music gives the impression of clarity, repose, balance, lyricism, and restraint. The Classical period is one of the high points of musical history and is marked by a number of important developments in the patronage and the function of music, developments that have continued to influence music in the nineteenth and twentieth centuries.

In the eighteenth century, Austria and Germany became the center of vital musical activity. It was in these countries that a large number of principalities and duchies were able to maintain a measure of political independence. In France and England, on the other hand, almost all aristocratic life had come under the influence of a central power. The small courts in Austria and Germany were gradually forced to give up much of their political and economic independence, but they were able to maintain their artistic and social positions. There was often considerable rivalry among them in these matters. A long tradition of instrumental music, an abundance of talent, a natural love of music among all classes of people, and artistic ambition combined with great wealth produced an exciting atmosphere in which eighteenth-century music flourished.

Composers of the time depended upon the patronage of an aristocratic society discriminating in its taste. This society was not only sophisticated and elegant, but it felt no need to try to be profound or to show emotion. There was a general decline in the patronage of serious music by the churches. While certain reform movements did take place in both Protestant and Catholic churches during the eighteenth century, none of them provided for a continuous growth of religious music. It is also evident that the pleasure-loving aristocracy did little to maintain religious music at the high level of the Baroque period.

The function of music in the Classical period was to provide pleasurable entertainment for a sophisticated aristocratic society and for a larger but still discriminating audience which patronized public concerts of orchestral music and opera. The concert hall and opera house became established institutions, and their existence made it possible for all classes of people to enjoy creative music. Publishing houses were well established and exerted a strong influence both on composers and on the public. Printed music became readily available to a large number of people which resulted in an increased number of musical performances. It also placed publishers in a position to champion some composers at the expense of others.

Music also grew more important in the home, where amateur performances were popular. Many composers of both vocal and instrumental music wrote chamber music for this amateur field. Chamber music was suitable for performance in a relatively small hall or in the main room of a house, in contrast to music suitable for a church or large concert hall. At one time the form included one player assigned to each part. Although a wide variety of instrumental groups are used to play this music, many of them using piano accompaniment, the most representative is the string quartet, consisting of two violins, viola, and cello. Music for dancing was also in popular demand in this society which loved gayety and entertainment. The church was not a major "consumer" of serious music during the eighteenth century; it still rewarded composers who wrote sacred music for its services, although they often reflected the secularism of the time.

A new and simplified type of musical form, known as the ABA form, came into popular use. In this form, a first melody is stated; a second, contrasting melody appears; and the first is repeated. The ABA form created a simple type of structure which could be understood and enjoyed by all and was symptomatic of the widespread resistance to the complicated polyphony so widely used in the Baroque period. Other characteristics of the Classical style were: (1) precise and clear forms with sections marked off by cadences, (2) characteristic symmetry and form, with musical periods usually balanced in four-measure phrases, (3) introduction of folk melodies and idioms into serious music, (4) popularity of instrumental music—orchestral compositions and chamber music for both winds and strings as well as solo instruments, and (5) the division of instruments of the orchestra into four major groups: strings, woodwinds, brass, and percussion. With the exception of the percussion section, each group became a complete choir in itself. With this enlarged orchestra, the harpsichord was no longer used or needed for the bass line or to fill in the harmonic texture.

There were many important composers at work in the eighteenth century, but probably Franz Joseph Haydn (1732–1809) and Wolfgang Amadeus Mozart (1756–1791) were the two who exerted the greatest influence upon the musical trends of their time and of the future.

Franz Joseph Haydn

Haydn was one of the most prolific composers of all time. Born in lower Austria, he received early training at a choir school at the Cathedral of St. Stephen in Vienna. He was largely self-taught, however, and carefully studied the styles and techniques of such composers as Karl Philipp Emanuel Bach and Christoph Willibald Gluck, who had initiated several reforms in the opera of the day.

Haydn's career is a good example of the patronage system functioning at its best. He was given a post as assistant Kapellmeister at the court of Prince Esterházy in 1761, where he enjoyed an ideal patronage for a period of more than thirty years. His duties were to provide music requested by the Prince for all ocasions. Consequently, he was called upon to write in a variety of musical forms, from sonatas through opera, including all the forms of Catholic religious music. He had an orchestra at his disposal at all times which enabled him to experiment with various orchestral instruments and techniques. In this way, he brought unity to late eighteenth-century music and contributed greatly to the perfection of the Classical style. He played an especially important part in the development of the symphony, which emerged about 1760 as an independent piece of music for orchestra. A minuet was added to the three-movement sonata form, thus creating the four-movement symphony which became widely accepted.

Haydn's main contributions to the Classical style were: (1) the use of a slow introduction to the first movement of the symphony, (2) the enlargement of the development section in the first movement, (3) the use of the variation form for the slow movement of symphonies and quartets, and (4) flexible orchestration that permitted melodies to be freely imitated in contrasting tone colors.

Although he did not start composing until his late twenties, Haydn wrote an enormous amount of music. Much of it has been lost, but among his more important works we have 104 symphonies and 82 string quartets. His compositions in other forms include operas, oratorios, solos for various instruments with piano accompaniment, usually in three movements, and a wide variety of chamber music. His most representative compositions are: (1) The London Symphonies (Nos. 93 and 104); (2) the later string quartets, especially The Emperor (Opus 76, No. 3) and The Lark (Opus 65, No. 1); (3) two oratorios, *The Creation* and The *Seasons,* and (4) his piano sonatas.

The long career of Franz Joseph Haydn spanned the critical decades of the Classical period. He absorbed all that the eighteenth century had achieved and succeeded in bringing its diverse elements together in a remarkably unified style. The importance of his contribution to the development of music cannot be overestimated.

Wolfgang Amadeus Mozart

Wolfgang Amadeus Mozart was a composer whose creative inventiveness and. genius for melody have ranked him among the greatest of musicians. Born in Salzburg, Mozart showed evidence of great creativity from early boyhood. His youth was spent in the atmosphere of the Salzburg court, where his father, Leopold Mozart, was a violinist. His genius was recognized at a very early age, and his talents as a performer and a composer were displayed over much of Europe on tours to important courts and musical centers. Despite almost ideal conditions for a successful career and despite his superior talent, Mozart's life was one of struggle and disappointment. In contrast to Haydn, Mozart never really had a patron. He was one of the first independent composers, living without the security of a permanent position. Lacking security, Mozart was forced to write music in every popular form of his day in order to interest a large number of people. His death came at an early age, just as he was gaining public acclaim for his opera *The Magic Flute*.

In style Mozart was a conformist. He refined and polished the Classical form, but made no major innovations. Mozart was well acquainted with Haydn, and their friendship probably influenced Mozart's mature works. While there are many similarities in their styles of composition, Mozart is distinctive in several ways: (1) in general, his melodies are more extended and more subtle in their lyric expressiveness; (2) he seldom repeats phrases, note for note, but makes minute changes in rhythm, dynamics, or harmonic structure; (3) he seldom uses a slow introduction to his symphonies; (4) his music comes closer to the Romantic style by using chromaticism in both melody and harmony; (5) in his chamber music all parts became equally important; one instrument no longer played the melody while others furnished an accompaniment.

Mozart did not follow the patterns of Gluck's reforms in opera; his refined Classical taste and his innate feeling for the theater led him to superior achievement in combining pure music with extra-musical ideas. One of his most obvious contributions to music is his development of the orchestra. To the typical orchestra of Haydn, which consisted of flutes, oboes, bassoons, trumpets, horns, strings, and kettledrums, he added clarinets and trombones, thus preparing the way for the great Wagnerian orchestras of the nineteenth century. He wrote equally well for all of the orchestral instruments. Until its introduction into the symphony by Mozart, the clarinet was considered a vulgar instrument, fit only for the lower-class dances and weddings where it was commonly used. The use of the clarinet was a distinctly modern step, somewhat like the use of the saxophone in the serious music of the twentieth century.

It is difficult to select the major works from Mozart's more than six hundred compositions. There are a few, however, that stand out from the rest as monuments to his creative genius. Special attention should be called to his last three symphonies: Nos. 39, 40, and 41. While he wrote a number of religious works, his *Requiem Mass* is his crowning achievement in this medium. Among his many string quartets, there is a group known as the *Ten Celebrated Quartets* which is truly outstanding. The Köchel * numbers are: 387, 421, 428, 458, 464, 465, 499, 575, 589, and 590.

Audiences of the Classical era differed from those of our time in one important respect. Their attention was directed mainly to the hearing of new works by living composers; our public today shies away from contemporary music, but goes eagerly to hear the standard repertory, reinterpreted by one virtuoso after another. The star of the Classical scene was the composer and creator of music. In the musical scene today, we turn the spotlight upon the performer. Eighteenth-century eagerness for new music may be compared to the present-day demand for new motion pictures or television programs.

Summary

1. Classical is a term used to describe a style of artistic expression which is concerned with form, logic, balance, and restraint.
2. The Classical period is one of the high points in music history.
3. During this time, Austria and Germany became the center of musical activity.
4. Composers depended upon the patronage of an aristocratic society, notable for its sophistication and its discriminating taste.
5. There was a general decline in the patronage of serious music by the church.
6. Opera houses and concert halls, as well as publishing houses, were well established and exerted a strong influence upon music.
7. The chief function of music in the Classical era was to provide entertainment for a sophisticated society.
8. Some characteristics of the Classical style in music are: clear forms, well-defined cadences, and balanced phrases.
9. Franz Joseph Haydn was the most prolific of the many outstanding eighteenth-century composers.
10. Haydn enjoyed the patronage of Prince Esterházy for over thirty years.
11. The orchestra became an independent musical unit.

* Mozart did not number his works in a chronological order using the usual opus numbers; fifty years after his death, Ludwig von Köchel compiled a chronological catalog of all of Mozart's works. This was recently revised and brought up to date by the late Alfred Einstein. A Mozart composition is now commonly designated by its number in Köchel's compilation.

12. Wolfgang Amadeus Mozart was a composer of rare creative genius, but was unlucky in finding patrons.
13. Mozart enlarged the orchestra; the orchestra of today is basically the one Mozart developed.   *Why?*
14. Mozart's music is distinctive in several ways: his melodies are extended and expressive, he seldom uses exact repetition, the chromaticism in his work points toward the Romantic style, and in his chamber music all parts are equally important.
15. The star of the Classical scene was the composer of music; in the twentieth century, the spotlight is on the performer of music.

Examples of Music

Haydn

1. *Symphony No. 104 in D* ("London"). Columbia (ML 5349).
2. *Divertimento No. 1 in B♭ for Flute, Oboe, Horn, Clarinet, and Bassoon.* Epic (LC 3461).
3. *Concerto in D for Cello and Orchestra,* Op. 101. Angel (35725).
4. *Concerto for Trumpet in E♭.* Vanguard (VRS 454).

Mozart

1. *Requiem Mass in D Minor,* K. 626. Vox (DL 270).
2. *Symphony No. 41 in C Major* ("Jupiter"), K. 551. London (LL 3002).
3. *String Quartets* (complete). Vox (VBX 12).

11 ∿ Ludwig van Beethoven

There are several musical terms with which we should be familiar before we start a discussion of the musical development that came with the nineteenth century.

There are four basic terms which refer to *tempo* or *movement* in music. These may be taken to represent the various phases of life: *presto* can be illustrated by the quick, short movements of a young child or animal at play; *allegro,* by the more deliberate but impatient movement of the teenager; *andante,* by the strong, firm movement of a middle-aged person going about his daily work; and *largo,* by the movement of an old man using a cane to walk slowly but firmly along. There is a long list of tempo markings, most of them more explicitly descriptive of the four we have just mentioned.

Four hundred years ago, the term *cantata* indicated music for singing, the term *sonata,* music to be played upon instruments. As instruments were developed and perfected, so the form of the sonata was also developed and structured. This sonata form proved to be a flexible and highly desirable medium for presenting the musical thoughts of the nineteenth century. The four kinds of sonatas most commonly used will be discussed later, but we should list them now: (1) the concerto; (2) the solo sonata; (3) the string quartet; and (4) the symphony. All of these forms were balanced by the principles of unity and contrast.

The smaller sonata forms comprised only three movements, the symphony traditionally used four. The first movement of the symphony is fast; it is usually called *allegro.* The second movement is slow and expressive, usually called *andante,* or possibly *largo.* The third movement is a dance form characteristic of the time in which the music was written. Eighteenth-century Mozart used a *minuet,* a formal dance of French origin favored in the courts of Europe during his lifetime. Nineteenth-century Beethoven used a rollicking, boisterous *scherzo* (sker'-tzo), a dance with a vigorous driving rhythm; and twentieth-century Harl McDonald used a *rhumba,* a Cuban dance with a complex rhythm that attained great popularity during the 1930's. The fourth movement of the symphony is vigorous and spirited. It may be called an *allegro moderato,* or "moderate" allegro. Together these movements make a symphony which is in sonata form. If the themes of the first movement are used again in successive movements, we say that this sonata form is cyclical in structure.

There is also a special pattern which is applied only to the first —or allegro—movement of the symphony. This pattern is called the *sonata-allegro* form. The sonata-allegro form has three essential parts: (1) the first section, called the *exposition,* presents the theme or themes to be used; (2) the second section, called the *development,* works out some of the possible variations upon these themes; (3) the third section, called the *recapitulation,* is a summary or a replaying of the material already presented—sometimes in a different key. In addition to these three divisions of the sonata-allegro form, the composer may use an *introduction* at the beginning to set the mood and anticipate the themes. If he does this, he will also write a special ending to the movement, called a *coda,* which, in effect, balances the introduction.

The modern symphony emerged between 1730 and 1750 as an independent musical form, modeled after the Italian overture. At that time, a minuet was added to the three movements of the overture. After 1780, the form became well established in the hands of creative men such as Haydn and Mozart. By the turn of the nineteenth century, Beethoven found the symphony most suitable for his creative efforts. It is interesting to note that the great German composers tended to follow the thoughts and the seriousness of purpose voiced by their leading philosophers; this was not so true of other European countries. The temper of Romanticism in Germany had a strong national flavor.

The spirit of Romanticism was the spirit of men giving voice to their passions, fears, loves, and longing. New sources and subjects for music were given artistic expressions, including subjects and experiences previously considered in bad taste by Classical artists. Because Romantic music expresses the temperament of its individual creator, the personal lives of artists took on a new, public importance. Biographical details can serve as keys to the motivating experiences into a composer's music. Composers' lives came to be as "romantic" as their work. Their love affairs, relations with publishers, financial problems, and individual eccentricities all became an integral part of the record of a composer's work.

There was also a change in the patronage of Romantic music. No longer were artists attached to courts for the purpose of providing entertainment in keeping with courtly customs. The Romantic artist depended upon his ability to arouse the interests of the "common people." Composers and writers depended upon the sale of published works. Because of this close economic tie with the general public, they were very sensitive to public reaction. A large part of European society accepted Romanticism, and the artist of the period expressed the thoughts and hopes of large numbers of people. This new patronage also brought a change in the social status of the creative artist. He was no longer a servant, but held a place on the social ladder fairly commensurate with his artistic and financial success. The day had passed when the artist musician in livery waited in the antechamber for his instructions.

All Romantic music is based on the premise that a feeling of musical tension is necessary to achieve a corresponding intensification of emotional response. Romantic music, therefore, concerns itself with the problem of achieving this tension. This means that the problem of sonority and dynamics, or the exploration of sheer masses of sound, is of deep concern to the composer. The composer creates tension and, of course, its ultimate release in the development of formal structure. Apart from these few common aspects, the structure of Romantic music is difficult to generalize.

There were Romantic idealists and Romantic realists. The idealists insisted that music could exist for its own sake. The realists insisted that music must tell a story that could be verbalized or possibly visualized. There were Romanticists who excelled in spectacular virtuosity, dazzling the listener by the brilliance of their technique or by the power of large orchestras and complex orchestration. Then, there were those who, emphasizing intimacy as the best approach to personalized feeling, wrote chamber music and solo songs. Others again combined literature and landscape with music in the invention of the *tone poem*, in which the development of the music depicts moods suggested by its title. This variety of musical concepts shows common characteristics in all periods of music; the difference between them is a matter of emphasis.

There were three favorite media of expression for the romantic composer: the orchestra, the piano, and the human voice. Most nineteenth-century composers wrote for all three. The orchestra grew into the favorite large performing group of the century—its resources surpassed those of even the largest organs. Its possibilities of massiveness, color, and brilliance were well suited to Romantic expression. It could run the gamut of musical ideas from a whisper to an overpowering thunder, and therefore lent itself well to the descriptive needs of Romantic composers. The piano could do much the same in more confined quarters and, what was more, it could be played by a single person. Consequently, the piano became almost a musical symbol of the Romantic spirit of freedom and individualism. The voice also became a symbol of the personal, for it combined the literary elements of Romanticism with the musical to give added intensity to the poetic text. Of course, other instruments were also used during the period, particularly those that could be exploited by the virtuoso performer.

The changing times which we have just described at the turn of the nineteenth century made a place for a strong leader in the world of music. Thirty-year-old Ludwig van Beethoven of Vienna, already established as a popular concert pianist, was the one to assume this important role and to hold it unchallenged until his death in 1827. While arguments can be made for placing Beethoven in the Classical period or between the Classical and Romantic, it is clear from an analysis of his music that he is the one whose compositions first reveal those characteristics generally recognized as Romantic. Beethoven belonged to a generation that received the full impact of the French Revolution. He was nourished by its vision of the freedom and dignity of man. He created the music of a heroic age and, in accents never to be forgotten, proclaimed a faith in the power of man to shape his destiny.

His powers as a pianist took the music-loving aristocracy by storm. He was made welcome in the great houses of Vienna by the powerful patrons whose names appear in the dedications of his works —Prince Lichnowsky, Prince Lobkowitz, Count Rasoumovsky, and many others. To this "Princely Rabble," as he called them, the young genius came, in an era of revolution, as a passionate rebel, forcing them to receive him as an equal and friend. "It is good to move among the aristocracy," he observed, "but it is first necessary to make them respect you." When a nobleman at the home of Count von Browne persisted in talking during his performance, Beethoven stopped playing and in a loud voice remarked, "For such pigs I do not play!" When Prince Lichnowsky, during the Napoleonic invasion, insisted that he play for some French officers, Beethoven stormed out of the palace in a rage, demolished a bust of Lichnowsky that was in his possession, and wrote to his exalted friend, "Prince, what you are, you are through the accident of birth. What I am, I am through my own efforts. There have been many princes and there will be thousands more. But there is only one Beethoven!" It would be difficult to put the spirit and temper of Romantic music in more forceful words than these.

Beethoven's creative life falls into three periods. The first period extends from 1792 to about 1802. This was the period of the popular pianist-composer; and while the works written during this period exhibit the seeds of growing Romanticism, they still carry the trademark of the Mozart-Haydn period. The composition of the Third Symphony in the years 1802–1804 ushers in the second period of Beethoven's career, which is truly Romantic in character. The Third Sympony was written as a tribute to Napoleon Bonaparte; but, when in 1804 Napoleon took the title of Emperor of France, Beethoven blotted out his name as it appeared on the score and said, "He is nothing but an ordinary man, now he will trample on the rights of other men to gain his own ambitions." He renamed the work *Sinfonia Eroica,* with the subtitle "to celebrate the memory of a great man."

If Beethoven had never written more than his First and Second Symphonies, we would consider him just another competent composer who rounded out the Classical period in an acceptable Classical style. But in his Third Symphony we find the real genius of Beethoven. No one has ever been able to surpass him in combining simplicity and complexity. The "Eroica" Symphony is distinguished first of all by the type of thematic material it contains. Instead of rather complete melodies such as Mozart usually employed, Beethoven introduces a number of fragments, each one capable of suggesting a different emotional state (Fig. 11–1). Those fragments are then developed. New melodies grow out of them, and they are combined in a variety of ways. His introduction to the Third Symphony is two sharp, startling chords. Then follows a little melody reminiscent of a

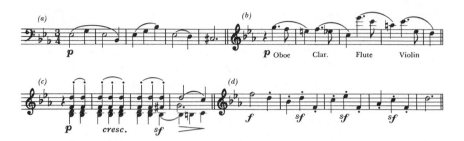

Fig. 11–1. Themes from Symphony No. 3 ("Eroica"), Beethoven

bugle call. He then gives us another surprise, this time in the rhythm. It has been flowing along smoothly enough in three-quarter waltz tempo, but suddenly it erupts and places accents on different beats of successive measures, for example, 1 2 3, 1 2 3, 1 2 3. This leads to a highly complex development of the little bugle call. As he continues, Beethoven repeatedly brings in a harsh sound or a rhythmic disturbance, but he gives the feeling that that is the proper way.

In the second movement Beethoven continues to be unpredictable. For his slow andante movement, he composes a funeral march in the form of a fugue drawn from the period of Bach and Handel. No other composer would attempt such a thing, but Beethoven did, and he made it work. In the third movement the traditional minuet is dropped in favor of the scherzo. The scherzo is not a well-defined dance form. It is very fast and exciting in sharp contrast to the funeral dirge of the second movement. The fourth movement, or finale, is a set of variations on a theme that Beethoven had used before in his ballet, *The Creatures of Prometheus.* Discussing his works at a time before he had finished his Ninth Symphony, he declared the Eroica to be his favorite.

In the third and final period of Beethoven's career, he withdrew from the world, he became more profoundly spiritual, and his music seemed to know no bounds. He composed his most sublime music during this period—five great piano sonatas, five of his greatest string quartets, a Mass in D (also known as the *Missa Solemnis*), and his colossal Ninth Symphony. The Ninth (also known as the "Choral" Symphony) was completed and performed in 1824, three years before his death. As the culmination of this monumental work, Beethoven integrated a chorus to sing several verses of Schiller's poem "Hymn to Joy" into the final movement. Following repeated discords at the beginning of the movement, a baritone voice sings "O friends, no more these sounds continue! Let us raise a song of sympathy, of gladness. O joy, let us praise thee!" * Then the first four lines of the poem sung by the chorus continues:

> Praise to Joy, the God-descended
>   Daughter of Elysium!
> Ray of mirth and rapture blended,
>   Goddess, to thy shrine we come.

Other verses are sung by full chorus, quartet, and solo voices, tied together by the refrain, "O ye millions, I embrace ye, With a kiss for all the world!" and other variations on the theme of joyful brotherhood.

At the first performance in 1824, Beethoven, who was by this time quite deaf, and no longer conducting, sat in the middle of the orchestra watching the score and the players with keen interest. The concert hall was crowded and the music highly successful. Everyone was pleased with the performance, except Beethoven, who felt cheated when he received only 412 gold florins while the total receipts of the concert amounted to 2700. Critics were not unanimous in their praise of the Ninth Symphony. One said, "A masterpiece of composition, but the use of the voices creates a beautiful white marble statue with a red head." Most critics today agree that the unity of the symphony is clear. Beethoven wrote in all of the musical forms of his time, but is best known for his symphonies.

Summary

1. Cantata and sonata were terms originally used to indicate vocal and instrumental music.
2. The four kinds of sonatas most commonly used are: the concerto, the solo sonata, the string quartet, and the symphony.
3. The Romantic symphony is usually in four contrasting movements: Fast—*allegro;* slow—*andante* or *largo;* a dance form—*minuet* or *scherzo;* and moderately fast—*allegro-moderato.*

* Translation by Natalie Macfarren, in Robert Bagar and Louis Biancolli, *The Concert Companion* (New York and London, Whittlesey House, McGraw-Hill Book Company, 1947), pp. 51–52.

4. Sonata-allegro form refers to the structure of the first movement of the symphony.
5. The spirit of Romanticism inspired the use of new sources and subjects for music.
6. The periods of Classicism and Romanticism have common musical characteristics; the difference between them is a matter of emphasis.
7. There were three favorite media of expression for the Romantic composer: the orchestra, the piano, and the human voice.
8. Beethoven emerged as the musical leader of his time. His life may be divided into three periods of creativity: 1792–1802—brilliant pianist-composer, still under the Classical influence; 1804–1813—productive composer, developing orchestral forms in spite of growing deafness and many worries; 1814–1827—composer of his most profound works, withdrawn from the world.
9. Beethoven excelled in many forms of composition, but is probably best known for his nine symphonies.

Examples of Music

Beethoven

1. *Symphony No. 3 in E♭* ("Eroica"). RCA Victor (LM 2387).
2. *Symphony No. 9 in D Minor.* RCA Victor (LM 6066).
3. *Piano Sonatas,* Op. 27 ("Moonlight") and Op. 13 ("Pathetique"). Angel (35025).
4. *Piano Concerto No. 2 in B♭,* Op. 19. Angel (35672).

Part Three ～ 1800 = 1900

12 ∼ The Romantic Century

Romanticism originated in the medieval spirit of troubadour poetry and song. To be "romantic" was to be original, modern, national, popular, down-to-earth, not abiding by the rules and regulations of religion or the prevailing social institutions.

The Romantic symphony orchestra was a highly structured organization. It provided for four well-defined choirs of instruments, which we call the string choir, woodwind choir, brass choir, and percussion. Each choir, except percussion, was capable of singing all four choir parts as we know them: soprano, alto, tenor, and bass.

Since the early development of the orchestra in the seventeenth century, the strings have furnished the main body of the orchestra, producing a predominantly string type of sound. However, with the rapid development of woodwind and brass instruments in the nineteenth century, new concepts of orchestration became evident. In contemporary symphonic writing there is a tendency to make the brilliant, brittle tones of the woodwind sections increasingly more important. This tendency can first be seen in the late Romantic symphonies.

In order to explore the sounds and techniques developed after Beethoven, we should contrast his music with that of the late nineteenth century. To do this, we will examine briefly the musical scene in the United States in 1890.

Mrs. Jeanette Thurber, wife of a wealthy New York wholesale merchant, had a dream. In 1885 she launched two of the most ambitious musical ventures that this country had ever seen: The American Opera Company and The National Conservatory of Music of America. The Opera Company was an artistic success, but a financial failure; it ended two years later in 1887. Undaunted, Mrs. Thurber kept the National Conservatory going. What the institution needed, in Mrs. Thurber's opinion, was a "Name." Accordingly, in 1891 she invited one of Europe's most famous living composers—Antonin

Dvořák, of the Prague Conservatory of Music—to become Director of the National Conservatory.

Antonin Dvořák

Dvořák was no globetrotter, but the salary that Mrs. Thurber offered—$15,000 a year, which meant much more then than it would today—seems to have been too much for him to refuse. Also, Bohemia was causing him discomfort for his political views at that time, so after a year of farewell concerts he arrived in New York late in 1892. He was a modest man and, apparently, had no expectation of being known on this side of the Atlantic. He was, therefore, quite overwhelmed with astonishment and delight to be greeted by a chorus of three hundred voices singing *America,* the New York Philharmonic Orchestra, speeches of welcome, and the presentation of a silver wreath. He stayed in the United States for two and a half years.

There is a tendency among his biographers to disparage his influence on the National Conservatory and to assume that he was a sort of amiable figurehead. The root of this disparagement may lie in the fact that, because he managed to compose seven important choral and orchestral works during his term at the Conservatory, his critics found it difficult to believe he could pursue a full-time career as a composer and still perform his duties as head of a Conservatory; but he could and he did. This was demonstrated when he instituted a complete reorganization of the method of instruction. The most fortunate result of Dvořák's American visit had nothing to do with his influencing anything or anybody. It was on December 19, 1892, in his apartment at 327 East 17th Street in New York that he began the first sketches for a new symphony. At Mrs. Thurber's suggestion he named it A Symphony from the New World.

This symphony is Dvořák's fifth, and it is by far his best work in that form. Whether it is predominantly American or Bohemian has been much discussed, but it really makes little difference. The important point is that Dvořák expressed himself in an individual fashion under new conditions, producing something that pleased—and still pleases—his American listeners. He suggested enough of the Negro idiom to give it a native touch, and sacrificed nothing of his instinct for melody or of the excellent musicianship that characterized all his work. Actually the New World Symphony is far more American in spirit than many compositions written by American-born musicians of the time, enslaved as they were by European traditions and too timid to try to express what the average hearer would recognize as belonging to the United States.

Dvořák had some distant relatives in the Bohemian community of the small town of Spillville, Iowa. In order to visit them, Dvořák and his entire family—his wife, six children, a cousin, a maid, and a secretary—migrated to Spillville for the summer of 1893; and there he was very happy. He played the organ in the town church while his wife sang in the choir; he played string quartets with the local schoolmaster and two of his children; he could inspect and criticize pigeon lofts as an expert. So proud were his neighbors of their illustrious visitor that they named a road for him, the Dvořák Highway.

As one travels the road leading into Spillville, one crosses a small river. A sign on the bridge tells of Dvořák's visit in 1893. A park bench in a small park by the bridge displays a sign that says, "Dvořák sat here as he worked on portions of his New World Symphony." A small brick house across the street bears the sign, "Dvořák lived here when he composed his immortal Humoresque." A town pump, carefully fenced, is identified as the place where Dvořák came to slake his thirst on hot summer evenings in 1893. It was in this rural setting, as well as in his New York apartment, that Dvořák composed his New World Symphony.

The symphony is cyclical in form. That means the same thematic material is used throughout all four movements (Fig. 12–1). There is a substantial introduction, mostly to create an atmosphere, and the opening theme sounds with an upward thrust and an immediate touch of ragtime syncopation; it continues in a very dramatic fashion, with woodwind and brass voices predominating. The second theme is a plaintive melody of Bohemian folk character. The third is a song-like theme that suggests Dvořák's favorite Negro spiritual, "Swing Low Sweet Chariot." The development is comparatively simple, dealing entirely with the first melody, which reappears in the recapitulation, along with melodies which were introduced later. The coda is a further treatment of the first theme. The slow movement of the symphony is the famous Largo in 4/4 time. Out of the remote chords of the introduction comes a haunting melody assigned to the English horn. As the folk song Going Home, this melody is

First Theme

Second Theme

Third Theme

Principal Theme, Second Movement

Principal Theme, Fourth Movement

Fig. 12–1. Themes from New World Symphony, Dvořák

known throughout the world. The third movement is a lively dance pattern based upon the themes heard in the first and second movements. The finale is marked "allegro con fuoco" (with fire) and, after a stormy introduction, leads to a vigorous, march-like melody counterposed to the more lyrical themes of earlier movements. A grand procession of all themes leads the symphony to a rousing close.

As one listens to the New World Symphony, one hears a variety of instrumental voices and sounds which the mighty Beethoven did not have at his disposal. In addition to his use of new instrumentation, Dvořák makes a most notable innovation in his use of the Negro musical idiom.

The Romantics

Now that we have briefly discussed symphonic music from the early and late nineteenth century, we should acquaint ourselves with some of the men who made its development possible. In 1803 Ludwig van Beethoven was thirty-three years old; Franz Schubert was six; in the ten-year period which followed, a remarkable number of musical giants were born. This list includes Robert Schumann, Frédéric Chopin, Franz Liszt, Hector Berlioz, Johann Strauss, Felix Mendelssohn, Richard Wagner, and Giuseppe Verdi; these men are called the first generation of Romantic composers. Born a few years later were Johannes Brahms, Peter Ilyich Tchaikovsky, César Franck, Camille Saint-Saëns, and Gustav Mahler. We hardly need to describe the outpouring of music which resulted from the genius of these men. Each of them was searching for and finding a way to express himself that was uniquely his own.

Nineteenth-century Romantic music still dominates concert and recital programs of today, even though the Romantic period ended more than seventy years ago. It is questionable whether symphony orchestras as we know them today would or could be maintained without the rich resources of nineteenth-century music.

Robert Schumann, Felix Mendelssohn, and Frédéric Chopin are each representative of the general Romantic trends. Although we think of Schumann primarily as a composer, he was also a con- servatory director and music journalist. Both occupations became possible in the nineteenth century, which saw the founding of the first state music schools or conservatories in the face of the withdrawal of the church and the aristocracy as patrons of music. Mendelssohn, privately wealthy, founded one of the first public orchestral societies and served as its director. Chopin, the master pianist, made his living through widespread concertizing, in which his own works were largely featured.

Perhaps Schumann's most typical Romantic expression comes in his composition for piano. In these he employs the small forms such as the two- and three-part song forms. A two-part song form is the pattern used in songs like America. The melody is divided into two parts, A and B, without repetition. The three-part song form is the pattern used for Way Down Upon the Swanee River. The melody of the first phrase A is repeated, almost unchanged, in the second phrase A'. The third phrase B is different. The fourth and final phrase is again a repetition of A. This three-part form is often called an ABA form.

Schumann wrote an interesting composition, *Carnival*, which serves as a good example of Romantic mood music. This work is a series of short works held together by an extra-musical idea; it is a musical representation of a pre-lenten carnival ball. Most of the twenty-two short pieces are in dance rhythms, many of them using the waltz. The individual names of the pieces are suggestive of Schumann's desire to characterize certain individuals. Besides this descriptive quality, Schumann set himself the task of using the notes A, E-flat, C, and B, which in German represent the letters ASCH, the name of a town where an early sweetheart lived. They also represent the four letters of his own name which could be musically stated. Practically every one of these short pieces is based on the use of those four notes in one order or another. Each of the sections is simply constructed, most of them in the three-part song or simple rondo form. Harmonies are enriched with chromatically altered tones, lending color through dissonance. There is no actual program to give specific meaning to the individual numbers other than ambiguous titles. Ernestine von Fricken was the girl who lived in ASCH, but Clara Weick was the girl whom he later married.

Mendelssohn was more interested in serving the Classical tradition than was Schumann. The bulk of his great works—the symphonies, the piano and violin concerti, as well as his oratorios—show a deep regard for Classical form. Romanticism is apparent, however, particularly in one specific musical mood—his fanciful, fairylike scherzo movements. In fact, this particular stylistic invention of Mendelssohn is often the distinguishing feature of many of his compositions even where the term scherzo is not used. A good example of this romantic contribution is the scherzo from *A Midsummer Night's Dream,* written to be used with the performance of Shakespeare's play. It has become one of the great orchestral virtuoso pieces of symphonic literature. Mendelssohn's scherzo was no longer a piece of boisterous humor, such as those Beethoven wrote, but imagistic, lilting melody, in which the actual tones seem to dance as if they were indeed imaginative sprites. The short movement is based on the alternation of two closely related themes, both of which are developed briefly and then restated. This work represents another facet of nineteenth-century musical Romanticism, the invoking of literary fantasy through musical technique and invention.

Frédéric Chopin was a poet of musical fantasy. With the exception of a few songs scarcely known today and two piano concerti,

Chopin composed exclusively for the piano. The fact that a composer of such enormous talent could find realization through a single instrument gives evidence of how greatly the piano had expanded its expressive qualities. This was not accomplished merely by mechanical perfection but by newer concepts and exploitation of pianistic composition and performance. When the short piano piece is discussed in Chapter 14, we will become further acquainted with Chopin and his music.

Franz Liszt was one of the most influential musical figures of his time. He not only enjoyed a fabulous career as piano virtuoso, teacher, and composer, but he was influential in securing performances for many controversial works by other composers. Aspiring young composers and pianists flocked to him for encouragement and assistance. Wagner and Grieg, among many others, received his blessing. One of Liszt's daughters became the wife of Wagner. Although only a few works are still programmed regularly from the reams of piano and orchestral music that Liszt composed, his popular reputation is largely maintained by some of his most trivial works such as Liebestraum. He deserved a better fate, for he has a long list of worthy compositions to his credit.

Liszt first used the term *symphonic poem*, in 1848, as a title for an orchestral work of symphonic proportions, but of only one movement. Within this form, he developed one or more themes at great length and in a free style. Liszt's purpose was to paint a picture in music of some historical or fanciful subject. His twelve symphonic, or tone poems, of which Les Preludes is best known, inaugurated this form. His nineteen Hungarian rhapsodies for piano, some of which he transcribed for orchestra, popularized *rhapsody* as a designation for a musical work. His piano music is brilliant, if somewhat bombastic. His star, which burned brightly during his lifetime, has faded but continues to glow.

Johann Strauss, popular composer of waltzes and dance band leader of Vienna, was better known in his time than his Vienna contemporary, Franz Schubert. Richard Wagner and Giuseppe Verdi, along with Hector Berlioz, complete the list of first-generation Romantic composers. Their contributions were primarily in the field of opera, and they are more fully discussed in later chapters dealing with opera.

Summary

1. The Romantic symphony orchestra is a highly structured organization consisting of three complete choirs and percussion.
2. The nineteenth-century development of brass and woodwind instruments added new resources to the orchestra.
3. Jeanette Thurber founded the National Conservatory of Music in New York.
4. Antonin Dvořák became its Director in 1892. He composed seven major choral and orchestral works, including the New World Symphony, during his two and a half years in America.
5. Dvořák exerted a great influence upon American music and pointed to the resources later identified as our national music.
6. Eight great composers of music were born between 1803 and 1813.
7. Two- and three-part song forms were developed.
8. New career opportunities were available to musical leaders such as Robert Schumann, Felix Mendelssohn, and Frédéric Chopin.
9. Franz Liszt—piano virtuoso, teacher, conductor, composer—was one of the most influential musical figures of his time.
10. Liszt inaugurated a new musical form with his twelve symphonic poems.

Examples of Music

1. Dvořák, *Symphony No. 5 in E Minor,* Op. 95 ("From the New World"). Epic (LC 3575).
2. Schumann, *Carnival,* Op. 9; Guiomar Novaes, piano. Vox (PL 7830).
3. Mendelssohn, *A Midsummer Night's Dream.* RCA Victor (LM 2223).
4. Liszt, "Man's Life: A Prelude to Eternity," from *Les Preludes.* Columbia (Masterworks ML 5198). (This is the third and the best known of the tone poems by Liszt. Much of the *Lone Ranger* music, well known to the older generation, was drawn from this source.)
5. Dvořák, *Humoresque.* Gold Label Series (DL 9780). (This recording of *Humoresque* shows Dvořák's use of the lyric song form, and the incomparable violin playing of Jascha Heifetz.)
6. *Rubinstein Plays Liszt.* RCA Victor (Red Seal LM 1905).

13 ⌐ The Art Song

Franz Schubert

In April, 1826, Franz Schubert applied for the position of Vice-Kapellmeister at the court of Austrian Emperor Francis I. It would be difficult to sketch Schubert's life and experience any more concisely than he has done in the six statements that make up his letter of application. It is short and to the point:

1. The undersigned is a native of Vienna, a son of a schoolmaster, and twenty-nine years of age.
2. As a court chorister, he enjoyed the supreme privilege of being for five years a pupil at the Imperial Choir School.
3. He received a complete course in composition from the late First Court-Kapellmeister, Anton Salieri, and is thereby qualified to fill any post as Kapellmeister.
4. Through his vocal and instrumental compositions, his name is well-known—not only in Vienna, but also in all Germany.
5. He has in readiness, moreover, five Masses for either large or small orchestra which have been performed in various churches in Vienna.
6. Finally, he now enjoys no appointment whatsoever, and hopes in the security of this permanent position to be able at last to attain completely the artistic goal which he has set for himself.

Your Majesty's most obedient humble servant,
Franz Peter Schubert *

His final statement, that he "enjoys no appointment whatsoever," is a revealing one. Schubert, with his great genius, was never to receive a musical appointment. He did teach elementary children in his father's school for a period of four years, but he admits this

* Otto Erich Deutsch, ed., *Franz Schubert's Letters and Other Writings* (London, Faber & Groyer, 1928), p. 116.

was mainly to avoid conscription into the army. Otherwise, his income was derived from giving a few music lessons, occasional honoraria received for his musical works—particularly his songs, and the memorable single concert of March 26, 1828, the year of his death at the age of thirty-one.

The inexpensive and convenient living conditions in Vienna and Schubert's friendship with other struggling musicians, poets, and artists enabled him to live from day to day, enjoying life as best he could. This mode of life in itself was strongly characteristic of the Romantic influences unfolding in the nineteenth century. Such a way of living would have been unthinkable in the days of Mozart and Haydn just a few years earlier.

In contrast to the misfortune of his short and troubled life, full of poverty, humiliation, and disappointment, Schubert found joy and rich, profound satisfaction in his music. As a musician, Schubert came into the world at exactly the right time. He was able to enter into a rich and active musical inheritance from the Classical century, and he was great enough to use it in helping to create a new world of music. This inheritance is the basis of his lonely position as the "Romantic Classicist." When Schubert began to create, Mozart's and Haydn's work had been completed; and in the same city as Schubert, honored by him timidly from afar, the great Beethoven lived and worked.

Schubert occupies a unique place in music history. The transition to Romanticism seems concentrated in his music. Elements that have come to characterize Romantic music—harmonic boldness, extremes in the size of performing groups, subjective expression, and the advantageous use of instrumental tone color—were all fully exploited in his work, but for the most part within the musical forms which the Classical masters had perfected. In Schubert's larger works we do not find the perfect balance of emotion and intellect that distinguish the music of the great Classical composers. Schubert is perfectly willing to let emotion dominate and express itself in the most wonderful melodies that have ever been composed.

During the seventeen years between 1811, when he was fourteen, and 1828, the year of his death, Schubert composed about one thousand works. These include nine symphonies; about fifty chamber music works and piano sonatas; a very large number of short piano pieces and works for the stage, including several operas and operettas; six masses, as well as about twenty-five other works for the church; nearly one hundred choral compositions of various kinds; and most remarkable of all, over six hundred *art songs*, or *lieder*. Only a fraction of this music was published during his lifetime, and much of it was not discovered until many years after his death.

Schubert felt strongly that no improvement could be made on the symphonic form as it had been developed by Beethoven. He was at times almost apologetic for his own symphonic works, but he did not take into account the magic touch of melody which distinguishes his symphonies. A good example of his lyrical treatment is found in his Symphony No. 8 in B Minor, the so-called "Unfinished Symphony" (Figure 13–1). A century later he probably would have subtitled it "a symphony in two movements," with no question about it being finished. This music was written in 1822 when Schubert was twenty-five, but it was not performed until 1865, forty-three years after his death. The strong, melodic themes contrast sharply with the little bugle calls that Beethoven used in his Third Symphony.

Schubert is known to have composed 603 works in the special category of art song. Their unique qualities set them apart from the songs of other composers. Songs for voice and piano had existed long before Schubert's time, but they were written to focus attention upon the vocal part. The piano was subordinate and provided only necessary harmonic and rhythmic support. With composers who came after Schubert, the song became a miniature drama. The piano part be-

Fig. 13–1. Themes from Symphony No. 8 in B Minor, Schubert

came so descriptive it often gained ascendancy over the vocal part. Thus, the songs after 1840 completely reversed the principle upon which the eighteenth-century songs were composed.

The art song, also known by its German name, *lied* (pronounced leed, depends for its success upon the performance itself—the fusion of the text with the music. It must express all shades of emotion, yet retain a simplicity and directness comparable to folk music. There may be a tendency for one of the three—the voice, the poetry, or the piano—to become dominant, but it is the purpose of the composer to achieve an artistic balance in the union of all three. The art song, in order to avoid this imbalance, must be "through-composed," or "composed throughout": each verse is set to its own music.

In Schubert's works the melody and accompaniment are always well balanced and entirely suitable to the text. The piano established moods either in an introduction or in suggesting an appropriate atmosphere throughout the composition. It is often able to go beyond the power of words to express emotion. This is well illustrated by his song, "Gretchen at the Spinning Wheel," in which the piano suggests the sound of the spinning wheel while Gretchen sings of her love for Faust (the song is from Goethe's play, *Faust*).

The Romantic poets tended to encourage the use of their poems as texts for songs. Tennyson, however, is known to have voiced some irritation when musicians occasionally repeated phrases or added words when setting his poetry to music.

In the nineteenth century the common man, as well as the creative musician, often played the part of Romantic philosopher. Schubert demonstrates this in his poem and song, *Die Forelle* (The Trout). The English translation of the text follows:

> Within a sparkling streamlet that sang its merry song,
> I marked a silver trout
> Like an arrow, speed along.
> Beside the brook I lingered
> And watched the playful trout
> That all among the shadows
> Was darting in and out.
>
> With rod and line there waited
> An angler by the brook,
> All eager, he, to capture
> The fish upon his hook.

While clear the water's flowing,
So thought I to myself,
His labor will be fruitless:
I'm sure the trout is safe.

The angler loses patience,
He stirs the stream,
And makes the limpid, shining water
All dull and muddy seem:
"I have him," quoth the stranger
As swift his line he cast:
And heeding not the danger,
The trout was caught at last.*

It is interesting to note the variety of ways in which Schubert could and did use his melodies. One of his friends was an amateur cellist; Schubert was often a visitor in his home and many of his compositions were first performed there. For one of these occasions, Schubert prepared his Quintet in A Major for Piano and Strings. This was done in good Classical form, except that a special movement was inserted which presents the trout melody and a series of variations in which each instrument has a part. It is interesting to listen to the part given the cello as it appears in the fourth movement of this work.

One of Schubert's best known songs is part of a song cycle or series of songs using the poetry of Sir Walter Scott's "Lady of the Lake." The final number in this group is called, "An Apostrophe to the Virgin Mary," better known as Schubert's "Ave Maria." Seldom has any composer been able to capture such a deeply religious spirit with a more perfect fusion of words and music.

Schubert was primarily a creator of melodies, expressing all shades of emotion and yet retaining a simplicity and directness comparable to folk music. Built upon this foundation, the art song was carried to new heights by the greatest composers of the next generation.

Robert Schumann

Robert Alexander Schumann (1810–1856) was born when Franz Schubert was thirteen years old. Surely no one was more in the fore-

* Charles R. Hoffer, *The Understanding of Music* (Belmont, Cal., Wadsworth, 1967), pp. 245–246.

ground of Romantic music in Germany than Schumann, not only because of his own compositions, but also his critical writings, personal encouragement, and active aid to worthy young composers, among them Brahms and Chopin. In a characteristic way he created an imaginative private society which he called the Davidsbund (League of David). The object of this society was to champion the principles of the Romantic style against the traditionalism of the old school, whose followers Schumann grouped under the name Philistines. When Schumann was thirty years old, he received an honorary degree of Doctor of Philosophy from the University of Jena. This was in recognition of his literary as well as his musical achievements.

Schumann's piano music embodies many of the traits which became the idioms of the piano style of the Romantic period. These can be identified as: (1) rhythm expressed in syncopation (where the accent is placed on a usually unaccented part of the measure); (2) new effects resulting from sudden changes of harmony and sonority; (3) heightening of interest through literary elements related to the music.

In Schumann, more strongly than in almost any other composer, we find the stimulus of some particular interest affecting his composition during a period of years. His first twenty-three compositions were all for the piano. In 1840 he married Clara Wieck and, in that year alone, he composed more than one hundred art songs including the song cycle, *Woman's Love and Life*. This was to be a wedding gift for Clara, who was one of the great concert-pianists of the nineteenth century. No actual story links the eight songs of the cycle, but it depicts the happiness of a maiden who, in the first song: (1) loves from afar; (2) dreams about her young man; (3) gets a ring. The cycle continues: (4) "help me my sisters to become a beautiful bride"; (5) the wedding; (6) a child is born and all is joy; (7) "here on my breast lies my treasure"; and (8) now for the first time he has made me grieve. She goes on to say her husband is wrapped in the sleep of death. As the song ceases, the piano plays a quiet little epilogue that each listener may interpret as his own.

Names which should be associated with the art song are: Franz Schubert, Robert Schumann, Hugo Wolf, Johannes Brahms, and Robert Franz. These men are called the "great five of the lied."

The beauty of the art song is in the subtle artistry of combining a nation's best language and music. This is the basis of that intangible something that makes Schubert and Schumann so German, Debussy so French, and Stephen Foster so American.

Summary

1. Franz Schubert lived a short and troubled life, but derived much satisfaction from his musical ability.
2. Schubert lived at just the right time to use the rich inheritance of Classicism in a way that opened up a new world of music.
3. Schubert's greatest genius was in his ability to create and use melodies.
4. The *art song*, or *lied*, is a perfect fusion of a nation's best language and music.
5. Schubert wrote more than six hundred art songs.
6. Romantic poets usually cooperated in furnishing texts for art songs.
7. The piano generally furnished the accompaniment for art songs.
8. Lieder melodies expressed all shades of emotion, yet retained a simplicity and directness comparable to folk music.
9. The "great five of the German lied" are: Schubert, Schumann, Hugo Wolf, Johannes Brahms, and Robert Franz.
10. Art songs after 1840 completely reversed the principle upon which the eighteenth-century songs were composed.
11. Robert Schumann was honored for his literary and musical achievements.
12. His music established idioms of piano style in the nineteenth century.
13. Schumann wrote more than one hundred art songs in the year 1840, including the song cycle *Woman's Love and Life*.

Examples of Music

1. Schubert, *Symphony in B Minor* ("Unfinished"). Angel (35524).
2. Schubert, *Gretchen at the Spinning Wheel*. London (5258).
3. Schubert, *Die Forelle* ("The Trout"). RCA Victor (LM 2003).
4. Schubert, *Quintet in A Major for Piano and Strings*. Westminster (XWN 18264).
5. Schubert, *Ave Maria*. RCA Victor (LM 1800).
6. Schumann, *Woman's Love and Life*, Op. 42. RCA Victor (Red Seal LCT 1126).

14 ～ The Short Piano Piece

Nineteenth-century Romanticism sought and found an attractive way of escaping from the formal eighteenth-century sonata and symphony. This was by way of the short lyrical forms—the art song and the short piano piece. These came to occupy a central place in the first phase of the Romantic movement when there was a strong desire for individual lyrical expression. The Romantic interest in tone color led to rapid development in the size and importance of the orchestra, but the desire for individual expression focused attention on the piano and the short piano piece.

The Piano

The short piano piece was the instrumental equivalent of the art song and was chiefly responsible for the piano's growing popularity in the early nineteenth century. Its literature far surpassed in interest and variety that written for any other instrument. The piano itself was developed from a notable group of ancestors given the general name of clavier instruments.

The keyboard or clavier instrument dates back about six hundred years, when it had too many limitations to be taken seriously. The *clavichord* seems to be the first really functional ancestor of the piano. It was developed in Germany about 1533, with a key mechanism which used small metal hammers to strike the strings. The clavichord resembled a writing desk in appearance and had at most twenty keys. Its limitations were that it had a small range, a lack of volume, no dynamic variation, and no way of sustaining a tone.

The *harpsichord* was invented in the fifteenth century but was developed as a solo instrument in Italy about 1680. In appearance, this instrument looked like a grand piano and was played by means of a key mechanism which plucked the strings with quills or small leather picks. The harpsichord extended over four or five octaves and had two or three strings sounding each tone. It was a much improved instrument, but still lacked dynamic qualities of tone (Fig. 14–1).

Another small instrument called a *virginal* was widely used on the Continent and in England during Elizabethan times. This was a miniature harpsichord with a small, thin sound. In their day the limitations of these instruments were not particularly a handicap since they were used mostly for chamber music (Fig. 14–2).

In 1710, an Italian named Bartolomeo Cristofori, one of the best harpsichord makers in Europe, invented an instrument with a key mechanism which struck the strings by means of a felt-covered hammer. Pedals were also used to damp the strings and to regulate the action of the hammers. This instrument was a great improvement over others of its time because it could be played softly or loudly; for this characteristic, Cristofori named it *pianoforte,* which literally means soft-loud. Within the next few years, instrument makers in both France and Germany laid claim to similar inventions, but their instruments were inferior to the Italian model. Cristofori's principle is the one which has been in use since that time.

There was immense interest in the piano and it developed rapidly. By the close of the American Revolutionary War, a very large number of excellent instruments had been brought to America. The piano of that time, however, was a fragile instrument under great stress of string tension and was not particularly suited to the pioneer conditions of America. An important American contribution to the improvement of the piano was the development and successful application of an iron frame, which increased its sturdiness and added greatly to its life and dependability. This was the type of instrument Americans took to pioneer communities and moved across the continent by covered wagon.

We have already noted the Romanticist's interest in the tone color and the technical possibilities of musical instruments. This probably explains the intense effort to perfect the piano. This effort brought about close cooperation between the performing artist, the composer, and the craftsman who built the instrument. The result was a highly satisfactory instrument available to a large number of nineteenth-century people who were anxious to develop some skill upon it. In this way the piano became the instrument of the common man. The harpsichord remained the instrument of the kings, but

Musical Instruments *by A. J. Hipkins:*
A & C Black, Ltd., London

Fig. 14–1.   The Empress Harpsichord

*The time this instrument was built for Empress Maria Theresa in 1773, the harpsi-
chord was generally being replaced by the pianoforte. The Empress Harpsichord is of
the largest size, 8 feet 10 inches in length and 3 feet 4 inches in width at the keyboards. It is the culmination of an instrument that had remained in use for nearly
three hundred years. There are four registers and six stops included on this instrument which was one of the first to use the Venetian Swell pedal invented for the
harpsichord and patented by Burkat Shudi in 1769. The Venetian Swell uses the
principle of the Venetian blind to control the volume of sound coming from the
instrument. It was later transferred to the organ, where it is still widely used. Special
effects which could be achieved by stops were: (1) "lute," where the jacks or plectra
strike only the first of the unison strings; these are struck near the bridge for a more
reedy sound; (2) "octave," where the plectra act upon strings tuned an octave higher;
(3) "buff"—sometimes called "harp"—where the second unison strings are partly muted
by contact with small pads of leather. The machine stop permits an agreeable combination of lute and buff by using the left pedal and both keyboards. Handel and
Scarlatti are among the composers who have best understood the resources of the
harpsichord.*

128

Musical Instruments *by A. J. Hipkins:*
A & C Black, Ltd., London

Fig. 14–2. Queen Elizabeth's Virginal

An indistinct number on the case of Queen Elizabeth's Virginal indicates that it was built in 1570, but the Royal Arms of Elizabeth were emblazoned upon it and it was refinished in 1660. It is of very elaborate construction, inlaid with silver, ivory, and different woods; the entire case is 5 feet long, 16 inches wide, and 7 inches deep. These instruments were easily transported; and, in Italy, virginals were commonly taken in gondolas, played for pleasure, and used for the performance of serenades. The virginal was of the harpsichord family and was so closely allied that no clear distinction was made between harpsichord and virginal until after the sixteenth century. The name implies that it was an instrument favored by young ladies.

the piano reigned supreme in the concert hall and in the homes of middle-class families. It became especially popular as an instrument of the home after the "upright" model was developed in the 1850's.

There were five notable improvements added to Cristofori's piano which resulted in the instrument we have today:

1. The range increased from 2½ to 7⅓ octaves (its present range).
2. The new iron frame and reinforced sounding board increased its resonant tone and made it more dependable.

3. More intensity and volume was brought about by using heavier strings wound with wire.
4. The addition of a sustaining foot pedal (patented by Broadwood, 1783) gave it power to play melody with warmth and expressiveness.
5. An improved key action, called the "double escape type" (patented by Sebastian Arard in 1820), provided for almost unlimited technical facility.

In addition to the piano works of Beethoven, Schubert, Saint-Saëns and other great composers during the first half of the nineteenth century, a vast amount of inferior piano music had been composed and published. The major goal of piano literature of the day was to display virtuosity. It stressed a remarkable degree of technical brilliance but little else. Schumann, Chopin, and Liszt are the three musicians who were most important in saving piano composition from the shallowness into which it had fallen. When Henri Herz (1803–1888), one of the most popular composers of his day, presented his Second Piano Concerto, Opus 74, Schumann commented, "One can write about this music in three different ways: (1) sadly, (2) humorously, and (3) ironically; or possibly use all three at once. I hesitate to make these remarks about Mr. Herz, and must keep him at least ten paces away from me so as not to have to praise him too greatly to his face." This observation of Schumann's gives us something of an insight into the musical trends of the day. The influence of Romanticism set the stage for the virtuoso musician. Although this led at times to technical rather than artistic music, it also established inspirational goals of achievement which exerted a strong influence upon nineteenth-century music.

Niccolò Paganini

The musician who created a new ideal of virtuosity in the early nineteenth century was not a pianist, but a violinist, Niccolò Paganini. Born in 1782, Paganini belonged to an older generation, but he impressed the Romantics with his virtuosity and with his Romantic personality. His youth was shrouded in obscurity until 1805, when for three years he lived in the courtly household of a sister of Napoleon in the small Italian town of Lucca. After a series of concerts in 1813, his fame spread to all Italy. In 1828, he made a highly successful concert trip to Vienna, and in 1831–1832 his concerts in Paris and London aroused such enthusiasm that it was said his phenomenal playing bordered on sorcery. The musicians as well as the crowds of people who came to hear him were fascinated by his technical genius and also by the remarkably expressive power of his playing.

Paganini's effect upon Romantic music is all the more remarkable since his career lasted only a few years. In 1834 he retired to a villa near Parma in his native Italy; thereafter he played in public only on rare occasions, and then usually for charity. Paganini died in the solitude of his villa in 1840. The pianists of the day were even more interested in Paganini than were the violinists. The violinists could not imitate him nor could they add anything to the technical achievements which he demonstrated. An excellent example is his set of variations for violin and orchestra, *Le Streghe* (*The Witches*), 1813. The masters of the piano, however, could and did attempt to transfer these achievements to their instruments and to conquer the differences of technique between the two instruments.

Schumann, Chopin, Liszt, and even Brahms made highly successful transcriptions of Paganini's compositions. Schumann wished, in his own compositions, to combine certain academic qualities with the freedom of Paganini's expressive style. He was quite successful in achieving this ideal, as is demonstrated in works such as *Bunte Blätter,* Opus 99, and the *Waldszenen,* Opus 82.

Schumann and Liszt

Schumann introduced the first piano masterworks in the true Romantic style. His Piano Concerto in A Minor is one of the finest piano concertos since those of Beethoven. In typical fashion, he often gave pictorial titles to many of his compositions although most of the names were affixed after the compositions had been written.

Liszt took a different position with regard to virtuosity. He severely criticized the musicians of his day, such as Sigismund Thalberg, who seemed to do little more than display technical skill. In order for his criticism to be meaningful, Liszt outdid his contemporaries in virtuosity while adding artistic qualities as well. Like Paganini with his violin, Liszt drew from the piano possibilities of sound that no one had ever before achieved. He developed a variety of technical features which class him as a Romantic innovator, but his art also consisted of new techniques, especially in harmony and repetition of his motifs.

Chopin and Brahms

Frédéric Chopin (1810–1849) was born and educated in Warsaw, Poland. He left his native land at the age of twenty and spent most of the rest of his short but creative life in Paris. He composed almost exclusively for piano and was most successful in the shorter forms, such as étude, nocturne, impromptu, mazurka, and polonaise. He exploited the melodic and harmonic possibilities of the piano to a greater degree than any other composer had done. He concentrated on melody, which he decorated with delicate embellishments and graceful harmonies. He used new dissonances which often prolonged the harmonic tension, and he increased the number of tones which could be sounded in a chord by skillful use of the sustaining pedal. He was also responsible for the development of new types of left-hand figuration (rhythm patterns). Chopin's music is often associated with Polish nationalism because of his fondness for the Polish folk melodies and national dances, the polonaise and the mazurka. Today his best known piano works are his twenty-four preludes and impromptus and a large number of waltzes and ballads. These continue to hold the interest of present-day pianists and their audiences. Chopin's first impromptu (A-flat Major, Opus 29), composed in 1838, is an excellent example of the winged lightness he achieves in much of his writing. This kind of intimate composition which represents a mood rather than a general idea is known as a *character piece.*

The short piano compositions of Johannes Brahms (1833–1897) are in a direct line of descent from the lieder of Schubert and Schumann. He handled the form with ease and craftsmanship and recaptured for the piano piece something of the quality it had achieved during the first part of the century. His Waltz in A-flat is an excellent example of the charm of his writing.

Summary

1. Romanticism escaped from its Classical heritage by way of the *art song* and *short piano piece.*

2. Romantic interest in tone color and virtuosity led to rapid development of the piano and orchestra.
3. Keyboard instruments, as we know them, were called clavier instruments.
4. The first such instrument to be really functional was the clavichord, which was developed in Germany in 1533.
5. The harpsichord was an improved instrument developed in Italy about 1680.
6. The pianoforte was also developed in Italy by Cristofori in 1710.
7. Pianos arrived in America following the American Revolution. An American improvement was the development of an iron frame.
8. Both piano and orchestra developed rapidly in the nineteenth century.
9. Improved mechanism of the piano provided for unlimited technical facility by the virtuoso. Technical virtuosity was developed rapidly during the years 1830–1850.
10. Names most often associated with the short piano piece are Schubert, Schumann, Chopin, Liszt, Brahms, Saint-Saëns, Mendelssohn.

Examples of Music

1. *2000 Years of Music: Harpsichord and Clavichord.* Folkways (FT 3700).
2. Mendelssohn, "Spring Song," from *Songs Without Words.* RCA Victor (LM 6128).
3. Chopin, *First Impromptu in A♭,* Op. 29, from *Piano Music.* Vox (BVX 402).
4. Saint-Saëns, "The Swan," from *Carnival of the Animals.* Capitol (G 7211).
5. Beethoven, *Minuet in G.* Capitol (PAO 8422).
6. Liszt, *Six Paganini Etudes.* Westminster (XWN 1807).
7. Beethoven, *Variations on a Theme by Diabelli,* Op. 120. Columbia (Masterworks ML 5246).

15 ∿ The Concerto

In the modern sense, the word *concerto* indicates a composition for solo instrument and symphony orchestra that affords the soloist ample opportunity to display his virtuosity. The word was used in older musical writings to describe a performance in which musicians joined forces in a united or concerted effort.

The form of the eighteenth-century concerto was established largely by three composers of the Italian School: Arcangelo Corelli (1653–1713), Giuseppe Tartini (1692–1770), and Antonio Vivaldi (1676–1741). In this form there was not one soloist, but a group of soloists. They might play any combination of instruments, either singly or together, as a contrasting element to the orchestra as a whole. This small group of soloists was called the *concertino;* the remainder of the orchestral players were called the *ripieno;* together, they were known as the *concerto grosso.* The form of the music they played came to be known also as the *concerto grosso,* and as such flourished throughout the eighteenth century. It depended for its effect on the interplay and contrast of the two groups: the concertino and the ripieno.

An excellent example of this musical form is the Concerto Grosso in D, Opus 6, by Corelli. A master composer and violinist, Corelli crystallized the form and delivered it to posterity. In this composition the concertino consists of two violins, cello, and harpsichord. These instruments furnish an interesting contrast to the orchestra and later add greatly to the rich tone color when the two forces are joined together.

With the rise of the sonata form in the period of Haydn and Mozart, the concerto grosso gradually receded in popularity and was supplanted by the solo concerto, where the concertino part was taken by a single instrument. This form naturally focused attention on the solo instrument and its interplay with the orchestra. This interplay was heightened as a dramatic element when, instead of two groups balanced against each other, a single instrument carried the action against the background of the orchestra, just as in Greek tragedy the single character is pitted against the chorus. One might say that the solo concerto drew inspiration not only from the concerto grosso traditions but also from the opera, in which the solo singer alternated with the interludes of the orchestra. In the late eighteenth and early nineteenth centuries, these influences combined with the new virtuosity of the solo instruments to produce a flexible, varied, and highly imaginative form. The emergence of the concerto was closely coordinated with technical improvements in the solo instruments themselves, and in the technical mastery of those instruments.

Mozart played a decisive role in the rise of the solo concerto during the Classical period, developing it as an effective dialogue between soloist and orchestra. He left the form basically as we know it today: the basic sonata form (fast–slow–fast) with a brilliant *cadenza*—usually in the first movement and sometimes in the last— while the orchestra maintains silence to focus attention on the soloist. A *cadenza* is a short, tcehnical passage performed without accompaniment, designed to show the virtuosity of the performer. In the days of Mozart and Beethoven, when the artist was often also the composer, the cadenza was a free improvisation upon the themes of the movement; but as the art of improvisation waned, the cadenza was written out by the composer or by another soloist who had a flair for improvisation. Mozart wrote between forty and fifty concerti for various instruments; these became the foundation upon which later composers constructed their works. In the piano and violin concerti of his mature period, we find revealed his mastery of the style of each instrument and his sensitivity to the possibilities of each.

In most nineteenth-century concerti, especially those written under Romantic influence, one can find evidence of highly personalized expression. This Romantic type of music makes frequent use of national characteristics of melody, rhythm, and instrumental color. Often there is an adaptation of actual folk tunes and native peculiarities, even in the use of indigenous harmony and sound effects.

Few musical works have enjoyed such world-wide popularity and consistent favor as Mendelssohn's Concerto in E Minor, Op. 64, for violin and orchestra. This work is an excellent example of composition in the virtuoso style, yet it retains carefully considered content, form, and balanced structure. It is truly Romantic in its use of extended, lyrical melodies, its use of several contrasting themes in each movement, its connection of movements without a pause, and its warmth of feeling.

We should emphasize the short melodies that provide the basic material of the large forms. It is by their melodies that one comes to know them. When one can recognize one or two melodies or themes from each movement, one is in possession of the points of contact which create familiarity. The melodies are the characters in these dramas of absolute music: their development and treatment constitute the plot, conflict, and suspense.

In the Mendelssohn violin concerto, the first movement, "allegro molto appassionato" (very fast and impassioned), omits the customary orchestral introduction and the solo violin immediately announces the first theme in a very high register. The second is a lyrical theme of narrow range characterized by stepwise movement. The development section reaches true symphonic proportions and culminates in the cadenza which, instead of coming at the end of the movement as is customary, serves as a link between the second and third sections (development and recapitulation). The final theme is marked andante and follows without a break. (See Fig. 15–1.)

Mendelssohn created a remarkable fusion between Classical and Romantic concepts: his Classical forms are easy to follow and his

Fig. 15–1.   Themes from the First Movement of the
Violin Concerto in E Minor, Mendelssohn

Romantic melodies are beautiful and interesting. An excellent analysis of the Violin Concerto in E Minor may be found in the recording listed at the end of the chapter.

During the last half of the nineteenth century, the musical world was searching for composers who would give them a type of piano music suitable for use in the thousands of homes which were by that time equipped with upright pianos. Few musicians of the day were able to cope with the virtuoso music of Chopin and Liszt and more often than not they had to be satisfied with a superficial type of salon music. The large number of lyrical pieces composed by Edvard Hagerup Grieg (1843–1907) did much to meet the needs of the amateur pianist. His compositions were meant to be Norwegian music and they were written at a time when nationalism was at its height. But they have, in fact, become international in their acceptance. To the international music world, Grieg has come to represent the voice of Norway. The nationalistic movement of which his music was an expression had a political background. For some time there had been agitation for independence from Sweden, and much to his satisfaction he saw this become a reality in his lifetime.

Until the time of Grieg, Scandinavia's "serious" music remained under the influence of the German. Her composers studied at Leipzig or Weimar and came home to continue the traditions of Mendelssohn, Schumann, Wagner, and Liszt. Grieg's first attempts at composition, after studying several years at the Leipzig Conservatory, clearly followed the familiar pattern, but after he returned to Norway he found his personal idiom, which was both Norwegian and international.

Copenhagen was the home of his cousin, Nina Hagerup. It was to her that he wrote his most famous song, "I Love Thee" (Ich liebe dich), using the verses of Hans Christian Andersen. Grieg and Nina were in their early twenties when they were married; and for more than forty years, they were constant companions in a happy marriage. He traveled to Italy at the age of twenty-five, shortly after having completed his masterpiece, the Piano Concerto in A Minor. While in Italy, he made the acquaintance of Franz Liszt, who read his manuscript at sight and encouraged him to "keep steadily on and don't let anyone scare you." At thirty-one, Grieg was granted a life annuity from the Norwegian government, which made it possible for him to devote all of his time to composing.

Grieg was one of a rather large number of artists who started their career with a composition they could never again quite equal. The Piano Concerto in A Minor was such a composition. The piano part is idiomatic throughout with a style that combines the brilliance of Liszt with the romantic lyricism of Schumann. It is in turn dramatic and pastoral. However, the most important characteristic of Grieg's music is the refinement he added to his Norwegian musical heritage.

The first movement of the concerto, which is marked "Allegro molto moderato," is in sonata form. It opens with a dramatic roll on the tympani; after descending octaves in the solo part, a melody descriptive of a northern scene enters (Fig. 15–2). An animated

Fig. 15–2.   Theme from Piano Concerto in A Minor, Grieg

bridge passage leads to a contrasting idea which shows the same construction from fragments of the first theme. The development section is brief and intense. The recapitulation is climaxed by an impressive cadenza that presents the main theme embellished in a variety of ways. The middle section is characterized by very delicate work on the piano, after which the first theme is repeated with Romantic intensity. The finale is marked "Poco animato" (somewhat animated). This movement uses song-like and dance-like themes which give it a vigorous, rhythmic, folk-dance character, ending in the usual triumphal Romantic close.

Grieg's incidental music for Henrik Ibsen's play *Peer Gynt* did more than any of his other compositions to spread his name and musical reputation throughout the world. He arranged this music in two concert suites, each containing four numbers. Although both suites were well received and have continued to be important examples of Grieg's creative work, the first remains the best known and most popular of the two. It opens with "Morning," a serene impression of day dawning over a Norwegian forest. The second section, "Ase's Death," is a dirge for the mother in the play. Then follows "Anitra's Dance," performed by an exotic beauty whom Peer meets during his travels. The final number, "In the Hall of the Mountain King," depicts Peer, lost in the mountains, surrounded by mischievous trolls and elves who perform their grotesque dances. The music is not incidental in the true sense of the term since it enters into the action of the play, but it seems to illustrate perfectly the story Ibsen wished to tell.

The final years of Grieg's life were spent at his villa Troldhaugen (Hill of the Trolls), overlooking the fiords and his native town of Bergen. All over Europe he was much in demand as a conductor and pianist; he received several offers to visit the United States but declined because of poor health. His death at the age of sixty-four was mourned throughout the world. He has often been overshadowed by great musicians of the nineteenth century, but his music continues to radiate warmth and charm.

Summary

1. A modern concerto is an extended composition for solo instrument and orchestra, each bearing an equal part of the musical responsibility.
2. The term was originally used to mean a piece of music in which all the musicians joined in a concerted effort.
3. Corelli, Tartini, and Vivaldi, of the eighteenth-century Italian School, crystallized the form of the concerto grosso.
4. The musical forces of the concerto grosso are the concertino and ripieno.
5. Mozart crystallized the form of the solo concerto, usually three movements (fast–slow–fast, based upon the sonata form); a cadenza is featured in the first movement and sometimes in the last movement.
6. The Romantic concerto was fused with nationalism.
7. Mendelssohn's Violin Concerto has enjoyed consistent world-wide favor.
8. Characteristics of the Romantic concerto are: three movements without a break; maximum use of melody and virtuosity; frequent emphasis on national characteristics.
9. The melodies in a concerto are treated as characters in a drama. Their relationship and destiny are worked out in the development of the music.

10. Edvard Grieg did much to fill the need for a type of piano music suitable for amateurs to play.
11. Grieg's music was both Norwegian and international.
12. While traveling in Italy, he made the acquaintance of Franz Liszt, who read the manuscript of his Piano Concerto and encouraged him as a composer.
13. Grieg's Piano Concerto is one of those most often performed by young musicians of today.
14. Peer Gynt is his composition best known throughout the world.

Examples of Music

1. Corelli, *Concerto Grosso in D,* Op. 6. Angel (35253).
2. Mendelssohn, *Concerto in E Minor for Violin,* Op. 64. Book of the Month Club, Music Appreciation Record (XTV 21789).
3. Grieg, *Piano Concerto in A Minor,* Op. 16. Angel (35561).
4. Schumann, *Piano Concerto in A Minor,* Op. 54. Angel (35561).
5. Strauss, *Two Horn Concertos in E♭* (dated 1883 and 1941). Angel (35496).

16 ∿ Italian Opera

An opera is a drama set to music. It combines the resources of vocal and instrumental music, soloists, chorus, poetry, dramatic action, pantomime, dance, scenery, and costume. To weld these diverse elements into a unity is a problem that has exercised some of the best minds in the history of music.

The word *opus* means composition. When applied to a musical composition, it is followed by a number which shows the place of this composition in a series of works by one composer. The plural of *opus* is *opera,* and therefore refers to a series of musical compositions, such as *overture, chorus, recitative,* and *aria.*

The general concept of opera dates back to the stadium pageantry of the Greeks and Romans; but opera as we know it today started just before the year 1600 with a group of Florentine noblemen known as the Camerata. This group, conforming to a concept of Greek drama, evolved a musical style which consisted of vocal declamation with careful attention to the natural rhythm, accent, and inflection of the text. This sort of intensified speech was carried out over a simple, instrumental, harmonic background. This concept was revolutionary at that time, and it had a strong influence on the course of music; but, after the novelty had worn off, the limitations of melodies bound so closely to natural speech were apparent. The main advantages of this style were that the text could be clearly understood and the action could proceed almost as fast as in spoken drama. Later attempts to increase the musical value with more appealing melodies and more expressive harmonies sacrificed something of these advantages. Arias, ballets, choruses, and instrumental interludes contributed to the musical interest of the performance, but only at the expense of the dramatic action.

We like to think that since opera combines the arts of music, drama, and dancing it is the most attractive form of stage entertainment; but this has not proved to be true. Each of the arts sacrifices something when combined with the others. Music tied to a text and the human voice lacks the freedom of absolute instrumental music. The orchestra in the pit supporting the singers on the stage lacks the eloquence of the symphony orchestra on the stage. The slow pace of singing compared to speaking causes the drama to suffer, as does the difficulty of understanding the words in song. Dancing in opera usually adds color and variety, but also slows down the action.

Opera, then, to be properly enjoyed must be accepted as a medium of entertainment separate and apart from its components; enjoyment is contingent upon accepting it as an art form in itself. It is not natural to sing a song when under great emotional stress or to use one's last dying breath to sing an extremely high note. The interested person, then, must be ready to accept the traditional conventions of opera.

The successful opera has remarkable qualities, its emotional conflicts are linked to universal types and are projected through the contrasting voices of soprano, contralto, tenor, baritone, and bass. In the traditional style of eighteenth- and nineteenth-century opera, the soprano is the heroine; the contralto, a relative or servant; the tenor will probably be the hero; the baritone, his good friend; and the bass must be the villain.

An important component of opera is the formal style. The pomp and splendor of its great scenes are survivals of a time when opera was the chief diversion of princely courts. To this studied majesty of movement and gesture has been added the supercharged atmosphere of poetic drama. The emotions are tense; everything is presented as either black or white, larger than lifesize. The drama will present a clash of ideas, but will concentrate on sentiments and passions. All of the resources of art are at the disposal of the opera composer and his challenge is to make the most of them.

Nineteenth-century opera experienced its major development in Italy, France, and Germany, and illustrations can best be drawn from these national schools. The rest of this chapter will be devoted to the most important, Italian opera.

Italy was less affected by the spirit of Romanticism than either France or Germany. Her Classical heritage weakened the impact of the movement and allowed her to maintain the continuity of her strong operatic tradition. The style of singing developed in early

Italian opera was called *bel canto,* which means "beautiful singing." Consequently, Italian opera of the nineteenth century primarily depends for its appeal on the power and beauty of the human voice. This preoccupation led, on the one hand, to exhibition pieces demanding the most difficult technique on the part of the singer; very often having little or nothing to do with the mood of the drama. On the other hand, it led to a style of flowing, sensuous vocal melody that is the glory of the Italian school. During the eighteenth century, drama had been so subordinated to singing that the plot of the Classical opera was little more than a framework for brillliant arias and ensemble numbers. This type of "prima donna opera" was the extreme of the bel canto style—little more than a vocal concert in costume. However, early in the nineteenth century, Italian opera, both *seria* (serious) and *buffa* (comic), returned to the dramatic principles upon which opera was founded. This change was largely brought about by three Italian masters of vocal melody: Gioacchino Rossini (1792–1868), Vicenzo Bellini (1801–1835), and Gaetano Donizetti (1797–1848). These are the earliest composers of Italian opera whose works are still regularly performed. Their style was immediately successful and so international in scope that Rossini's *The Barber of Seville* (1816) was produced in New York less than two years after its first performance in Rome. The libretto of this opera is based upon the first of a series of three comedies by the eighteenth-century French playwright, Beaumarchais (boh-mahr-shay'). The second play formed the basis of Mozart's *The Marriage of Figaro* (1786) and several characters in this opera also appear thirty years later in Rossini's work. The style of *The Barber of Seville* provides a welcome contrast to the gloom and despair which was common in the stories of most operas of the time. *The Barber's* Rosina is a new kind of heroine who is a gay, quick-witted little charmer that knows exactly what she wants. She gives a self-portrait in the aria "A Little Voice I Hear," in which she says that she is obedient, docile, and easy to get along with when she gets her own way; but let someone cross her way and she will turn into a viper. Lily Pons sings this aria beautifully, but Rossini's preoccupation with bel canto makes the words hard to understand and greatly slows the pace of the drama. The soprano voice is used in the same manner as the flute.

Vicenzo Bellini (1801–1835) proved himself to be a master of melody comparable to Rossini; his best known work is the opera *Norma* (1831). The Druids, about whom the story of Norma revolves, were members of a religious order which wielded great influence among the ancient tribes of Gaul, Britain, and Ireland. They were regarded as having the gift of prophecy, and all civil and military affairs required their sanction. The high priestess Norma betrayed her vows, married a Roman proconsul, Pollione, and bore him two children. At the time the story begins, Pollione has grown tired of Norma and has fallen in love with a temple maiden. The tragic ending of the opera shows Pollione and Norma ready to cast themselves into a sacrificial fire in atonement for their broken vows.

Bellini shows no capacity for humor, nor is he much better fitted to cope with the somber or heroic; but he was endowed with a gift for writing beautiful melodies with qualities of tenderness and emotion. The other member of this Italian operatic trio was Gaetano Donizetti (1797–1848), who wrote more than sixty operas during a period of twenty-six years. Among many great operas we should probably call *Lucia di Lammermoor* (1835) his masterwork. The *libretto* (script or story) of this opera is drawn from Sir Walter Scott's novel, *The Bride of Lammermoor*. Donizetti, working with a librettist, did a masterful job of compressing Scott's sprawling tale, with its many characters and wealth of local color, into suitable operatic material. Donizetti came honestly by his predilection for Scotland: his grandfather is said to have been a Scotsman by the name of Donald Izett. After moving to Italy and making a fortune there, he adopted the name of Donizetti.

In our discussion of the concerto and the symphony, we identified several themes in each movement which made up the material of composition. Each of these themes has a character which allows for the development of contrasts and unity in the music. We noted that the use of such themes was a characteristic of orchestral music in the Romantic period. This concept is also found in the operatic development of this period. A specialized example of this tendency —using several themes simultaneously—may be found in the second act of *Lucia di Lammermoor*. A sextet from scene two not only presents six separate themes, but gives each a different and an intensely dramatic character. They represent two men who are mortal enemies, the jilted lover and the villainous suitor; the domineering brother; the unfortunate heroine; her friend who is unable to help her; and her tutor. This also illustrates the rising nineteenth-century popularity of polyphony (the combining of several individual but harmonized melodies), which had been the dominant style about 1600.

There is an interesting anecdote which tells of both Rossini and Donizetti's attending a social affair given by a society matron. In the afternoon she gave each musician a paper and pencil and asked them to compose something on the spur of the moment. She was delighted when Rossini's and Donizetti's work proved to be almost identical. She announced it as a work of genius, to which Rossini replied, "Yes, Madam, it is a work of genius, but not as you think; we have both written down a delightful melody from Bellini's opera *Norma.*"

In the second half of the nineteenth century, the Italian operatic tradition was upheld primarily by one man. Giuseppe Verdi (1813–1901), in a long creative period that extended over more than fifty years, remained faithful to the bel canto tradition and kept the singer always in the dominant position, never allowing him to be submerged in orchestration. An outstanding characteristic of most Italian operas of the ninetenth century, and of Verdi's operas in particular, is the treatment of the characters in the drama. We feel they are real people, experiencing understandable emotions in the situations of the plot. Never does a person in these works become merely a symbol, as was so often the case in eighteenth-century operatic writing. In this way the Verdi opera traditions developed in a very different pattern from the musical drama of Richard Wagner. Although Verdi continued to use the recitative and the aria, he added to the orchestral accompaniment a lyrical quality in the recitative, which was joined to the aria without a break. An illustration of this can be found in Act II of his opera *Il Trovatore*. The music from this scene expresses the passion of Count di Luna for the beautiful Leonora. In "Per me ora fatale," he tells of his determination to invade the convent in which she has taken refuge and, if necessary, to take her away by force. In typical Verdi style, you can hear in the background the bells representing the convent.

Verdi aligned himself politically with the nationalists, who were working for a united Italian kingdom. For a time, he played an active part in politics; he was elected to the first National Parliament in 1860, but resigned five years later to devote himself to music. When

Aïda was produced in 1871, Verdi was fifty-eight years old and had been Italy's outstanding composer for over thirty years. An excellent example of the spirit of nationalism may be found in the stirring chorus from Act II of *Il Trovatore,* the "Gypsy's Anvil Chorus."

Several times we have mentioned the elements of nationalism that have been noticeable in late nineteenth-century music. Another influence on music became evident as the highly patriotic spirit of nationalism began to wane. This was *exoticism,* and referred to the power of music to transport the listener to another part of the world. Exoticism is prominent in several of the operas written by the last of the great Italian bel canto opera composers, Giacomo Puccini (1858–1924).

Puccini was extremely skillful in taking a tragic plot and combining it with music of the bel canto style within the framework of light opera and arriving at a sincere, down-to-earth result. By adding a touch of exoticism to his genius for melody, he was able to keep the bel canto tradition alive and healthy well into the twentieth century. The locations of his major operas are in distant parts of the world, such as Paris (*La Bohème*), Japan (*Madame Butterfly*), Peking (*Turandot*), and California in 1849 (*The Girl of the Golden West,* with Dick Johnson as the hero).

Puccini once said of himself: "The finger of God pointed at me and said write music for the theater; mind you, only for the theater; and I have obeyed his supreme command."

In the latter part of the nineteenth century, Italian opera achieved a better balance between the voice and the instruments of the orchestra; however, the orchestra still served as an accompaniment, not as an equal partner. Eighteenth-century opera, wherever found, was dominated by the Italian style, but in the nineteenth century, France and Germany each developed and maintained its own style of musical drama. These should be considered separately in their now national atmospheres.

Summary

1. An opera is a drama which is set to music.
2. Opera is the plural of the word *opus.*

3. The Camerata, which laid the foundation for modern opera, was a group of sixteenth-century noblemen in Florence.
4. In opera, each of the arts sacrifices something when combined with the others.
5. Enjoyment of opera is contingent upon accepting its traditions.
6. Opera experienced its major development in Italy, France, and Germany.
7. Italy was less affected by Romanticism than were France and Germany. The bel canto style of opera was developed in Italy.
8. Men associated with nineteenth-century opera were Rossini, Bellini, Donizetti, Verdi, and Puccini.
9. Nationalism was apparent in late nineteenth-century opera in that the characters became increasingly more lifelike.
10. Verdi added a lyrical quality to the recitative, and joined it to the aria without a break.
11. Puccini left the fanciful and imaginative and turned to everyday life for his subjects, but used exoticism to stimulate the imagination.
12. Puccini was extremely skillful at interrelating two seemingly contradictory elements of music. He could take a tragic plot and combine it within the framework of light opera and arrive at a sincere, down-to-earth result.

Examples of Music

1. Verdi, "Per me ora fatale." RCA Victor (Red Seal LM 1932).
2. Verdi, "Anvil Chorus." RCA Victor (LM 1827). (The "Anvil Chorus" is a good example of Verdi's strong nationalistic feelings.)
3. Gioacchino Rossini, "A Little Voice I Hear," *The Barber of Seville.* Columbia (ML 5073).
4. Giacomo Puccini, *Madame Butterfly.* Angel (2XBA 148).
5. Gaetano Donizetti, *Lucia di Lammermoor.* RCA Victor (LM 6055). (Donizetti wrote more than sixty operas during a period of twenty-six years; *Lucia di Lammermoor* is unquestionably his masterwork.)

17 ∾ Opera in France and Germany

Eighteenth-century opera was dominated by the Italian style, but in the nineteenth century, France and Germany each developed and maintained its own style of music drama.

Grand Opera

The name *grand opera* had been used sparingly in France during the eighteenth century. With the production of Auber's opera, *The Dumb Girl of Portici,* in 1828, a new style was created, French grand opera. This style concerned itself with subjects drawn from history; it portrayed violent action, extreme emotion, and sharp contrasts of mood. It was longer than earlier opera and was filled with much detail. Elaborate ballets, crowd scenes, colorful complex orchestration, a great variety of vocal styles and effects contributed to the novelty of this new type. The total result well deserves the name "grand opera."

The most dazzling of grand opera composers was Giacomo Meyerbeer (1791–1864), whose *Robert the Devil,* produced in 1831, created a sensation. Born and educated in Germany, he moved to Italy and mastered the Italian style of opera with moderate success. He then moved to Paris and was influential in establishing the new and exciting grand opera. Five acts were standard and the ballet, which had formerly appeared near the end of an act or between acts, now took a prominent place within the act. The main arias were carefully distributed among the leading singers, and under no circumstances was a minor character given a part that could possibly outshine the opera star. Most grand operas catered to public taste rather than to artistic judgment, so when musical tastes and styles changed, grand opera passed from favor somewhat in the manner of current American popular songs.

Meyerbeer's masterful use of the aria in grand opera is well illustrated by the "Shadow Song" from his opera *Dinorah,* where equal demands are made on the soprano voice and the flute. His watchword was success at any cost, and his method was to achieve it by cunningly devised sensations rather than by the innate power of his music. His works, however, did have a powerful and on the whole a beneficial influence on the course of dramatic music. They placed living human beings on the stage in place of the cold abstractions of mythology; the singer was forced to impersonate as well as to sing. The insistence on all means of expression, whether vocal, instrumental, or scenic, was often exaggerated, but led to an extension of technical ability in all these directions. During his lifetime, Meyerbeer held the French public so completely under his spell that other composers of grand opera gained but little attention. Even the mighty Richard Wagner met a cool reception in Paris.

Comic Opera

Comic opera in France admitted dialogue and spoken passages, which were more expressive than the intoned recitative of grand opera. The comic style was not allowed to be performed at the Paris opera, but comic operas were played in other theaters of France. Light orchestral writing, very different from the massive sounds of Wagner, was also characteristic of French opera. George Bizet's masterpiece, *Carmen,* belongs to this category and recent surveys have shown that the American people rate *Carmen,* along with *Aïda, Il Trovatore,* and *Lucia di Lammermoor,* as the four best-known and best-loved operas. *Carmen,* like many other highly successful *opéras comiques,* was later entirely set to music, thereby gaining the additional prestige and status of a grand opera.

Other successful French composers of grand opera are Charles Gounod (goo-no′) (1818–1893), best remembered for *Faust,* and Camille Saint-Saëns (san-sahng′) (1835–1921), noted for *Samson and Delilah.* The characteristic conservatism of the French school resulted in retaining well into the nineteenth century the style which had been fixed for generations; only gradually was the nineteenth-century Romantic spirit allowed to make itself felt. Set forms were closely joined with a melodious declamation which resembles the song-speech of Wagner's music drama. "The Soldiers' Chorus," from the third act of Gounod's *Faust,* is a good example of the French style of writing at this time.

German Opera

Carl Maria von Weber (fon vay'-ber) (1786–1826) is usually thought of as the "father" of German opera. He was very responsive to the musical tastes of his time and played an important part in the unfolding of musical Romanticism in Germany. His songs of war and fatherland inflamed a nation that was discovering its identity in the face of a war with Napoleon. Weber produced three major operas: *Der Freischütz,* one of the most spectacular successes in operatic history, *Euryanthe,* and *Oberon.* All three sought to reconcile German Romanticism with the bel canto tradition of Italy. They were neither strictly German nor strictly Italian. This probably explains why, despite much fine music in these operas, they have never established themselves very strongly in the international repertory. Despite the bel canto influence in his three operas, he is ranked as one of the great German composers.

Richard Wagner summed up what Weber meant to his compatriots eighteen years after his death when he said: "Never was there a more German composer. In whatever fathomless realms of fantasy genius bore him, he remained bound by a thousand tender links to the heart of the German people, with whom he wept or smiled like a believing child listening to the legends and tales of his country." *

The Music Drama of Richard Wagner

Although only thirteen years old when Weber died, Richard Wagner lost no time in assuming the role Weber had created in Romantic opera. Wagner looms as probably the single most important phenomenon in the artistic life of the later nineteenth century. It is hard to know where to begin or end in discussing Wagner's life and music. Entire books have been written about each of his opera dramas. His music is profound and awe-inspiring, fantastic and forceful. He was a complex musician with a complex personality and one of history's greatest egotists.

* Joseph Machlis, *The Enjoyment of Music* (New York, Norton, 1955), p. 217.

Wagner tried very hard to achieve a balance between the music and the drama of his opera. He often indicated the belief that poetry and music should be one and to this end he called his works *music drama* rather than opera. He wrote his own librettos and usually used mythological characters, thinking that these subjects have the greatest emotional appeal. Wagner began his operatic career by writing conventionally enough, but his mature works differ from Italian and French opera in almost every detail. With his early opera, *Rienzi,* a grand opera in the French style, he had hoped to conquer Paris. Failing that, he moved to Dresden where his work was accepted and produced.

Wagner refined a technique that Weber had used earlier and that Richard Strauss was to make use of a generation later. He wrote his tone poems with literary programs, especially *Don Juan* and *Till Eulenspiegel.* This technique associates a musical motive with a particular character, emotion, or idea. The musical motive is called a *leitmotiv* (Fig. 17–1). As soon as various motives are established, Wagner weaves them in and out of the music at appropriate times to enhance the intrigue of the plot and to provide unity. This use of the *leitmotiv* also enhances the role of the orchestra. With the greater prominence of the orchestra and with the use of leitmotifs, Wagner eliminated the breaks in the forward motion of the drama caused by the traditional recitatives, arias, and choruses.

Wagner's music dramas differ from conventional operas in another important respect. He was more interested in expressing the interaction of universal forces than in musically working out indi-

Fig. 17–1. Leitmotifs from Wagner's Music Drama

vidual human emotional problems. The conflict between divine love and insufficient faith, or the forces of creativity opposing those of human tradition, offered him his greatest musical challenge.

Of the many opera dramas that Wagner produced, his most ambitious is *The Ring of the Nibelung*. It is a *tetralogy*, a set of four music dramas taken from a story in Norse mythology, the search for the magic gold at the bottom of the Rhine River. The names of the four operas are *Das Rheingold, Die Walküre, Siegfried,* and *Die Götterdämmerung.* The English musicologist, Ernest Newman, has compared the Ring to a symphony. *Das Rheingold,* he suggested, resembled the first or expository section; the main motives, both psychological and musical, are set forth to be worked out in detail. The movements are blended, contrasted, and at last brought triumphantly to their logical conclusion. In this scheme, *Die Walküre* is the slow movement by reason of its strong sweeping melodies and qualities of suspense and emotion. *Siegfried* is the scherzo, and *Die Götterdämmerung,* the overwhelming finale.

We have Wagner's own record of his feelings on completion of the first "movement" of the *Ring.* In a letter to Franz Liszt, dated January 15, 1854, he writes:

> Well, *Rheingold* is done; with what faith, what joy I began this music! In a real frenzy of despair I have at last completed it. Alas, how I too was walled in by the need of gold! Believe me, no one has ever composed like this. I fancy my music is fearful—a pit of terrors and grandeurs. *

The story of the *Ring* begins at the bottom of the Rhine River. There, a large deposit of gold is being guarded by three mermaids, known as the Rhine maidens. The crafty Nibelung dwarf, Alberich, steals this precious gold and fashions a ring from it which has magic of boundless power. Meanwhile, the great god, Wotan, has commissioned the brother giants, Fafner and Fasolt, to build a magnificent home for the gods, a palace towering amid the clouds, which will be called Valhalla. As a reward for their work, Wotan has promised to give them Freia, the sister of his wife and the Goddess of Youth and Love. When the giants come to claim their pay, Wotan is unable to make good his promise—his wife won't let him.

* Quoted in Robert Bagar and Louis Biancolli, *The Concert Companion* (New York and London, McGraw-Hill and Whittlesey House, 1947), p. 820.

A quarrel is starting when Loge, the God of Fire, returns to report Alberich's theft of the Rhine gold. The giants gloat over the prospects of magic gold and agree to accept that prize instead of Freia. By trickery, Wotan obtains the ring from Alberich, who in a rage over his loss, lays a curse of fear, suffering, and death over anyone who possesses it. Soon the curse of the ring begins to work: in a struggle for its ownership Fafner strikes his brother dead while the gods look on horrified.

Thoughts are now turned toward Valhalla, the new home of the gods, which is still shrouded in storm clouds. Donner, the Storm-God, mounts a huge rock and begins to swing his hammer. Lightning flashes and thunder roars from his blows but in a short time the cloudburst ends, the sky clears, and a rainbow is seen, arching its brilliant span like a bridge to the portals of Valhalla. The gods begin their march over this rainbow to their new home while from below can be heard the mournful song of the Rhine maidens lamenting the loss of their gold. One can readily see that all is not well in the land of the Nibelungs, and it requires four complete operas to resolve the problems of the gods and their mortal friends.

Wagner did not create a school of music, but his influence was felt in all the schools of Europe and America. He was offered large sums of money to take his work to London and Chicago but he chose to remain in Germany. He was the greatest of the masters of his brand of opera, but there were also those who were very critical of his music drama. The great Russian writer, Leo Tolstoi, attended a performance of *Siegfried,* but apparently was unable to accept the conventions of Wagner's opera; in one of his letters he described his experience in these terms: "Yesterday I was in the theater and heard the famous new opera *Siegfried* by Wagner. I could not sit through the first act to the end but sprang up in the middle of it like a madman, and even yet I cannot speak quietly about it. That is a stupid Punch-and-Judy show, which is much too poor for children over seven years of age; moreover, it is not music. And yet thousands of people sit there and pretend to like it." * Similar judgments were made by others who had grown up in the tradition of Gluck and Mozart.

* Alfred Einstein, *Music in the Romantic Era* (New York, Norton, 1947), p. 254.

Probably the greatest aspect of Wagner's musical genius is found in his remarkable ability to suggest every degree of human moods and feeling. All emotions, including boredom, are expressed at some time in his music. Wagner's chief aim was to create a balance among all of the art forms represented in his music drama. In this, time has proved that he was not entirely successful, since his music far overshadows the dramatic concepts of his work. Others who followed Wagner have attempted to use his methods, but none has achieved comparable success. There were many in Wagner's time who were highly critical of his music dramas, but there is no doubt that he commanded a greater international audience than any musician before him.

Engelbert Humperdinck (1854–1921) was the only one of Wagner's successors to develop a new phase of music drama. This he did in 1893 by applying Wagnerian techniques in a miniature form to a fairy tale in his opera, *Hänsel und Gretel*. This work soon found its way into all the theaters of the world, the first German opera to have such success since the death of Wagner.

Summary

1. Grand opera emerged in France in 1828.
2. Meyerbeer (1791–1864) was the most dazzling composer of French grand opera, a grand spectacle of lavish proportions. The music was composed for public consumption and was therefore transient in nature.
3. French opéra comique developed under Georges Bizet, Charles Gounod, and Camille Saint-Saëns.
4. Carl Maria von Weber (1786–1826) is usually thought of as the founder of Romantic German opera.
5. Weber's three major operas were highly successful in their time, but failed to establish themselves strongly due to the mixture of German and Italian characteristics.
6. Richard Wagner assumed the leadership in Romantic opera through his music dramas.
7. The chief objective of the music drama was to achieve perfect balance between music and libretto.
8. In music drama, a *leitmotiv* was associated with a particular character, objective, or emotion.

9. No other composer has been able to successfully use Wagner's philosophy and practices.
10. *The Ring of the Nibelung* is a tetralogy consisting of four operas: *Das Rheingold, Die Walküre, Siegfried,* and *Die Götterdämmerung.*
11. Wagner commanded a greater international audience than any musician before him.

Examples of Music

1. Meyerbeer, "Ombre Légère" (Shadow Song) (*Dinorah*), from *The Art of Lily Pons.* RCA Camden (CBL 101).
2. Gounod, "Soldiers' Chorus," *Faust.* Capitol (GDR 7154).
3. Wagner, *Das Rheingold.* London (A 4340).
4. Weber, *Oberon: Overture,* and *Euryanthe: Overture.* Angel (35754).
5. Saint-Saëns, *Samson and Delilah.* Angel (3639 C/L).

18 ～ Descriptive Music

After the Napoleonic Wars, a peace conference was held in Vienna, called the Congress of Vienna, in 1814–1815. There are two major reasons for remembering it: (1) it arbitrarily fixed boundary lines of small nations, and (2) it generally interfered in the political and social life of Western Europe, particularly of the less powerful nations.

A natural result of this international tampering was an awakening of national pride, and an awareness of the rich heritage of the folk music, legends, and history that gave people a sense of national importance. In the 1830's, while Franz Liszt was developing the tone poem, with its patriotic overtones, most of the smaller countries were turning to their folk culture in music and literature, both as a means of self-expression and as an expression of the denial of any national inferiority.

There were two reasons why Russia pioneered the nationalist movement: (1) middle-class Russians resented the music of Italy, France, and Germany that had been commonly imported by their rulers, and (2) a series of revolutionary movements was climaxed by the freeing of the serfs in 1861. Nowhere did nationalism acquire the intensity that it did in Russia at that time. When the serfs became free citizens, no longer legally bound to the land, there was a great increase in national pride and out of these years of revolutionary atmosphere emerged Mikhail Glinka and the "Russian Five," whose aim it was to develop a musical consciousness which would not be dependent upon musical traditions of other countries.

Mikhail Glinka and the "Russian Five"

Mikhail Glinka (1804–1857) wrote his opera *A Life for the Czar* in 1836. This was probably the first major musical work that was highly nationalistic. Glinka was followed by another generation of composers, a group usually known as the "Russian Five." A leading member of this group was Alexander Borodin (1833–1887), a chemist, who wrote the opera *Prince Igor* which is not so much a drama as it is a series of scenes or tableaus. In Act Two there appears a section called "Polovtzian Dances" (poh-loft'-zeon), which in itself is only distantly related to the story line. After a short introductory section, a haunting melody is heard, in a section called "Dance of the Young Girls." (It was incorporated into the Broadway musical *Kismet* as the song "Stranger in Paradise.") (See Fig. 18–1.) Other members of the group were Cesar Cui (1835–1918), a soldier, writer, and music critic; Mily Balakirev (1837–1910), leader of the group, pianist, composer, and teacher; Modeste Mussorgsky (1839–1881); and Nicholas Rimsky-Korsakov (1844–1908), a naval officer. The activities of these men centered in St. Petersburg; and though all were trained for some profession other than music, they managed to pool their musical resources; working through the St. Petersburg Conservatory, they became masters of orchestration and composition, completely dedicated to their homeland.

After the performance of Richard Wagner's music dramas in St. Petersburg in 1888, Rimsky-Korsakov began to write for a larger orchestra and to develop the ideas on orchestration which were published in his *Principles of Orchestration* (English translation by E. Agate, 1912).

Alexander Borodin's tone poem *On the Steppes of Central Asia* is a good example of what these masters of orchestration produced. In this instance a color tone of very high pitch is sustained through the first section to establish the mood or feeling. This is an oriental device used cleverly by Borodin, since he is about to introduce an "Oriental Camel Caravan." In this way he sets the atmosphere of early morning on the high, desert-like central Asian plains. The Russian cavalry is waiting to meet the caravan from the Orient, and a Russian song, sounding first high and then low, is heard in the distance. As the caravan approaches, we hear a song of an oriental

Fig. 18–1. *"Stranger in Paradise" Theme from*
Polovtzian Dances, *Borodin*

quality, first in a high and then in a low register. The two themes converse, then join, and move off into the distance toward the great cities at the heart of Russia.

Modeste Mussorgsky (1839–1881) was probably the most brilliant and creative of the "Five." But he lacked the purpose and discipline of the others, and his early death was probably caused by malnutrition and excessive use of alcohol. His best known works are probably his opera *Boris Godunov* and a set of piano pieces later transcribed for orchestra, *Pictures at an Exhibition*. Much of his work was left unfinished and was completed and published by his good friends, Balakirev and Rimsky-Korsakov. Such was the case of his *A Night on Bare Mountain,* also known as *St. John's Eve* (comparable to the Anglo-Saxon Halloween), when all spirits and ghosts meet on Bare Mountain, located in south Russia. Mussorgsky, with the support of Rimsky-Korsakov's superb orchestration, gives us a description of what happened on these occasions. Walt Disney used this music to make his color and sound experiments which resulted in the moving picture *Fantasia*.

Rimsky-Korsakov (1844–1908) is credited with writing the first Russian symphony. He was appointed Profesor of Instrumentation and Composition at St. Petersburg Conservatory in 1871, a position he held until his death. In spite of his lack of early formal training, he progressed rapidly and in his later years wrote Russia's classical textbooks of music, particularly *The Principles of Orchestration,* with examples from his own compositions. One of his most widely performed pieces is "The Flight of the Bumblebee," a very realistic and difficult composition written for his opera *The Czar Sultan,* which is based upon a fairy tale. The story tells of a princess who has been changed to a swan by a witch. A bumblebee carries a message from the princess to a certain prince who alone can set her free.

Much of Rimsky-Korsakov's music is based on Russian folk-idiom and on the oriental melodic patterns which led to his mastery of exoticism. He possessed a remarkable ability to bring legends and fairy tales to life, to make magic carpets fly through the air, transporting his audience to "far corners of the earth." The Italian composer, Puccini, discussed above, used this concept of exoticism in his operas a generation later. Rimsky-Korsakov can be credited with initiating exoticism and providing added interest and understanding to that form of music. His best-known orchestral works include *Scheherazade* and the first Russian tone poem, *Sadko*. During our Civil War period in the 1860's, Rimsky-Korsakov, the naval officer, spent a year anchored off our Atlantic coast as a Russian military observer. He also visited London and South America on his three-year voyage. In 1902 he met Stravinsky, who became his pupil and who followed the clear, brilliant musical style of the Russian master. It was largely through Stravinsky that Rimsky-Korsakov was to influence the orchestral writing of many contemporary composers.

A very active conservatory of music was centered in Moscow during the nineteenth century. It developed under the leadership of Anton Rubinstein, the virtuoso pianist of his team, who staffed it largely with German professors of music who were loyal to the Romantic tradition.

Peter Tschaikovsky (1840–1893) was a notable exception to the Moscow tradition and served as a bridge between nationalistic program-music and Romantic absolute music. The genius of Tschaikovsky is shown in a wide variety of musical styles. However, in his later years, he composed more highly nationalistic compositions. Probably the best known is his Overture 1812. The Overture 1812 is a remarkable musical picture of the battle near Moscow in which Napoleon's armies were defeated. Folk material, along with national hymns and anthems, represent the French and Russian armies in battle; as the battle subsides, the Russian national anthem prevails and the bells of Moscow ring in the distance. It is very noisy but the cannons, bells, bombs, gunfire, folk music, and national anthem are all combined into remarkable orchestration.

Bedřich Smetana (1824–1884) represents a very competent group of Czech composers which includes Antonin Dvořák, whom we have already discussed. Smetana wrote a number of folk operas and incidental compositions, but his tone poem *The Moldau,* which belongs to a series of works entitled *Má Vlast* (My Fatherland), is a masterpiece of orchestration as well as inspiring nationalism.

The Moldau is a river with its source in the mountains of Bohemia, the section of Czechoslovakia in which Smetana lived. Two little mountain streams come together and grow to form the mighty river flowing through the heart of Smetana's native land. He has chosen eight scenes which he describes musically (Fig. 18–2).

1. The sparkling streams which join together.
2. The flowing river.
3. A hunter's horn in the forest.
4. Peasants dancing on the banks.

5. Moonlight on the water (water fairies).
6. Dashing rapids.
7. An ancient castle near Prague.
8. The river majestically flowing on to the sea.

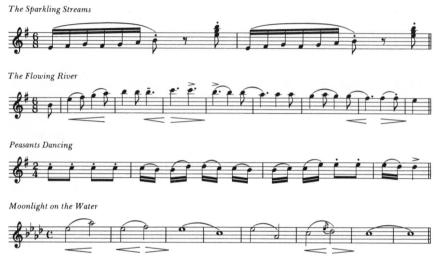

Fig. 18–2.   Themes from The Moldau, Smetana

The Czechs regard this symphonic landscape as a national tone poem which mirrors the soul of their country. The rest of the world sees it as an excellent example of late Romantic tone painting.

It is difficult to give an exact definition of what makes a musical work nationalistic. One needs to know the stimulus of the composer in writing the music since nationalism is not so much a matter of fact as of intention. Composers consciously used folk melodies, stories, and legends because they were representative of patriotic feeling for their country. They placed a heavy reliance on programmatic music and no new forms were needed or developed in the schools of this period. The forms most useful for nationalistic music seemed to be opera, tone or symphonic poems, ballet, and dance forms.

Italian Nationalism of Giuseppe Verdi

The music and ideas of German composers dominated Western music throughout the nineteenth century just as the music of Italy had done in the seventeenth. But the history of Europe during this period is marked by growing nationalism in culture as well as politics. Everywhere there was a mounting enthusiasm for native folk songs, rhythms, and musical traditions. While no two countries carried out this musical nationalism in exactly the same way, the movement in Italy was represented and carried on almost exclusively by the personality and operas of one man, Giuseppe Verdi. Throughout his life he was a patriot and fighter for the unification of his country, and his artistic fame coincided with the events that led to the realization of Italian nationalism. Verdi's nationalistic work was not in discovering or working with folk material but in renewing and strengthening Italian opera, an art form that had been closely associated with Italian life for three centuries. Since Verdi accepted the traditions and tenets of established opera, he applied himself to the task of refining and invigorating its long-standing conventions and forms. The wide range of Verdi's operatic subjects show the wide range of Romantic literary taste. They range from the plays of Schiller, Alexandre Dumas, and Victor Hugo to the medieval romance, *Il Trovatore*. Above all these stand his adaptations of two Shakespeare plays: *Otello* in 1886 and *Falstaff* in 1895. Verdi asserted his national pride by bringing a native art form to a peak of perfection that challenged the supremacy of Wagner's music drama.

General Characteristics of Romantic Music

1. Use of national legends in "Program music" and symphonic tone poems. Examples: Saint-Saëns, *Danse Macabre;* Dukas, *The Sorcerer's Apprentice;* Tschaikovsky, *The Sleeping Beauty* and *Nutcracker Suite;* Humperdinck, *Hänsel and Gretel;* R. Strauss, *Till Eulenspiegel;* Rossini, *William Tell;* Sibelius, *The Swan of Tuonela;* Wagner, *Die Meistersinger, Tannhäuser, Lohengrin,* and *The Ring of the Nibelung.*
2. Use of geographic associations. Examples: J. Strauss, *Blue Danube* and *Tales of the Vienna Woods;* Grofé, *Grand Canyon Suite* and *Mississippi Suite.*
3. Use of folk tunes and dances. Examples: Chopin, *Mazurkas* and *Polonaises;* Liszt, *Hungarian Dances;* Brahms, *Hungarian Dances;* Enesco, *Roumanian Rhapsodies;* Dvořák, *Slavonic Dances;* Smetana, *The Bartered Bride;* Grieg, *Norwegian Dances;* De Falla and Albeñiz, *Spanish Dances;* Vaughan-Williams, *London* and *Pastoral Symphonies.*

Summary

1. The Napoleonic Wars resulted in a national awakening in European countries.
2. Nationalism was a means of self-expression as well as a denial of national inferiority.
3. Mikhail Glinka pioneered the way for the "Russian Five."
4. Activities of the "Russian Five" centered in the St. Petersburg Conservatory.
5. Russian nationalism brought the art of orchestration to new heights.
6. The musical effectiveness of the "Russian Five" was enhanced by their mutual cooperation.
7. Tschaikovsky was a product of the Moscow Conservatory, which was largely staffed with German professors. He became highly nationalistic in later years.
8. Rimsky-Korsakov initiated exoticism.
9. Bedrich Smetana wrote *The Moldau* and other nationalistic works celebrating his homeland, Bohemia.
10. Nationalism is not so much a matter of fact as it is a matter of intention.
11. The most useful forms of music in nationalism were dance forms, opera, tone or symphonic poems, and ballet.

Examples of Music

1. Borodin, *On the Steppes of Central Asia* (tone poem). RCA Victor (1816).
2. Mussorgsky, *A Night on Bare Mountain*. RCA Victor (1816).
3. Rimsky-Korsakov, "Flight of the Bumblebee," *The Czar Sultan*. Capitol (P 8339).
4. Tschaikovsky, *Overture 1812*. Columbia (ML 5392).
5. Smetana, "The Moldau," *Má Vlast*. Columbia (ML 5261).
6. Brahms, *The Gardener*. Westminster (XWN 18062).
7. Mahler, *Symphony #1*, third movement. Angel (35180). (Themes are "Are You Sleeping" and "London Bridge Is Falling Down.")
8. Tschaikovsky, "The Dance of the Mirlitons," *The Nutcracker Ballet*. Columbia (ML 5171).
9. Sibelius, *Finlandia* (tone poem), Op. 26. Epic (LC 3477).
10. Sibelius, *Night Ride and Sunrise*. London (LL 1276).
11. Rimsky-Korsakov, *Scheherazade*, Op. 35. Epic (LC 3300).

19 ∿ Abstract Music

In the last half of the nineteenth century, the majority of composers concerned themselves with programmatic or nationalistic music, which necessarily is related to something external to the music. Its form is likely to be free or vague in outline and it often bears only a casual relationship to the traditional form. These works are filled with the special effects that would result from distinctive uses of melody, chord progressions, national idioms, as well as unusual qualities of sound to illustrate a program or national element. Emotional reaction to this music is influenced by the events, objects, or ideas which it describes; the title is expected to call attention to extra-musical events, objects, or ideas which inspired the composer.

Although this is the usual type of musical composition for this period, there were a number of outstanding composers who developed and maintained an interest in absolute or abstract music. An abstract composition contains musical material which is chosen for its musical characteristics. The composer is concerned for purely musical reasons with a particular melody and its rhythmic and harmonic components. This material is manipulated and developed according to musical laws and practices, and the forms in which it is cast are most often the traditional forms that served earlier composers. The emotional reaction to abstract music arises from the music itself—there are no descriptive titles or extra-musical suggestions to influence the listener. The title of such works will probably be a type identification and an opus number (e.g., Sonata No. 5).

Johannes Brahms

Johannes Brahms is the composer who best represents the field of abstract music in the late nineteenth century. Programmatic elements may occasionally appear in his vocal or choral work, but this is largely to carry out the meaning of the texts. Nationalistic elements are also evident in a few of his compositions, for Brahms remained close to the spirit of German folk music. He sometimes employed Hungarian gypsy idioms, which he knew well. With these exceptions, however, Brahms remained the champion of abstract music.

Brahms was born in 1833 in Hamburg, the son of a professional string bass player. The boy's musical talent revealed itself at an early age. He was given the best musical education his home town had to offer; by the time he was fourteen he had already distinguished himself as a pianist. At the age of twenty, he became the accompanist for an excellent Hungarian violinist named Remenyi, with whom he made a rather extensive concert tour. He became acquainted with Franz Liszt and Robert Schumann and played his own compositions for them during the course of that tour. Schumann, at that time editor of a music periodical known as the *Neue Zeitschrift für Musik,* wrote so enthusiastically about the young Brahms that public attention focused upon him before he had achieved maturity. Schumann assumed that his young friend would align himself with the group of composers headed by Franz Liszt and Richard Wagner, who called themselves the Neo-German Party and whose purpose was to further this "music of the future"—that is, program-music of the day. Brahms, however, chose another and very different means of expression.

The composers of the Neo-German Party took it for granted that they spoke for all composers. This position irritated Brahms. In 1860, he helped draw up a petition protesting their principles and practices. However, this proved embarrassing when the petition was discovered and made public when it had only four signatures. After this experience Brahms withdrew from the Neo-German Party and became a conservative champion of Classical musical ideals. Brahms' principal objective seemed to be the restoration of abstract music, the practice of austerity and economy in the choice of material, and an attitude of objectivity toward all musical composition. He was aided in carrying out these principles by a sense of self-criticism and a capacity for self-discipline seldom matched by other composers. Brahms' friendship for Schumann was at the time of the older composer's mental collapse in 1854. An acquaintance with Schumann's wife, fourteen years older than Brahms, developed for a time into a romantic infatuation, but after Schumann's death in 1856, the emotional involvement seems to have ended, in a life-long friendship between the two. Brahms never married, probably fearing that domestic responsibilities would interfere with his composing.

His professional activities included many concert tours as a pianist and several important positions as a conductor. However, when Vienna became his permanent home in 1878, he devoted himself almost entirely to composition. Brahms' fame spread rapidly throughout Europe and he was in demand as a conductor of his own work. He died in 1897, a month before his sixty-fourth birthday. Foreign countries sent representatives to his funeral, which was attended by thousands of people who honored him as one of the greatest masters of all time.

Brahms' relationship to the past is seen especially in his fondness for four-movement instrumental forms. Of his chamber music, a major part of his creative work, only three of his twenty-four compositions depart from the Classical forms. In the writing of his four symphonies, he restored the objectively written symphony in four movements to its high place in musical literature. He did not use the minuet or scherzo. His third movements are moderately vigorous movements which fit perfectly into their setting. All four of the Brahms symphonies have demonstrated their lasting qualities and are considered as great as those of Beethoven. His symphonies are technical masterpieces which may prove difficult for the listener who has not made a study of the complex techniques of Brahms' composition. Probably the Symphony No. 2 is the most easily understood of these four giant works for orchestra.

César Franck

In the early part of the nineteenth century, French composers concerned themselves mainly with opera or choral music. After about 1875 and continuing into the twentieth century the balance shifted to instrumental music. French symphonies, symphonic poems, chamber music, and similar forms took on an importance they had not had earlier. César Franck, more than any other, was responsible for this shift. Franck was born in Liège, Belgium, in 1822; he prepared for a career as a concert pianist at the Paris Conservatory. But, against his family's wishes, he chose to teach organ and to devote himself to composition. After becoming a resident of Paris in 1844, he was a church organist and a teacher of organ at the Paris Conservatory. His organ lessons eventually became equal to a complete musical education and later were considered as a composition class for conservatory students. In this way, Franck exerted a profound influence upon the future of French music.

His life was spent in complete devotion to his music. He received virtually no public recognition until he was sixty years old. Most of his works heard today were written in the last ten years of his life. They include a symphony, a set of variations for piano and orchestra, a violin sonata, a string quartet, several organ compositions, and several choral works. Franck's larger works are distinguished by his use of the cyclical form. He shows great skill in employing his theme in the different movements in a way which gives him a high degree of unity. His Symphony in D Minor, written in 1888, provides an excellent example. The first movement, in sonata-allegro form, begins with a short section in a slow tempo. Its theme reappears in the body of the movement as well. Each of the other movements is provided with its own themes, but also includes a clever development of the first theme.

There was almost no point of contact between Brahms, the composer of Vienna, and Franck, the teacher and composer of Paris. However, we consider them together since each remained aloof from the popular concepts of program-music. In all other respects, Franck was a man of his time, strongly influenced by Liszt. The emotional tone of his music was consistently religious and sometimes mystical. In spite of what his critics have called harmonic sweetness and lack of rhythmic vitality, Franck's compositions have continued to occupy a high place in the musical repertoire.

Anton Bruckner

Anton Bruckner (1824–1896) was an Austrian composer, a contemporary of Brahms, whose serious and profound symphonic style is evidenced in all his works. He was a deeply religious man who spent most of his life as a church organist in Vienna. He wrote a number of religious works for the Catholic Church, including three excellent masses. His nine symphonies are characterized by their great length and massive structure. He used song-like themes as a basis for his symphonic writing and achieved great climaxes by using them in a choral manner. His instrumentation suggests an organ sound. Bruckner is considered a nationalist in his native Austria, where his work is very popular; but only the Fourth and Seventh Symphonies are performed regularly outside Austria.

Gustav Mahler

Gustav Mahler (1860–1911) was the last of the great line of Viennese composers that included Haydn, Mozart, Beethoven, Schubert, and Bruckner. He was born in Bohemia and educated mainly in Vienna. He became one of the great conductors of all time; first as director of opera in Budapest, Hamburg, and Vienna; later as guest conductor of the Metropolitan Opera and the New York Philharmonic Society. His reputation as a composer rests primarily upon nine massive symphonies and a symphonic song cycle, *The Song of the Earth*. This symphony for solo voice, chorus, and orchestra was composed in 1908, but received its first performance under the direction of Bruno Walter in 1911, after Mahler's death. Mahler's symphonies represent a type that had become common in the late nineteenth century. Older symphonies had been based upon contrast between themes and between the thematic and lyrical elements. In the works of the minor composers of the time and to some extent in the massive works of Anton Bruckner and Mahler, the symphony form became a loosely constructed composition made up of an endless stream of motives or melodic fragments. A clear distinction between the thematic and transitional material, or even between one section and the next, was not always discernible. This characteristic may have been developed from Richard Wagner's "endless melody."

Mahler, in typical Romantic fashion, tried to compose music that reflected the whole world, that is, music that expressed every facet of life. He included folk songs and elaborate musical symbolism along with choral passages and music of all shades between these extremes. Several of his symphonies include parts for singers, either as soloists, or in chorus. Folk songs are used in his Second, Third, and Fourth Symphonies; a portion of Goethe's *Faust* and a Latin hymn appear in his Eighth; and a cycle of Chinese poems is employed in *The Song of the Earth*. The quality of Mahler's orchestral sound is unique; instruments are used as individuals, and it is common for a hymn to alternate between a light transparency and a great sonority of sound. His harmonies are often dissonant and point the way to the polytonality of the twentieth century. Mahler's symphonies are among the longest that have ever been written. His Symphony No. 3, for example, contains six movements, the first of which lasts forty-five minutes. Considering these characteristics, it is not difficult to see why this music has its champions and its opponents, and why it is not performed as often as Mahler enthusiasts would like.

Nationalism and Impressionism

In the last years of the nineteenth century, there were two factors that played important roles in the stylistic changes which took place in music: (1) the surge of nationalism embodies the desire to make music express nationalistic concepts; this spirit first arose in Russia, then spread through all of Europe and the United States; and (2) a strong French challenge for musical supremacy, called *Impressionism,* pointed the way to modern twentieth-century music.

The transitional years leading into the new century and the years immediately after 1900 saw the development of Impressionism, which sought to provide an antidote to German-dominated Romanticism. It became an international movement and, although it did not last beyond the life span of its innovator, Claude Debussy, it established a climate in which many young composers began experiments that led to truly non-romantic music. Composers such as Schönberg, Bartók, Stravinsky, and Hindemith made significant contributions to the "new music," as it came to be called.

Summary

1. In the last half of the nineteenth century, many composers concerned themselves with programmatic or nationalistic music.
2. A number of gifted composers did not follow this mainstream, but turned toward abstract music.
3. Johannes Brahms best represents this group.
4. Brahms refused to join the Neo-German ("music of the future") Party headed by Liszt and Wagner.
5. His compositions were models of excellence and he favored the Classical forms.

6. After 1875 French composers shifted their interest from choral to instrumental music.
7. César Franck, more than any other, seems responsible for this shift. Recognition came to him after he was sixty years old.
8. Bruckner, a deeply religious church organist in Vienna, was an Austrian contemporary of Brahms.
9. His nine symphonies and other major works are characterized by their great length and massive structure.
10. His Fourth and Seventh Symphonies are widely performed outside his native country.
11. Gustav Mahler was the last of a great line of Viennese composers.
12. He became one of the great conductors of all time.
13. His reputation as a composer rests primarily upon his nine symphonies and his long cycle, *The Song of the Earth.*
14. Two stylistic changes appeared in the final years of the nineteenth century: Nationalism and Impressionism.
15. These movements died early in the twentieth century, but they set a climate for a school of new composers such as Schönberg, Bartók, and Stravinsky.

Examples of Music

1. Bruckner, *Symphony No. 4* ("Romantic"). Capitol FDS (P 8352).
2. Brahms, *Symphony No. 2 in D Major.* Angel (35532).
3. Franck, *Symphonic Variations.* Everest (LPBR 6036).
4. Mahler, *The Song of the Earth.* Vox Box (115).
5. Brahms, *Academic Festival Overture.* Epic (LC 3586).
6. Brahms, *Piano Trio in E♭.* Boston (B 209).

Part Four ～ *The 20th Century*

20 ～ Musical Impressionism

The decade just before 1900 may be called a period of culture-weary art. In the previous fifty years there had been such a concentration of emotional forces that people's feelings were almost immune to further excitement. It was natural, then, that new music which promised a smooth transition into the unknown twentieth century would be eagerly received. This new style was known as impressionism and it stands as a short connecting link between the extremes in nineteenth- and twentieth-century music.

Impressionistic composition is realistic in that it attempts to portray the subject as the artist sees it under particular conditions. The composer gives only a fleeting glance of the subject. The listener must supply the details and complete the picture. In this lack of detail, Impressionism becomes a sensuous art without moral quality: make of it what you will.

Claude Debussy

There were many experimenters in this field of musical suggestion, but most of them failed to produce anything of more than passing interest. However, impressionism finally found a successful champion in Claude Debussy (deh-boos-see') (1862–1918). Like other composers of his time, Debussy raised his voice against the exuberance of Romanticism and reflected the oversensitive, restless mind of the late nineteenth century. In his music he avoided the passion and sentiment of earlier composers; at the same time, there is little of the harsh, brittle, and dissonant materialism which was to come later.

Impressionistic music can be examined in two ways: (1) for what it tries to do; and (2) how it does it. The actual aims of Impressionistic music are well expressed by the name. The composer does not want to either tell a definite story or describe a scene in clear-cut musical colors as the Romanticist would have done. He prefers to give a vague impression of that scene which will leave to each listener his own interpretations. Debussy was not merely the successful founder of musical Impressionism, he was the whole movement. No other composer, with the possible exception of Maurice Ravel, was able consistently to create works in this style. It was extremely popular in its day; but because it was lacking in vitality and spiritual ideas, Impressionism as a style in music, as well as in painting, was destined to be short-lived.

Impressionism in music is characterized by a beautiful sound. The nationalistic sounds of battle and adventure gave way to a perfume-in-the-night concept of sound liberally influenced by dreams and wishful thinking. The delicate qualities of Debussy's Impressionistic music are well illustrated by his nocturne, *Prelude to the Afternoon of a Faun.* The faun, a mythical animal, half man and half goat, has been taking a nap on the flowery bank of a beautiful stream. He sees some nymphs bathing in the stream; he dreams on, or does he dream? Is he awake or is he asleep? It was a wonderful experience, so what does it matter?

This first triumph of musical Impressionism was composed in 1892, when Debussy was thirty years old, and it has remained his most popular work. Inspired by a prose poem by the symbolist poet Mallarmé, which has been termed a "miracle of unintelligibility," the music is a model of clarity, uniting in a remarkable fashion the simple sensuous tonal beauty of Impressionism and the richness of Debussy's imagination functioning at its most poetic level. He is able to take this primitive creature—half man, half goat—and transport him from antiquity to the artistic atmosphere of twentieth-century Parisian life.

Another well-known piece is the set of three symphonic sketches called *La Mer.* Every major period or style in music has produced its opera, so we would surely expect Debussy to write one in the Impressionistic style. His opera is *Pelléas et Mélisande* (pel-lay-ahss' ay may-lee-zahnd'), first performed in Paris in 1902. It is composed in five acts, which are performed in an unbroken flow, bridged by orchestral interludes. This is a Wagnerian characteristic, as in the leitmotiv concept which Debussy develops in complex harmonies to identify the characters and motivate dramatic situations. There are no set arias; most of the singing is done in the form of a flexible recitative; and although the story develops normally, it is subtle and symbolically charged. At the time of its first performance, it was called an important development in opera, but paradoxically it represents a return to the simple lyricism of the Florentines who had invented opera three hundred years earlier.

In Debussy's opera, Prince Goland goes hunting. He gets lost in the forest—his hounds get lost also and we never find out why. He comes to a stream, and sitting by the stream is the beautiful maiden, Mélisande. Together they find their way back to the palace and are eventually married. Later, she meets Pelléas, half-brother of her husband, and they fall madly in love. In the second act, Pelléas and Mélisande are seated together by a well in the garden; Mélisande is playing with a ring her husband has given her—a symbol of his affection. She drops the ring and his affection into the well; then turns to Pelléas and asks, "What shall I do; what shall I tell my husband?" Pelléas answers her, "Tell him the truth," and this sets up the eternal operatic triangle. Prince Goland kills Pelléas; Mélisande dies from a variety of tragic natural causes; and Prince Goland lives unhappily ever after.

Debussy was a skilled pianist and a talented composer who wanted to break with the Romantic past. His music is different; and regardless of how critics feel about Impressionistic music, his works are still held in high regard. His musical style is reminiscent of Chopin, although he freely added parallel chord movement, which is forbidden in conventional harmonic writing. He also extended chords and created new tone colors that were unmistakably his. Many of these tone colors and special effects were accomplished by his use of the whole-tone scale, which is a device for avoiding traditional concepts of key feeling. Since there are twelve half-tones in the octave, it follows that there are six whole tones, equidistant from each other and equally important in the whole-tone scale. (See Fig. 20–1.)

Fig. 20–1. Whole-Tone Scale

Maurice Ravel

Maurice Ravel (1875–1937), a countryman of Debussy's, was earlier influenced by the Impressionistic style, but he developed an individual style in his use of form and a well-developed melody line. He was also master of orchestration. Toward the end of his life he seemed more interested in displaying the dazzling technique he had developed rather than furthering any musical style. Without question, we should classify Ravel as the second musical Impressionist, but never at any time was his work in that field comparable to that of Debussy. Ravel, like Debussy, used the whole-tone scale a great deal, disregarding the well-tempered intervals of the major and minor system. Both of these composers have always been popular in the United States. The harmonies and orchestrations of Ravel in particular have had an attraction for jazz arrangers and moving picture and television composers. As a result of this popularity, his idiom has become part of the listening experience of millions of Americans. His *Bolero* is a study of crescendo for orchestra. It illustrates how a composition may be continued with no development of the melody or theme and although we expect it to be monotonous, we enjoy it because it has a magic—Impressionistic—quality.

As is often the case in the development of art, music was just one phase of Impressionism; the first Impressionists were painters. The name itself was originally derogatory; it was first used when French art critics harshly criticized some of the pictures in an exhibition of young and daring artists. One artist, Claude Monet, had entitled a picture *Impression of a Sunset;* the critics wondered why he could not have painted a sunset rather than his impression of one since the sunset was so much more obvious. However, the idea of the impression—rather than the object itself—stayed, and Impressionism became popular in music as well as in painting.

Other characteristics of musical Impressionism are that the rhythm, indefinite and subtle, attains flexibility by the use of patterns which obscure the feeling of a downbeat—there is a tendency to group 5, 7, 9, or 11 beats in a measure of music; traditional devices of variation and development are seldom used; phrases are usually irregular with their cadences or endings concealed, thereby rendering the internal structure deliberately indefinite and vague.

American Impressionists

An American composer, Charles Tomlinson Griffes (1884–1920), received his musical training in America and in Germany, after which he came under the spell of French Impressionism. Griffes, however, by some trick of creative magic, managed to avoid the pitfall common to most composers who experimented with Debussy's style of writing. Most of these experimenters ended by making unsatisfactory copies of Debussy's music. Griffes, on the other hand, retained some measure of individuality while working in the patterns of Impressionism. His composition *The White Peacock,* based upon a poem of the same name by William Sharp, is a good illustration of Griffes' work.

John Alden Carpenter (1876–1951) was another American who followed the Impressionistic trend but who was not above allowing an occasional bit of realism to predominate in his work. At one time he wrote: "My music, in effect, is often a light-hearted conversation, as between two friends. The rules of polite talk are not *strictly enforced*. Often in animated moments they talk both at once. Presently a moment comes, as always between friends, when no conversation is necessary." * Carpenter employed this charming literary style when writing his *Adventures in a Perambulator*. This is a tone poem done in six parts; the setting of each part is an impression or an experience, seen through the eyes of a baby.

> Part I: "The Voyage in a Perambulator." The baby, with a strap buckled over his stomach, is being pushed in his perambulator by his nurse. "Every morning after my second breakfast, if the wind and sun are favorable, I go out. My nurse is old and very powerful. She stands firmly behind the perambulator and we are off."
> Part II: "They meet a policeman." He is "a man round like a ball, blue and taller than my father. I feel him before he comes and see him after he goes. He walks like doom."
> Part III: "The Hurdy-Gurdy." "My ear is tickled to excess. I have a wild thought of dancing with my nurse and my perambulator —all three of us dancing together. I tug at the strap over my stomach but it is no use."
> Part IV: "The Lake." "The nurse finally pushes on, but soon

* From the notes prepared by John Alden Carpenter on the record jacket of Mercury record, Olympian Series MG50136A.

the land comes to an end and I see the lake with little waves as they escape from the big ones and come rushing up over the sand."

Part V: "Dogs." "We pass on and probably there is nothing more in the world, but there is! It is dogs! We come upon them without warning. One by one—in pairs—then in societies. They laugh, they fight, they run and play *follow the leader*. It's tremendous!"

Part VI: "The dogs have gone." "I have a sudden conviction that it is well I'm not alone. It is pleasant to lie quite still and close my eyes. How very large the world is and how many things there are."

Impressionism makes no philosophic pronouncements of ethical values or intellectual ideals; it portrays no striving of man against evil, fate, or tragedy. Impressionism is a world of art not struggling with reality; the purpose is to entrance.

The favored performance medium of Impressionists is instrumental. The quality of the sounds is of utmost importance. The orchestra is relatively small; a hazy musical quality is created by such means as muted strings and brasses and delicately handled percussion instruments. Subdued solo woodwind voices and the blending of individual instrument voices are more useful than blocks of choir sound. The great number of Impressionistic works for the piano reflect this ethereal quality especially clearly. Considerable experimentation was carried on in attempting to blend the senses of sight, sound, and smell (as the poetry of Baudelaire and Rimbaud). These experiments with color and perfume were interesting but not far-reaching in their results.

As a pure style, Impressionism began and ended with Debussy. Features of the style, however, have been adopted by other composers. Those most influenced by the movement were: Frederick Delius (1862–1934), English; Alexander Scriabin (1872–1915), Russian; Manuel de Falla (1876–1946), Spanish; Ottorino Respighi (1879–1936), Italian. Impressionism was not without influence on the musical leaders of the next generation such as Stravinsky, Schönberg, and Bartók. The musical resources available to Impressionist composers were relatively limited; by the twentieth century it became practically impossible to write Impressionistic music without sounding like Debussy. Composers were consequently forced to seek other idioms.

Impressionism valued elegance above emotion and refinement above intellectual content; but it created a finely wrought, highly decorative art which rescued a vision of fragile beauty from the twilight of European culture.

Summary

1. Impressionism provided welcome relief for "culture-weary" art in the last decade of the nineteenth century.
2. Impressionism stands as a connecting link between the extremes of nineteenth-century and twentieth-century music.
3. Impressionism was largely a one-man movement centered around the French composer, Claude Debussy. Debussy's *Pelléas et Mélisande* was the major opera to come from the Impressionistic movement.
4. His best known compositions are his orchestral nocturne, *The Afternoon of a Faun* and *La Mer*.
5. Maurice Ravel is the second most creative composer in the movement, although not all of his works were in this style. His later compositions were influenced by American jazz.
6. The term "impressionism" came from a painting by Claude Monet entitled *Impression of a Sunset*.
7. The American composer, Griffes, was more successful than most in avoiding a close imitation of Debussy's music.
8. Another American, J. A. Carpenter, effectively combined the styles of Realism and Impressionism in his later work.
9. The purpose of Impressionism is to charm, not to advocate or even depict struggle with reality.
10. The piano and the relatively small orchestra are the favored media of performance.
11. Composers outside France and America who were most influenced by impressionism were Frederick Delius, Alexander Scriabin, Manuel de Falla, and Ottorino Respighi.

Examples of Music

1. Debussy, *Prelude to the Afternoon of a Faun.* Epic (LC 3636).
2. Debussy, *Pelléas et Mélisande.* Angel (35478, 3580).
3. Ravel, *Bolero.* London (CM 9256).
4. Griffes, *The White Peacock,* Op. 7, No. 1. Mercury (Olympian Series MG 50085).
5. Carpenter, *Adventures in a Perambulator.* Mercury (Olympian Series MG 50136).

21 ∿ Folk Music

Mark Twain once said, "A folk song is a song that nobody ever wrote." There is much truth in what he said; good folk music has been tempered, brushed, polished, and fitted to the needs of a cultural group of people. Folk music is a popular music that is made by the people who sing it or play it or dance to it. They make it because they want to achieve a group expression of their loves and interests, their loneliness, the things they have and the things they have lost, and often the things they long for or hope to get. Sorrow and despair may well be tempered with hope and purpose when it is expressed in music.

One of the characteristics of our modern world is to emphasize the development of all patterns and forms which come to us by way of study, careful planning, and research. It is something of a blow to our ego to discover that for hundreds of years the people who have given us folk music have used a natural or unconscious sense of musical design and balance. They have used a great many of the professional tricks of formal composition without knowing the why or how of what they did, but because of this naturalness, they have created a great art.

Folk music is created to meet the needs and desires of the particular section of society that created it. In the Pacific Northwest of North America there was a time not long ago when it was common for two or three men, loaded with lunch buckets and the tools of their trade, to walk several miles out into the forest to lay siege to a giant fir tree. After several back-breaking hours of work, a rest in the shade stimulated their imaginations, and it was easy to talk about how wonderful it would be if a man could fell that tree with one stroke of his axe; there would also be a need for oxen strong enough to immediately haul it away to the mill. In this atmosphere of wishful thinking, Paul Bunyan and Babe, his blue ox, were born. They performed the same function for men of the north woods whether in Washington, Minnesota, or Michigan.

Today, Paul Bunyan and Babe are a reality, but not in the form of superbeings; Paul is a yellow chainsaw that weighs about forty pounds and Babe is a truck and tractor combination that efficiently does all the work assigned to it. With the noise of this machinery there is no chance for singing or storytelling, and when the motors are turned off, the conversation is likely to be limited to some uncomplimentary remarks about the weather.

Paul Bunyan was a logger, a man of the north woods, and it just wouldn't do for him to go down south to assist the work gangs that built railroads. So, it was necessary for John Henry to take over the duties of railroading and he was just as effective at laying tracks and driving steel as Paul Bunyan was in bucking logs. We will not take time to follow the career of John Henry, but it is interesting to notice how folk music keeps up to date. When modern machinery became available for building railroads, it was inevitable that John Henry would lose face but folk art came to his rescue and a competition was planned where John Henry was pitted against a steam-hammer. They were each to break rock and see who could get to the top of the hill first. Of course, John Henry won but then he "laid down his hammer and he died." About thirty-five verses are required to tell the entire story of the *Death of John Henry* but in it a true folk hero is described and respectfully disposed of.

Folk art is made of simple things. It takes whatever is at hand and fashions it artistically to reflect the temper and the feelings of the people. Folk art mirrors history at its romantic best. Every country in the world has developed a characteristic folk music of its own, yet a surprising number of elements will be found to be fairly common in all. Even so limited a melodic pattern as the five-tone scale appears in the folk music of almost every race. Strongly marked rhythm, simplicity of melody (but with a tendency toward embellishment), exaggerated tone color, and the spirit of improvisation may be considered vital characteristics of folk music all over the world.

Naturally, one finds primitive folk song emphasized in countries that still have a peasantry, like Spain, Russia, Hungary, Czechoslovakia, the Balkans, and parts of Italy and France. In Germany and the Scandinavian countries, folk music survives because of its originally strong foundation, and this is true also of England, Scotland, and Ireland.

In North America a great mass of true folk music has gradually been discovered, although much of this represents importations or adaptations of foreign material. The music of the American Indians is now of little more than historical importance. Negro spirituals and secular songs have contributed enormously to the popular as well as to the serious music of America; these may properly be considered native materials, influenced to some extent by African tradition. The mountain music of the South came largely from British sources; this is also true of many of the Western cowboy songs. We have borrowed Creole, French-Canadian, Spanish, Scandinavian, and even Oriental materials, and placed them in a melting pot—creating a brew that has an American flavor. Within all of this material one occasionally finds a piece of pure Americanism, like "The Arkansas Traveler," "Frankie and Johnny," "The Little Mohee," "Peter Gray," or the songs written about such legendary figures as John Henry and Paul Bunyan.

If it were possible to tell the complete history of folk music, it would be the history of the human race. Every experience a nation goes through comes out in some way in its songs. Folk music records the wars, the struggles, the migrations, the revolutions, the droughts, the famines, and the hours of triumph and emancipation. It records the great deeds of heroes and the love affairs of ordinary people. The words, melodies, stories, and dance steps are often inseparable and, in many cases, cannot be detached from acts of life of which they are a part. Music that was used for railroad work was suitable for railroad work. Other music must be used for household chores, or working in the field.

The folk song is a product of the mind, orally preserved and, until recently, seldom written down. As such, it is subject to change and is always in a state of flux. The very conditions under which folk songs exist encourage change and growth which leads to numerous variations by individual musicians. However, only those variations will survive which are adopted by other musicians and are imitated by them. In this way, it continues to accurately express the taste and feelings of a community; that which is purely personal will gradually but surely be eliminated.

Perhaps the greatest change which has been accepted in the world of folk music during the last two or three generations has been in styles and forms of accompaniment. Instruments of all kinds are more readily available today than in the past. A good example of this is a dramatic African song, "A Lullaby to a Hungry Child When There Is No Food." The background which heightens the emotional effect is furnished by a highly competent jazz trumpeter who has obviously acquired his skill from American artists, but the song is African in every respect. Interesting as this cultural interchange is on some occasions, there are other times when it just doesn't work out.

The folk music of the Orient cannot be played on the instruments of Western culture, such as the piano; an imported keyboard cannot reproduce their monodic music. The Arabs may play sketches of their melodies on the piano and the Hindus may sustain notes, as color tones, on the organ, but the right notes for the melody are simply not there. Oriental stringed instruments are without frets or are fitted with movable frets which may be shifted, like the Indian *vina;* or they may have several loosely set bridges, like the Japanese *koto.* The Oriental concept of tone quality is completely different from ours. They are overwhelmed by the massive chords of our Western music, and they wish to remain sensitive to the flexible intervals of their characteristic music. The nasal quality of the voice, they feel, is a very natural sound.

About halfway between the traditional folk song and the so-called "art song," there stands what is known as the "composed folk song." Certain composers are so thoroughly in tune with the spirit of their people and their native musical idioms that their creative efforts are adopted, loved, and used as traditional folk songs. Such men as Dvořák, Sibelius, Grieg, and Stephen Foster are representative of a large group of talented composers who have given us excellent composed folk music. Since this type of song is the product of a single creative personality, it allows for a wider range of subject and technical perfection than does the traditional folk song. It is also probable that this product of a trained composer will have smoothness of style and subtlety of effect that may be lacking in the traditional folk song. In any case, the composed folk song has become an integral part of national folklore.

Folk music is usually discussed in very general terms. It is easy to say that folk music is a natural expression of a cultural group, but it is more difficult to understand how this natural expression comes about, and how it continues to express the feelings and moods of a society as it undergoes dramatic changes in a scientific world. It may help our understanding to briefly discuss the history and some of the many factors which result in a representative expression of an area and its people.

Probably the best example of the development of a strong, highly representative music can be found in Hawaiian music. By tracing some of Hawaii's historical highlights during the past century, we can see a characteristic pattern of folk music that has crystallized, has taken a form uniquely Hawaiian, and has adopted instruments that were particularly appropriate to both the music and the dance.

Hawaiian Folk Music

The Hawaiian people have a mysterious past. Historians agree on one fact: they have lived for many centuries in the South Pacific area on lush, palm-shaded islands in a tropical climate. For many of these centuries, they had no written language, so their legends and traditions were handed down from one generation to another by singing, storytelling, and dancing. Music filled their lives and furnished the background for every function, whether joyous or sad. The beauty of their islands, the temperament of their people, and all the qualities which go to make up a true folk art are reflected and described in their music.

For hundreds of years Hawaiians used only chants of a wide variety. These seemed to serve the musical needs of their primitive society very well, until missionaries came to the islands shortly after 1800 and introduced part-singing in their Christian hymns and gospel songs. Solo and part-singing came naturally to the musical Hawaiians and many of their folk songs dating from the nineteenth century were done in harmony, showing a strong influence of the Christian gospel songs. They also readily adopted the guitars and ukuleles which were introduced to the islands in the mid-nineteenth century. These instruments were played impressively by the Portuguese, who came with the development of the sugar industry. Although some melody instruments such as violin, mandolin, and flute were also used, the performers found their voices to be the most effective agent in creating the peculiar character of the music of Hawaii. Singing enabled them to capture and convey the spirit and beauty of Hawaii in a manner impossible for European instruments and musical forms alone. Their songs permitted them to accompany and assist the dancers in their descriptive, storytelling *hulas*.

During the nineteenth century, the Hawaiians developed a written language with an alphabet of twelve letters, which included seven consonants and all five of the vowels used in the English language. This predominant use of vowel-sounds in the language is a distinct advantage for the singer and enables him to use many of the techniques of Swiss yodeling, with its characteristic changes from the natural to the falsetto voice.

In 1872 Captain Henry Berger came to the islands from Germany. He organized the Royal Hawaiian Band, which was highly successful from its beginning, and has remained a strong influence upon Hawaiian music since that time. The sounds and rhythms of European dance forms such as waltzes, schottisches, minuets, and marches which the Band played were imitated to some extent by Hawaiian composers as they broadened their approach to music.

In 1900 the United States Congress made the Hawaiian Islands a Territory of the United States. President William McKinley appointed the islands' former governor, Sanford B. Dole, the new governor of the Territory. This was an important milestone in Hawaii's change from a primitive to a modern society. Governor Dole and Mr. Berger both encouraged the development of a true Hawaiian style, which was achieved shortly after the beginning of the twentieth century. This style established the guitar-ukulele combination which has become the most familiar rhythmic sound in the history of Hawaiian music. This sound was refined and extended in 1916, with the introduction of the steel guitar which ultimately was designed for electrical amplification to provide the sound which to this day is recognized throughout the world as the signature of Hawaiian music.

In 1887 Princess Bernice Pauahi Bishop, great granddaughter of King Kamehameha the Great, endowed two schools, one for boys and one for girls. These were to be known as the Kamehameha Schools;

here Hawaiian children were to learn the skills of the Western world, and at the same time preserve the grace and traditions of their fore-fathers. Through classroom instruction and campus activities, they learn the dances, legends, games, and crafts of their ancestors. Every-one sings at school, at home, and at social gatherings; group singing is an old Hawaiian custom and an invaluable part of their musical heritage.

Charles E. King graduated from the Kamehameha School in 1892. He was a skillful musician with considerable training, and is best remembered for his work in compiling and arranging a large number of folk songs. King's *Book of Hawaiian Melodies* was pub-lished in 1948, and a companion book, King's *Songs of Hawaii* was published in 1950. His compositions include an Hawaiian opera, *The Prince of Hawaii,* from which is drawn the ever-popular "Hawaiian Wedding Song" (Ke Kali Nei Au). Among the outstanding per-formers of traditional Hawaiian music are: Mahi Beamer, the late Alfred Apaka, and Charles K. Davis. These men have demonstrated strong leadership in the best of Hawaiian folk traditions.

Many people today feel that the basic ukulele-electric guitar sound is the only true Hawaiian musical sound, but this is not neces-sarily true. Through the forties and fifties, little change was experi-enced in Hawaii's musical patterns; but when statehood was granted in 1959, there was a world-wide wave of interest in the music of Hawaii. In the 1960's a new type of island music began to emerge. Hawaii's youth accepted and imitated the rock-and-roll movement of the mainland, and the heavy rhythmic pattern of electrified guitars began to replace the graceful rhythm of the hula. The long-familiar brand of songs about swaying palms, grass skirts, and Hawaiian moon-light was not compatible with the accented beat and drive of rock-and-roll, so a modern and more personally emotional lyrical approach was sought and found in the Hawaiian compositions of the late Kui Lee and his colleagues. To thousands of Hawaiian visitors, the un-forgettable strains of the Royal Hawaiian Band playing *Aloha Oe* in a manner unchanged for half a century is the ultimate in Hawaiian music. To the purists, the ancient Hawaiian chants accompanied by nose flutes and pahu drums are the best in Hawaiian music. But to the young people of the late 1960's the pulsating, swinging sound of Don Ho, as well as the music of Kui Lee, is what Hawaiian music ought to be.

It is interesting to note that, to a large degree, modern mass communication is responsible for the sweeping wave of popularity folk music enjoys today. It also records for posterity that which has been established; but the question arises whether or not folk art and the folk process can survive under such exposure. The young people of Hawaii surely have the right to champion the current popular music of the mainland, but it will be a tragic loss if outside influences become strong enough to dominate or replace the unique artistry of traditional Hawaiian music.

Summary

1. Folk music has been tempered, brushed, polished, and fitted to the needs of a culturally unified group of people.
2. Folk music reflects natural artistry without the benefit of planning and research.
3. Folk heroes such as Paul Bunyan and John Henry are products of wishful thinking.
4. When John Henry and other folk heroes no longer serve a useful purpose, folk music gives them an honorable death and burial.
5. Folk art takes whatever is at hand and uses it in an artistic manner.
6. The piano can reproduce or accompany only a small portion of the world's folk music.
7. The social and economic problems of a country are reflected in its folk music.
8. The "composed folk song" stands about halfway between the traditional response of the people and the art song.
9. The composed folk song is usually more artistic than the traditional song.
10. The composed folk song has become as much a part of national folklore as the traditional folk song.
11. Dvořák, Sibelius, Grieg, and Stephen Foster represent the many talented composers who have provided us with excellent folk music.
12. Folk music is the most characteristic product of the cultural group from which it comes.
13. Hawaii has furnished an excellent example of the development of folk music.
14. Charles E. King has done much to organize Hawaiian music. His compositions include an opera, *The Prince of Hawaii*.

Examples of Music

1. *Folksong and Minstrelsy.* Vanguard (RL 7624); Book of the Month Club, Inc.
2. *Folksingers.* Elektra (157).
3. *Primitive Percussion, African Jungle Drums.* Reprise (R9-6001).
4. "Ngola Kurila," from *The Many Voices of Miriam Makeba.* Kapp (KL 1274).
5. *Hawaii's Mahi Beamer,* Authentic Island Song. Capitol (T 1282).
6. "Cossack Song" and "Kalinka," from *Russian Folk Songs.* Valiant (V 4935).
7. "Sakura Sakura" (Cherry Blossoms) and "Tanko Bushi" (Coal Miners' Song), from *Japan Revisited.* Capitol (T 10195).
8. *Swiss Mountain Music,* Alphorn with Cattle Bells, Appenzeller Yodel (With Moving Coins). Capitol (T 10161).
9. *Music of the Austrian Alps, The Tiroler Sänger- und Tänzergruppe Performs.* Capitol (T 10016).
10. *Hungarian Songs,* Kodály Girls Choir. Angel (36334).
11. Burl Ives, *In the Quiet of the Night.* Decca (CL 8247).
12. *Abe the Rail Splitter, The Life of President Lincoln in Song and Story.* 20th Century-Fox (FOX 3036).
13. *Music of Hawaii, The Twentieth Century,* Vols. I and II. Ala Moana Record, 4999 Kahala Avenue, Honolulu, Hawaii.
14. Charles K. L. Davis, *Hawaii's Golden Favorites.* Decca (CL 4214).

22 ∿ Early American Music

While Europe was struggling with the music of the Reformation and enjoying that of the Counter-Reformation, America was just beginning to change from a political experiment in the wilderness to a healthy, growing society with prospects of a future. Our nation started with a musical handicap. Although our Pilgrim fathers and their brother Puritans were not Calvinists in a true sense, their religious doctrines were fashioned largely from the same material. They felt that music of the church should be performed only in connection with the psalms which make up the Psalter. Their greatest fear was that the words of the Biblical text might be tampered with or rearranged when set to music.

English and Dutch traditions were combined in a Psalter which was brought out by Harry Ainsworth in Amsterdam in 1612. This was the Psalter widely used by the Pilgrims who brought it to New England in 1620. The Ainsworth Psalter was widely used in America for many years, although the first book to be published in New England was the *Bay Psalm Book,* printed on the Harvard University printing press in 1640.

The Pilgrims and Puritans of the first generation were well educated, some of them expertly trained in music. But the rigors of pioneer life, the rigid musical censorship, and the difficulty of obtaining a good education caused the quality of music to deteriorate rapidly with the new generations. Our forefathers came to America largely to escape two major forces in Europe: a dictatorial church and a pleasure-loving aristocracy. These were the same forces which had been mainly responsible for the growth and development of music in the Old World.

Due largely to the unfavorable attitude of our Pilgrim forefathers, American music was forced to exist and develop outside the church without the benefit of European aristocratic society to pay the bills. In the colonies, Americans no longer possessed the education and musical training which their forefathers brought with them from Europe. This lack of concern for music and for the serious study of it resulted in the deterioration of the amount and quality of music used in church services, and brought about a simplified singing technique. In this practice, there was no longer a need to depend upon reading the music or learning the song; you merely imitated the leader, who lined it out one short phrase at a time, to be repeated by the congregation.

The demand that something be done about this state of affairs came at the beginning of the eighteenth century when three young, energetic clergymen, recent graduates of Harvard University, started a singing school movement designed to upgrade the music of the church. These men were: Thomas Symmes (1677–1725), John Tufts (1689–1750), and Thomas Walter (1696–1725). They felt strongly about the cause of music and became leaders of the movement to reform New England singing methods. Strong support was given them by a number of the clergymen such as the Reverend Cotton Mather and the Reverend Nathanial Chauncey who preached and wrote in favor of "regular singing" or singing by note.

Thomas Walter asserts that he was thoroughly familiar with the common or country way of singing, and spoke of himself as one "who can sing all the various Twistings of the old Way." He adds a further description of the Psalm singing of his day,

> . . . the tunes are now miserably tortured, and twisted, and qua-vered, in some churches, into an horrid Medly of confused and disorderly Noises. . . . Our tunes are, for want of a Standard to appeal to in all our Singing, left to the Mercy of every unskilful Throat to chop and alter, twist and change, according to their infinitely diverse and no less odd Humours and Fancies. . . . *

Additional propaganda in support of the "new way of singing" was furnished by the Reverend Symmes, who wrote a pamphlet called "The Reasonableness of Regular Singing or Singing by Note." He subtitled the work, "An Essay Reviving the True and Ancient Method of Singing Psalm Tunes According to the Pattern of Our New England Psalm Books." Emphasizing this point further he writes, "There are persons now living, children and grandchildren of the first settlers of New England who can vividly remember that

* Gilbert Chase, *America's Music* (New York, McGraw-Hill, 1955), p. 26.

their ancestors sang by note and many of them can sing tunes exactly by note which they learnt from their fathers." *

The Reverend John Tufts published a small book called, "A Very Plain and Easy Introduction to the Singing of Psalm Tunes," which was probably issued around 1715. Tufts thought he had introduced "an easy method of singing by letters instead of by notes," but his system was never widely adopted. The sad state of musical affairs was meant to be remedied by implementing a system of singing schools designed by the clergymen to upgrade the psalm-singing in the Sunday service but they did not anticipate the social implications of a weekly evening singing school. It proved to be a very popular movement which spread rapidly throughout the colonies and was enthusiastically attended, but the lack of trained leadership in music was soon apparent. The quantity of music multiplied, but the quality was not improved as much as the churchmen had hoped.

Probably the best known musician to emerge from the singing school movement was William Billings (1746–1800). His home was in Boston; a tanner by trade, he was a prolific composer of music and, though he received little formal education in music, he made up in enthusiasm what he lacked in training. It is said of him that, "He spoke and sang with rare ability." Some of his compositions are still found in the repertory of choirs today. Another outstanding musician of the singing school movement was Oliver Holden (1765–1828), a carpenter in Charlestown who later transferred his musical activities to Boston where he became a highly successful real-estate broker. His best known work is the Coronation Hymn, which is included in most of the current Protestant hymnals.

The next group of men to forward the cause of American music was made up of Benjamin Franklin, Francis Hopkins, and Thomas Jefferson, who preferred to be known as "Gentlemen Amateurs." This group was led by the eminent Dr. Franklin, the outstanding music critic of his day, a capable performer upon the violin, and the inventor of several unique musical instruments. Francis Hopkins was poet, musician, and piano soloist. He called himself America's first native-born composer when in 1788 he wrote *Seven Songs for Harpsichord* and dedicated them to President George Washington. He also published several successful collections of psalms and an-

* *Ibid.*, p. 27.

thems. Young Thomas Jefferson, the Sage of Monticello, studied law, but practiced music. He writes of playing violin duets with Patrick Henry, and seems to be the first to notice and describe "the unusual musicality of the Negroes." He made plans to have a complete household orchestra, but never achieved what he felt was a full instrumentation.

These men were deeply involved in their business and professional occupations, but contributed much to the cause of music in early America, while protecting themselves from visiting Europeans and critical countrymen by maintaining an amateur status in music.

In the 1930's there were several laboratories in the United States which were experimenting with what was then known as picture transmission. Two decades later these experiments turned into a tidal wave of television. Just one hundred years earlier a comparable movement brought the piano, as we know it today, into common use.

Bartolomeo Cristofori, the Italian harpsichord maker, had invented the pianoforte in 1710 (see Chapter 14) but his instruments were delicate, required constant tuning, and they did not stand up well when they were shipped to the United States after the Revolutionary War. With the addition of an iron frame, the piano came to be a sturdy and dependable instrument; and soon Americans were sending these reinforced pianos, in new upright models, back to Europe.

America needed this type of instrument for several different reasons: (1) Urban tastes looked toward Western Europe, especially toward France in the 1780's. Gentlemen amateur musicians such as Thomas Jefferson, Benjamin Franklin, and Francis Hopkins agreed that we must have pianos to bring culture into American homes. (2) The churches of America were undergoing a great revival. The time of singing psalms was past. The religion of the day used hellfire-and-brimstone preaching and needed the stimulation of a virtuoso pianist to give the proper atmosphere. (3) Every saloon and gathering place in the American Westward-Ho movement had to have a piano and someone who could play it loud and long. The development of the upright piano reinforced with iron furnished the ideal type of sturdy instrument which could be carried hundreds of miles in a covered wagon and still remain reasonably useful.

Any survey of American music must at least mention the development of American bands. The band idea started with our military organizations following the Revolutionary War. In 1853, M. Jullien of France came to America and established the pattern from which the American band was further developed by Patrick Gilmore, John Philip Sousa, Victor Herbert, and many others. A hundred years later there were approximately seventy thousand such band organizations in the United States, mainly in the schools.

In the 1830's, music for the virtuoso soloists in the band rivaled the brilliance of the short piano piece for that instrument. A good example of this quick step type of music is "Woodup," written by John Halloway in 1835. It was composed to demonstrate the technique of the new piston valve cornet and compare its capabilities with the traditional keyed bugle.

The history of professional orchestras in the United States has followed the growth of the nation. As population frontiers have moved toward the west, the cultural movement within the community has carried the symphony orchestra with it. The first permanent orchestra in this country was the New York Philharmonic, which was founded in 1842. The development of most of our symphony orchestras since that time has followed the same basic pattern. Today there are more than eleven hundred professional symphony orchestras along with approximately nineteen thousand in the schools.

Since hymn tunes are preeminently the food of the common man, their importance in church history exceeds that of all other musical types in a nation so democratic as America. But during the last half of the nineteenth century, city churches began nearly everywhere to depend also on ensembles of paid soloists for their more pretentious music. The mixed quartet in a side gallery or above the pulpit became the norm in such churches, even in the newly settled West. As early as in 1856, the *San Francisco Bulletin* published a series of articles on local church music, and the reporter thought it odd that "The First Presbyterian Church has a choir of ten instead of the fashionable quartet so much in vogue in other churches."

It is interesting to note the influence of the great gospel singers during the past century. Some of the more important names are Philip P. Bliss, Ira D. Sankey, Homer Rodeheaver, and Beverly Shea, who is currently the soloist for the Billy Graham organization. These men formerly used the simple approach of country-style music and depended upon their sincerity and natural musicality to capture the hearts of the world. Today, however, Beverly Shea has a highly trained voice, a more sophisticated accompaniment and uses the approach of the professional light opera singer, but still his sincerity and the beautiful quality of his voice are his leading assets.

A study of gospel music made in 1960 shows "Blessed Assurance" as the all-time favorite. Following in close order are: "I'd Rather Have Jesus" (Shea), "What a Friend," "Near the Cross," "My Faith Looks Up to Thee" and "Nearer My God to Thee." The last two songs were written by Lowell Mason (1793–1873), who was a remarkable man. He received an excellent musical education, going to Germany for special study. He was a very competent composer who made a substantial fortune publishing music. His activity in the composing and publishing fields made him a leader in the nineteenth-century gospel song movement, which replaced the more formal psalms and hymn tunes. He also taught music in the public schools of Boston from 1838–1845, largely without pay since he was anxious to prove the value of music education in the public schools. He was the first to promote the idea of music for the masses by organizing conventions for the training of music teachers.

In 1829, twenty-six years after the Louisiana Purchase, Louis Gottschalk was born in New Orleans. Although his mother was French and his father English, he was an American citizen because of the Purchase. His mother started his musical education. At twelve years of age he was sent to live with relatives in Paris, where he became a gifted composer and a highly talented pianist—the first American pianist to be recognized on an international scale. Frédéric Chopin predicted he would become the "King of Pianists." He returned to America in 1852 and was hailed as the supreme pianist. He gave many sensational concerts in the following years, often playing his own compositions. Most of his own pieces remained popular only as long as he was alive to play them. In 1865 he set out on a Central and South American concert tour by way of California. The tour was highly successful, but he died of overwork in Rio de Janeiro, Brazil, in 1869.

Stephen Collins Foster (1826–1864) made a unique contribution to American music. In 1840, Americans had no heritage of folk music, so they were glad to select the best (verse and chorus) songs of the more than two hundred that Foster wrote, and call them their own. For more than one hundred years, "My Old Kentucky Home,"

"Massa's in the Cold, Cold Ground," "Oh Susanna," and many others have remained a part of American folklore.

In 1845, American-born Henry Fry wrote and produced his opera, *Leonora,* in Philadelphia. He tried to have it done in Paris, but was told: "Americans are political contrivers and inventors of gadgets, but they do not write operas so we could not think of performing it." *Leonora* was a creditable opera in the bel canto tradition; he might have done better if he had taken it to Italy. Shortly after this, George Bristow wrote an opera, *Rip Van Winkle,* with moderate success.

Late in the nineteenth century, a group of American composers living in and around Boston began to write longer and more sophisticated works. All of them had studied in Europe at one time or another. Consequently, their music sounded very much like that of their German and French teachers, but the work was of good quality and attracted serious attention in Europe. It is interesting that this group was able to keep Romantic music alive and healthy for more than a decade after it was dead in Europe.

The Boston classicists, or the New England group as they were called, included: John Knowles Paine, George W. Chadwick, Horatio Parker, noted professor of music at Yale University; and Edward McDowell, who exerted considerable leadership in the group. These men and their colleagues achieved international recognition for American music and did much to stabilize music in our country, though little of their music is heard today. The excellence of American music is often overlooked in search of something new.

John Knowles Paine (1839–1906) may be regarded as the ancestor of the New England group. He was born in Portland, Maine, in 1839, where his father had built the first organ in the state of Maine. After finishing his musical education in Germany, he returned to America in 1861, and the next year, he was appointed Director of Music at Harvard College, where he remained until a year before his death in 1906. His music has some qualities of workmanship and creativity that raise it above that of previous serious American composers. Nevertheless, it remains today primarily of historical interest. Professor Paine was most successful as an organist and teacher. At one time he was bitterly opposed to the Wagnerian school and even wrote several magazine articles against it, but age mellowed his views and he became a moderate conservative in music. He composed two symphonies, several symphonic poems, cantatas, other choral works, chamber music, and works for piano and organ.

George Whitfield Chadwick (1854–1931) was the oldest and most versatile member of the Boston group, although he did not have the advantage of a university education. Chadwick's first regular instruction in music began at the New England Conservatory in 1872. After graduation and a period of study in Germany, he became a teacher at the Conservatory; and, in 1897, he became its director. In his long tenure at the Conservatory, he made a name for himself as teacher, organist, conductor, and composer. His musical works include five operas of which *Tobasco* and *Judith* are probably the best known; three symphonies; five symphonic poems; six overtures for orchestra; five string quartets; six major choral works; and a wide variety of chamber music and songs—many of them with orchestra accompaniment. In a set of four orchestra pieces which he calls symphonic sketches: *Jubilee, Noel, Hobgoblin,* and *A Vagrom Ballad,* Chadwick becomes a truly American composer. In these sketches there is a vitality, a genuine and human emotional quality that keeps them from becoming museum pieces.

Among the American composers of his time, Edward McDowell (1861–1908) was the most important. He exerted a strong influence over the American musical scene at the beginning of the twentieth century. Though some of his works were based on American Indian themes, he cannot actually be called a composer of American music, since his training and early experience were in the true style of German Romanticism, somewhat affected by French Impressionism.

At the age of fifteen, after several years of piano study, McDowell, accompanied by his mother, went to Paris, where Debussy was one of his fellow students. He later moved to Frankfurt, Germany, where he began his professional career as a teacher and a composer. In 1882, he paid a visit to Franz Liszt, for whom he played his first *Piano Concerto* and his *Modern Suite.* Liszt encouraged the young composer and assisted him with publication problems and performance opportunities.

He returned to Boston in 1888, where he was active as a teacher and composer until 1896, when he became head of the newly founded Department of Music at Columbia University, New York. He resigned this position after eight years, due to ill health and differences

of opinion with the administration. His most characteristic compositions are those for piano and include four sonatas, two piano concertos, and a large number of smaller pieces. For orchestra he wrote
two suites and a variety of shorter works in addition to his many
songs.

Horatio Parker (1853–1919) made a place for himself which was
very near the top of musical achievement by the Boston group. In
1880, when Chadwick returned from Germany and opened a teaching studio in Boston, young Parker became one of his first pupils,
and two years later, he made the traditional pilgrimage to Germany
to finish his musical education. After three years abroad, he settled
in New York as church organist and teacher at the National Conservatory there; but in 1893, he transferred his activities to Boston;
a year later, he accepted the Battell Professorship of Music at Yale
University, where he remained until his death in 1919.

Parker's position at Yale and his activity as a choral conductor
removed him from Boston, but he definitely belongs to the group
because of his background, his training, and his associations. Although he wrote nine orchestral works, some chamber music, and
pieces for piano and organ, he is recognized and remembered as a
choral composer. His masterpiece was a sacred cantata, *Hora Novis-
sima,* for mixed chorus and orchestra. This has been frequently performed in America and England and, along with one of his later
works, *The Legend of St. Chistopher,* was responsible for his receiving a degree of Doctor of Music from Cambridge University in 1902.
Mona, one of his two operas, was awarded the $10,000 prize offered
by the Metropolitan Opera House for an opera by an American
composer. His opera *Fairyland* also received a $10,000 prize in 1913
from the National Federation of Music Clubs. This opera received
six performances in Los Angeles in 1915 and has not been heard
since. Many of his religious songs and anthems are currently heard
in American church music.

Summary

1. The forces which greatly assisted the development of art and music in
   Europe were not active in America.

2. The Pilgrims did not object to music as such; they objected to tampering with the scriptures to provide suitable texts.
3. The men most critical of the church music of their day were Symmes, Tufts, and Walter.
4. Church-sponsored singing schools became social institutions throughout the American colonies.
5. Native pioneer leaders were Billings and Holden.
6. Gentlemen amateurs were Franklin, Hopkins, and Jefferson.
7. Bands have played an important part in the development of American music.
8. Men who made unique contributions to American music were Lowell Mason, Louis Gottschalk, and Stephen Foster.
9. American nineteenth-century opera was moderately successful under great difficulties; early leaders were Henry Fry and George Bristow.
10. The Boston classicists were led by Edward McDowell. They were able to keep Romanticism alive in America for over a decade after it was dead or dying in Europe.

Examples of Music

1. *Music of the Pilgrims.* Haydn Society (HSL 2068–XTV 1945L).
2. *The American Harmony,* "Being a choice collection of the best and most approved fuguing and plain tunes, with a fine anthem." (Used in singing schools and church choirs in the United States, 1779–1813).
3. The Goldman Band, *Woodup* and *Chester.* Capitol (W 1688).
4. McDowell, *Piano Concerto No. 2 in D Minor,* Op. 23. Columbia (Masterworks ML 4638).
5. McDowell, *Second Suite,* Op. 48 (*"Indian"*). Mercury Classics (MG 40009).
6. Gottschalk, *Night of the Tropics.* Columbia (CS 9381).
7. Gottschalk, *Music in America.* An excellent anthology of early American music may be found in the set of MIA records, numbered from 96 to 111. These records are manufactured by the Society for the Preservation of the American Musical Heritage, Inc., founded by Karl Kruegar. No further address is given.

23 ～ Modern Music

The past century has seen many drastic changes in our way of life. Almost all of these changes were brought about, directly or indirectly, by technological and scientific advances. All of us are well aware that we live in an age devoted to technical experiments and other developments that have resulted in a scientific attitude toward life. But somehow we have expected our musicians to continue as they did in previous times, producing a music of romantic feeling and sentiment while we live in a mechanical world.

Music of the twentieth century held no future if it was only to become more nationalistic, more romantic, or more realistic—it must in some way reflect the age in which it is created. As music moved into the twentieth century, Debussy and his followers were leading the way with French Impressionism, which was soon to run its course. The German answer to this French challenge was Expressionism, which set up inner experiences as the only reality. It offered emotional release of more than normal intensity, a suppressed but desperate kind of Romanticism of an anti-Romantic age.

After two hundred years of musical endeavor, the twentieth century saw American composers finally rise above foreign domination and emerge with styles not derived from Europe. Technical elements common to international music were employed, of course, but the emotional content, rhythmic patterns, and harmonic color belong to this country.

In the history of music the element of change is always present. If this change comes about gradually, we accept it as natural progress; if this cultural progress moves very rapidly, we call it a revolution. There have been three such revolutions in the history of Western music. About A.D. 1300, the supremacy of polyphonic music was established. This arranged for two or more related melodies to be sounded simultaneously and was called "The New Art." Three hundred years later, about 1600, the style of homophonic music was developed. This style, called "The New Music," gave predominance to one melody, usually in the soprano or highest voice, and supported it with a chordal accompaniment. This is the type of music with which we are most familiar today. Another three hundred years brought a third revolution in music. This time, however, composers did not unite in following a single style or form which culminated in a period of music. It may be called, then, a time of contemporary individualism. The generally accepted name for twentieth-century music is "The New Music"—the same term that was applied three hundred years earlier.

There are three characteristics of Romantic music which twentieth-century composers particularly resisted: (1) the major and minor scale concept which resulted in a strong feeling of tonality or key—music of this type was too predictable, it restricted the creativity of the composer; (2) the powerful force of rhythm continually sacrificed to predominant melody; and (3) the beautiful, vibrant, sometimes overpowering sound, often highly charged with emotion, which did not reflect the twentieth-century machine age of electricity and jet propulsion.

Those twentieth-century composers who continued on in the nineteenth-century style are sometimes referred to as "The Lost Generation" of music, but there were also many talented and highly trained composers who dedicated themselves to the task of creating the "New Music" that would truly represent twentieth-century culture.

The musical concepts which seem most important for these twentieth-century composers are: (1) *Polytonality,* the simultaneous use of different key or tonal centers. Igor Stravinsky uses this in *The Rite of Spring* to suggest restlessness. (2) *Polyrhythm,* the simultaneous use of two or more kinds of rhythm such as duple in one part and triple in another. Paul Hindemith uses this device effectively in the second movement of his Third Quartet. (3) *Twelve-tone system,* the construction of music in which each of the twelve tones of the chromatic scale are equally important. The first step is to form a pattern or *tone-row* which uses all of the chromatic tones; no note is repeated until the entire pattern has been stated. Equal stress on each of the twelve possible tones dispenses with any tonal center or key feeling and thereby creates what is called *atonality.* (4) *The tone-cluster,* another device of atonality. It was first used by an American composer, Henry Cowell, in 1912. This special effect is produced by a group of notes on the piano played simultaneously with the forearm, elbow, or fist. (5) A *dominant, on-going, rhythm,* used as a unifying element of the music. (6) The high shrill sounds of the woodwind instruments, produced by a smaller orchestra, favored over the lush sound of the nineteenth-century strings. (7) The most radical of all: dispensing with traditional instruments and using machines such as the tape recorder as the musical medium.

Charles Ives (1874–1954) was an American composer who piled up compositions using advanced techniques commonly supposed to have originated in Europe a decade later. Ives seems to have been led to his extreme use of polytonality and polyrhythm by way of presenting American folk material in a way that does not rob it of its flavor. While his contemporaries in Boston were absorbing Brahms and Wagner and doing their best to keep Romanticism alive a little longer, Ives was absorbing the musical experiences provided by the New England village where he grew up. The concerts of the village band, the singing of the church choir, the fiddles and banjos of the barn dances, circus parades, and the religious camp meetings—all of these combine to give his music a feeling that is American, although he employed many of the new devices of experimental composition.

His Second Symphony is a good example of the unique style of his orchestration. The music is full of surprises. There are five movements instead of the traditional four. In the fifth movement his themes include the well-known melodies: "Camptown Races," "Long, Long Ago," the bugle call, "Reveille," and "Columbia, the Gem of the Ocean." His final chord for the composition is a dissonant tone cluster which sounds simultaneously the last note of each theme; all of these devices are used in good taste and the music is artistic and interesting.

Another example of this amazing complexity of orchestration is found in his New England Symphony, which he subtitles "Three Places in New England." The second movement, or place, is named, "Putnam's Camp, Redding, Connecticut." This was the site of General Israel Putnam's winter quarters in 1778–1779. The work is a musical fantasy, showing the camp as it might appear in dreams. Fragments of melodies are effectively used in a polyrhythmical way bringing about natural dissonances throughout this remarkable movement. A riot of march rhythms introduce several different tonalities at the same time with a variety of meters. When one listens to this music, one imagines the camp and parade grounds on the morning of the Fourth of July in 1779. This music is not only typically American but it is highly representative of music in a technical age.

One of the most important champions of the new music in Europe was Béla Bartók (1881–1945), born in a small Hungarian town where his father was director of an agricultural school. He studied at the Royal Academy in Budapest, where he joined the nationalist movement to shake off the domination of German musical culture. His interest in folklore led him to realize that the music which had been romanticized by Liszt and Brahms and had been universally accepted as Hungarian was really the music of the Gypsies, who had come from another, undetermined place. He decided the true Hungarian folk idiom was to be found among the peasants; in company with his fellow composer, Zoltán Kodály (koh'-dah-yee), he traveled widely throughout Hungary, devoting himself to the study and collection of genuine Hungarian folk music. He also studied Roumanian and Slovakian folk music.

In 1907 Bartók was appointed Professor of Piano at the Royal Academy in Budapest, where he remained for nearly thirty years. He received little recognition until the late 1920's, when his works began to receive recognition outside Hungary. In 1940, after the rise of Hitler and the subsequent collaboration of Hungary with Nazi Germany, Bartók felt impelled to leave his homeland and come to the United States to live. He was appointed to a position at Columbia University, primarily to continue his folk music research; but his last years in America proved to be a difficult period. He did receive a few commissions for compositions and played several piano concerts in New York. His health was failing and most of his worldly possessions had been left behind in Hungary. The American Society of Composers, Authors, and Publishers provided him with medical care; and jazz musician Benny Goodman also aided him financially. In 1945 he died of leukemia, with his stature as a composer still not fully appreciated.

Paul Hindemith (1895–1963) was a German composer, performer, conductor, teacher, and one of the dominant forces of the twentieth century. He was the most substantial figure among the composers who came up in Germany after the First World War. His early compositions were boldly experimental. When, in 1927, he was made Professor of Composition at the Berlin Hochschule, he put into practice his progressive theories of education. Although the Nazi regime was eager to encourage German art, Hindemith was too modern for those who felt that Wagner had provided the ultimate in music. Hindemith's works were banned in the Third Reich after Propaganda Minister Goebbels accused him of "atrocious dissonance" and "cultural bolshevism." He arrived in America in 1940 shortly before the outbreak of World War II and joined the faculty of Yale University. Later he lectured at Harvard and at the Berkshire Music Center in Tanglewood, Massachusetts, where he spent his summers. He returned to Europe in 1953 as Professor of Composition at Zurich University, Switzerland, where he remained until his death a decade later.

Hindemith was a prolific composer, writing in every conceivable field of composition, including solo works for most instruments. His best known works are a song cycle, *Das Marienleben (The Life of Mary)*; an opera, *Mathis der Maler (Mathis the Painter)*; and *In Praise of Music for Chorus and Orchestra*.

Arnold Schönberg (1874–1951) is probably the most controversial composer of the twentieth century. At first a vigorous follower of the Wagner tradition, he soon felt the necessity for a new system of composition. As a result, he devised a technique, the twelve-tone system, based upon the twelve tones of the chromatic scale. By arranging them in a particular order, a *motive* was created. This was not a melody or theme. It could be repeated in contrasting rhythms, started on any pitch in the chromatic scale, be inverted and used in a variety of ways. The order of the tones within the row, however, could not be changed or repeated in a given voice until the whole row had been "stated." By doing this, no note is stressed above the others, and the composer escapes the traditional patterns of harmony and key-feeling (see Fig. 23–1). The constant reappearance of this twelve-tone pattern serves as a basis for unity in the composition, and the variations built upon it furnish the variety. Despite the hostility of the public, Schönberg's music and ideas slowly made their way. When his symphonic poem *Pelleas and Melisande* was first performed in Vienna, one critic announced it to be "a fifty-minute-long wrong note." The tide finally turned, however, with the performance of his *Gurre-Lieder* in Vienna in 1913 when a band of

Fig. 23–1.   Tone-Row Forms in Suite, Op. 25, Schönberg

O = Original; I = Inversion; R = Retrograde; RI = Retrograde Inversion

enthusiastic disciples gathered about him. The most gifted were Alban Berg and Anton von Webern, who sustained their master in the fierce struggle for recognition that lay ahead. Among the most widely heard works of Schönberg are those of his early romantic period: *Verklärte Nacht (Transfigured Night)* for string orchestra; the *Gurre-Lieder* for chorus, soloists, and orchestra; a number of chamber music works; and a large quantity of songs. His most outstanding works in the twelve-tone system are his Piano Concerto, Violin Concerto and String Quartets Nos. 3 and 4.

Arthur Honegger (1892–1955) was of Swiss parentage, so it is not strange that his music occupies a place between French charm and German rigor. Honegger employs polytonal music practices and his music is therefore often extremely dissonant. He justifies this harshness of sound in the statement, "If your design, whether melodic or rhythmic, is clear, and if it commands attention, the dissonances that accompany it will not frighten the listener away." His composition *Pacific 231* is a remarkable study in rhythmic motion. The composer's prime objective is to give the feeling of mathematically accelerated rhythm, while the tempo itself remains fairly constant. The result is a description of a large steam locomotive; at first it is standing still; then starts to move, and gathers momentum.

Finally this large machine is traveling through the night at seventy miles an hour. Pacific 231 is the name of an actual Northern Pacific steam locomotive.

The music of Sergei Prokofiev (prock-off'-yeff) and Dmitri Shostakovich (shoss-ta-co'-vitch) is representative of Russia's contribution to twentieth-century music. Prokofiev (1891–1953) enjoyed an international reputation as a composer and concert pianist, which explains the large number of piano sonatas (eight) and piano concertos (five) among his works. *The Classical Symphony* and his opera *The Love of Three Oranges* (1921) were very well received, and his celebrated *Peter and the Wolf*, a symphonic fairytale, 1936, is known to thousands of school children as a means of identifying orchestral instruments. This number is one of the kind known as *Gebrauchsmusik*, a German word indicating music with a special purpose. Prokofiev is regarded as one of the important twentieth-century symphonists. Shostakovich (b. 1906) made a brilliant beginning with his first symphony at the age of nineteen. Since then, except for his Fifth Symphony, the quality of his music has been uneven. There are beautiful moments in his symphonies, but some of the movements are long, loud, and trivial in content. His recent chamber music is considerably more interesting.

Igor Stravinsky (b. 1882) is unquestionably the most successful of all twentieth-century composers in winning acceptance from the general public. Stravinsky neither followed nor formulated any set theory of composition. His music is characterized by a free use of dissonance, but rarely reaches the extreme of atonality, that is, music without a key-feeling. Rhythmic drive, often resulting in brutal repetition within very complex and irregular patterns, characterizes his works. Tonal qualities of great effectiveness are found, running the gamut from those of great beauty to those of just plain ugliness. We may understand his music better if we think of it in his terms; Stravinsky says, "The sole purpose of art is to establish order in things." Stravinsky is a master of orchestration. He led the way in selecting a variety of orchestral sounds; not nineteenth-century masses of beautiful sound, but single voices combined. He usually has woodwind instruments predominate. His composition, *The Rite of Spring*, furnishes a good example of his mastery of orchestral techniques.

In order to appreciate "machine music," we must disregard the nineteenth-century concept that rhythm, melody, and harmony must strike a balance. Electronic music is based on concepts of high and low, deep and shallow, and contrast and variation in the quality of sound. We must be willing to accept the idea that timbre, rather than melody, becomes the principal element of this music.

One of the most radical examples of machine music is called *Poème Electronique* (1958), by Edgard Varèse (vah-rezz') (1855–1968). Varèse came to the United States from France in 1915, and since that time composed largely in the field of machine music. His own reaction was, "This is not experimental music, for I know exactly what is going to happen, and I have planned it this way." His music was created partially with a stylus on electric recording tape, assisted by other electrically produced sounds. Of course, this system bypasses the need for traditional instruments and completely dehumanizes the whole concept of music; but in the technical world of generations to come it may find an important place.

The future holds the answer to the success or failure of this medium of musical expression. The performer and the instrument are eliminated, since the composer can create these sounds in a variety of ways or with a stylus marking directly on electric tape. Dancers find its rhythmic capabilities intriguing, and tape-music may find a considerable market in radio, television, and motion pictures. The dominant element of contemporary music is rhythm, which best represents the machine and mechanical devices, the concept of sports, ballet, and other dance forms; while polyrhythms and polyrhythmic concepts are not uncommon in today's writing.

The predominant style of modern art is a new realism which substitutes logic for emotion. It avoids overstatement, and tends toward abstraction, pure design, and symbolism. We find contemporary composers involved in a type of primitivism which thrives on shocking society, often using this as an escape from over-refinement. The emphasis in today's art is placed on techniques, and no effort is made to avoid ugliness. Until the emergence of an accepted style on the part of composers, there will be no general acceptance on the part of the listeners. As yet, such a unity of style—as is found in the styles designated Baroque, Classical, or Romantic—has not emerged in the twentieth century. It has been about sixty years since Romanticism, with its phases of realism, nationalism, and impressionism, was the accepted style. Most early twentieth-century composers seemed more interested in doing away with Romanticism than they were in creating expressive art works of their own.

A great deal of music written by composers of the past sixty years—many of them already forgotten—makes the evaluation of contemporary music extremely difficult. However, from this music some notable landmarks arise; if not for posterity, at least for us at this time. Composers do not set styles by themselves. Society as a whole sets a style; when there is no longer participation by society in this style, then the art form will die. The examples of contemporary music we have mentioned have been extreme and have not been widely accepted, but in each case they may serve as a resource for further development. There are other composers whose music reflects twentieth-century characteristics, and we cannot be sure which men of our day will be remembered by history.

Summary

1. Music of the twentieth century would have had no future if it were to become only more nationalistic or more Romantic.
2. Since 1900 we have seen more drastic changes in our way of life than man has yet known. Music of the twentieth century attempts to reflect these changes.
3. On three occasions, revolutions have taken place in the history of music, at approximately three-hundred-year intervals, 1300, 1600, and 1900.
4. A period in music history appears when an accepted style on the part of the composers is generally accepted by the listeners. No such well-defined period has emerged in the twentieth century.
5. The twentieth century saw American composers rise above foreign domination.
6. Twentieth-century composers particularly resisted major and minor scale concepts, rhythm sacrificed to melody, and emphasis on emotion.
7. In order to appreciate electronic music, we must accept the concepts of rhythm, timbre, contrast, and variation to be stronger elements than melody.
8. Igor Stravinsky is unquestionably the twentieth-century composer who has won the widest acceptance, although he has neither followed nor formulated a set theory of composition. At times, his music is atonal.
9. Musical concepts that characterize twentieth-century music are poly-

tonality and polyrhythms (Ives); atonality (Schönberg); dominant rhythm (Honegger); orchestral dominance of woodwind voices (Stravinsky); and machine music (Varèse).

Examples of Music

1. Charles Ives, *Symphony No. 2*. Columbia (ML 6289).
2. Charles Ives, *Three Places in New England, Symphony No. 3*. Mercury (Olympian Series MG 50149).
3. Igor Stravinsky, *The Rite of Spring*. Columbia (Masterworks ML 5277).

    Stravinsky's credo of modern music is a realism which substitutes logic for emotion. It includes a type of primitivism which thrives on shocking society and makes no effort to avoid ugliness. Stravinsky says the sole purpose of art is to establish order in things, and this is effectively done in his *The Rite of Spring*.
4. Arthur Honegger, *Pacific 231*. Westminster (XWN 18486).
5. Béla Bartók, *Music for Strings, Percussion & Celesta*. RCA Victor (Red Seal LM 2374).

    Bartók's music variously exhibits primitivism, neo-classicism and expressionism; it is usually polytonal, but sometimes atonal. The unique texture of his writing is illustrated by this short work for strings and celesta.
6. Edgard Varèse, *Poème Electronique*. Columbia (Masterworks ML 5478).
7. Arthur Schönberg, *Piano Concerto, Verklärte Nacht (Transfigured Night)*.

24 ～ Jazz and Popular Music

In the year 1894, Antonín Dvořák was teaching in New York City and urging the creation of an American "National" School of Music based upon the use of Negro and Indian melodies. Edward McDowell, wearing a derby hat and curled mustache, walked in Boston Common, musing upon Celtic lore and legends. He was soon to go to Columbia University and establish a School of Music there. Horatio Parker, academic, fastidious, Munich-trained, had just assumed his duties as Professor of Music at Yale University, and Charles Edward Ives, twenty years old, went to New Haven, Connecticut, to study music at Yale University. John Philip Sousa (1854–1932) was in the process of organizing his concert band, which set a pattern for the development of approximately seventy thousand bands in America today. Victor Herbert (1859–1920), although an army band master in 1894, was getting ready to go to Broadway to present a series of forty light operas, most of them highly successful. This tradition needed only slight changes to become the current Broadway musical show.

The clog dances of the nineteenth-century Irish emigrants had become ragtime dances of the American Negroes. They were often refined somewhat by the French influence of New Orleans and altered somewhat by the rhythmic agility of Negro dancers, but ragtime music had definitely entered the musical scene. Numerous small bands of Negro musicians traveled throughout the South, playing this kind of impromptu music wherever and whenever they could find someone to listen to them. The minstrel show, a combination of Negro music and comedy, was an extremely popular form of entertainment. The wail of frustration and sorrow that has been heard in one or another form throughout all of man's history, but which has quite recently been named the Blues, also found an audience.

All these sources came together in the popular music of the

First World War. In 1917 the now defunct but then widely read Literary Digest observed: "A strange word has gained widespread use in the ranks of our producers of popular music. It is *jazz,* used mainly as an adjective, descriptive of a band." This is rather vague, but it does establish the term *jazz* as being in general use by the end of the war. Jazz is the most controversial form of music that our country has ever known. Any one of the hundreds of would-be-authorities on jazz will glibly tell us that jazz came out of New Orleans about 1910, but few will talk about how it got into New Orleans in the first place.

The basic concepts of jazz come from ten thousand cabin homes throughout the South. It was practiced on the porches of these cabin homes, each evening of each hot summer day. When the family was seated on the porch, someone would sing, accompanied in a variety of ways. Some would tap on the porch with sticks, others would blow on a jug or some other improvised instrument. Possibly someone played a banjo, picking a plaintive tune or rhythm. A strong rhythm was set, a bass figure established, and anyone was welcome to play or sing some melody upon the pattern.

When these people moved to town, they managed to get some drums and trombones. They didn't have to beat on the porch any more; they made New Orleans jazz. The same rhythmic patterns were dressed up and made noisier as each instrumentalist expanded the possibilities of his own self-expression. There were few rules to follow, but the accepted ones were strict: all must play in the same key; all must keep the same tune in mind as each created his own variations and improvisations; members of the band might take turns, but the climax would come when they all played simultaneously.

As America was drawn into the First World War, a combination of Southern musicians made its way to Chicago to play an engagement at Lamb's Cafe. The four musicians were: Tom Brown, trombonist; Raymond Lopez, cornetist; Gus Miller, clarinetist; and William Lambert, drummer. Together, they were known as "Brown's Band from Dixieland." In 1916 Gus Miller formed his own band and named it the "Jazz Band from Dixieland." The Literary Digest picked up the name from this band.

The term *jazz* may have been borrowed from the name of Chaz

Washington, a talented percussionist who lived and worked around Vicksburg, Mississippi. If Chaz Washington did not originate the jazz style of drumming, there is no question that he was one of its early masters. The success of these jazz bands signaled the organization of many Dixieland combos that took the country by storm. As musicians approached 1920 and pulled out of this Dixieland tailspin, some of them attempted to write down the music they were playing. By reading notes it was possible to use large sections of instruments rather than carry out a variation with a single voice. In writing down the music, harmony became a part of jazz and the dance band of the thirties, forties, fifties, and sixties became the next step.

The "sweet" style of jazz was a natural reaction to the extremes that popular music had experienced. Under the direction of such men as Isham Jones, Vincent Lopez, and especially Paul Whiteman, came the development of "sweet" music (in contrast to "hot" music). There are many men who deserve mention in a review of popular music, but only a few of them brought about changes or new ideas in the jazz field.

Glenn Miller was constantly looking for a new sound with his orchestra. In his search, he changed the traditional harmony as well as the traditional style of early dance bands. Since the organization of the first Paul Whiteman orchestra of about 1920, there has been little change in the standard instrumentation of the dance band. Most of the experimentation has been done through the use of ensemble tone.

According to the new College Encyclopedia of Music, "Jazz is a musical form which uses improvisation in syncopated rhythms against a regular pulse. Its rhythmic style was inherited from ragtime and its melodic and harmonic style were affected by the minor thirds and sevenths of the 'blues.' " Almost every argument dealing with the values or lack of values expressed through the medium of jazz points toward the fact that jazz by the nature of its rhythm and by the style of its harmony and melody is limited to two types of expression: one of gay abandon, and the other of blue melancholy. Supporters of jazz, however, feel that there are lyrical qualities and various shades of emotion which can also be communicated.

Jazz is America's most specific contribution to world music. It invaded Europe immediately after the First World War and claimed serious attention in both Europe and America in the twenties. Jazz seems to thrive only in the hands of Americans and it is therefore still regarded as typically American. Its chief characteristics seem to be a duple rhythm, whether two or four beats in a measure. Upon this steady, machine-like rhythm is superimposed a syncopated melody that accents those beats and portions of beats that would not normally be accented. Instead of developing a theme in a regular way, some type of variation is improvised upon it. The subtleties of chamber music are difficult to impose upon the strict rhythmic framework of jazz.

The 1950's and 1960's will probably go down as the age of "rock 'n' roll." It is difficult to say exactly what the term indicates. When Louis Armstrong was asked to define it, he said, "Man, it is that mean music with those weird chords always hopping in the bass."

The crusade for what is called *progressive jazz* has been carried on largely by Dave Brubeck and his associates. If we listen carefully to Brubeck's music in a very determined effort to find out just what is implied by the term *progressive jazz,* it appears that the idea is closely related to the Dixieland music of 1910. However, the style of improvising is greatly refined and less noisy. Each member of the group has an opportunity to improvise while the others maintain a discreet accompaniment. The emphasis is placed on the performer's ability to improvise at the moment. Progressive jazz is not usually written down. The vague terminology of slang makes jazz even more difficult to characterize and analyze.

In the 1920's we had sweet jazz; violins were often part of the band, playing beautiful sweeping melodies. In the 1930's we had hot jazz, with rasping voices of muted trumpets and trombones supported by rhythm and five saxophones. In the 1940's we turned to *swing,* which was orchestrated and carefully written down. Its demand for talented, highly trained men brought about a degree of acceptance and respectability never achieved by earlier jazz musicians. This more sophisticated jazz closely paralleled a movement called *Neo-Classicism,* which received much serious attention. One way of rejecting the nineteenth century was to return to the eighteenth in a so-called back-to-Bach movement. This return to the Classical ideal was not mere imitation; it was more a borrowing of eighteenth-century patterns and forms and filling them with twentieth-century techniques and ideas. Neo-Classicism focused attention on elegance, craftsmanship, and taste. It pointed up the intellectual rather than the emotional elements of music.

George Gershwin (1898–1937) was the leading representative of a versatile group of young American composers in the 1920's. He was an American-born and an American-trained composer as well as a talented pianist. He used the concept of Neo-Classicism in his attempt to bridge the gap between "popular" and "classical" music. He came close to achieving this aim in 1925, when he composed his *Piano Concerto in F.* He used the form of the traditional piano concerto, with orchestral introduction and solo cadenza; but in the voicing and melodic style, he used the jazz idioms and techniques that emerged in the popular music of the 1920's. Gershwin was a gifted song writer and the composer of a highly successful folk opera, *Porgy and Bess,* which furnished a strong pattern for the later development of American opera.

By the year 1920, the United States had fought and won a world war. Almost everyone was trying very hard to be patriotic and do things American, but studiously keeping away from the fight-and-die-for-your-country kind of patriotism. American composers came under the influence of this new nationalism and turned their attention to music of their country, such as jazz and the music of the Indians, of the Negroes, and of cowboys and the West. The United States has produced a very large number of young and talented composers, but we have space to mention just a few.

Virgil Thomson (b. 1896) is the author of several books dealing with music and music criticism. He has written music for symphony orchestra, ballet, instrumental solos. He has written sonatas, concertos, and more than one hundred short pieces which he calls *Musical Portraits.* He has also written the music for several moving pictures. A suite drawn from one of them, *A Plow That Broke the Plains,* has a second movement called "Cattle," based upon three of the better known cowboy songs of the Old West. Listening to it, we notice that, as in the new nationalism, he chooses cowboy folk melodies; as in impressionism, he does not develop these themes, he repeats them many times; as in realism, he has added a guitar and saxophone to the orchestra to gain the true personal touch. These themes are (1) My Home's in Montana; (2) I Ride Old Paint; and (3) The Streets of Laredo.

We have already noted that understatement is one of the characteristics of contemporary music. Don Gillis is a talented composer who has written a very creditable symphony which he calls Opus 5½. Of course, it is difficult to take this work seriously. Another example of this is given us by Robert McBride, who has composed an excellent fugue in a good Neo-Classical style but has used two nursery rhymes, "Peter, Peter Pumpkin Eater" and "I Love Coffee, I Love Tea," as his theme material. He calls this work *The Pumpkin Eater's Little Fugue*. Again, it is hard to take this music seriously, but it is well written and makes interesting listening. Robert McBride is Professor of Music Composition at the University of Arizona.

Howard Hanson (b. 1896), renowned composer, conductor, and until very recently Director of the Eastman School of Music in Rochester, New York, is well known to most concertgoers for his four large-scale symphonies, his Chorale and Alleluia, and several other major works. In recent years, however, he has followed the trend, or perhaps we should say helped establish a trend, toward chamber music. His Serenade for Flute, Strings and Harp is a good example of his artistry in this style.

Aaron Copland (b. 1900) is an extremely well-known figure among present-day composers. His growth as a composer has mirrored the major trends in music for the past forty years. He achieved great success in writing for moving pictures and composing in various musical forms. Some of his most important music has been written for ballet. While writing in this form, he has been associated with Martha Graham, one of America's leading dancers and one of the first "interpretative" dancers. Miss Graham collaborated with Aaron Copland in producing the highly successful ballet *Appalachian Spring,* first performed on October 30, 1944. Their close collaboration is reflected in its subtitle, "Ballet for Martha." It tells the story of a pioneer couple making their home in the Appalachian Mountains. The music uses as a central theme an old religious song called "Simple Gifts." The words are these:

'tis a gift to be simple,
'tis a gift to be free,
'tis a gift to come down
where we ought to be.

In this case Copland's music is simple, but it is also beautiful.

The Association of Composers and Publishers lists a large number of talented and highly trained men in America who are registered as composers of serious music. Several hundred others are spending part of their time in composition. It is difficult to make a truly representative list from the many competent American composers but some of the better-known names which should be mentioned are Roy Harris, Douglas Moore, Walter Piston, Ernest Bloch, Roger Sessions, Randal Thompson, and William Schuman.

American musicians achieved a dominant place in the world of music about 1930. The evolution of Western music continues as it is guided by the tastes of the people. New music which cannot excite our enthusiasm has no claim to our sympathy or indulgence. All of the music that survives in the standard repertory has met this condition in its own time. We should therefore make an effort to acquaint ourselves with beautiful and artistic music and thereby gain in our appreciation of the magic that is music.

Summary

1. Antonin Dvořák urged the creation of a National School of Music based upon the study of Negro and Indian music.
2. Sousa's concert band, Victor Herbert's light operas, and Edward McDowell's musical genius influenced the trend of early twentieth-century music.
3. Jazz was a combination of musical sources, including ragtime, blues, and minstrel music.
4. Neo-Classicism was one way of rejecting Romanticism.
5. George Gershwin used the technique of jazz while composing in traditional forms.
6. Virgil Thomson uses folk material while composing in traditional forms.
7. Understatement and a flippant approach by the composer often interfere with the success and understanding of a composition.
8. American musicians achieved a dominant place in the musical world after 1930.
9. Howard Hanson is considered the Dean of American composers, while Aaron Copland is one of the most popular representatives of present-day composers.
10. Music is guided in its changes by public acceptance or rejection.

Examples of Music

1. Morton Gould, *Doubling in Brass*. RCA Victor (Red Seal LM 2308). (Marches by Sousa and other band music.)
2. "Gregorian Chant" and "Getting Together," from *Jazz Composers Workshop No. 2*. Savoy (MG 12059).
3. Virgil Thomson, *A Plow That Broke the Plains*. Vanguard (VRS 1071).
4. Howard Hanson, *Serenade for Flute, Strings, and Harp*. Mercury (Olympian Series MG 50076).
5. George Gershwin, *Piano Concerto in F*. RCA Camden (CAL 304).
6. George Gershwin, *Porgy and Bess*. RCA Victor (Red Seal LM 6033).
7. Aaron Copland, *Appalachian Spring*. Westminster (XWN 18284).

25 ∽ Afro-American Music

Throughout this book it has been necessary to be brief; to summarize and in some cases to outline material. Several areas of music have not been fully covered, but only in this way have we been able to present an overview of the men and music in Western culture. The final section dealing with Afro-American music must also be limited to certain aspects of the subject, and it seems that an appraisal of the Negro's position in the traditional business of American music would be appropriate. In a sense, this appraisal will show the way in which American Negroes have conformed to the music of white America and Western Europe. It will only partially explain the Negro's musical genius and creativity, which has contributed so much to the vitality of American music.*

Afro-American Musicians

When the Negro came to America, his racial heritage was taken from him. He had to adjust to a new country, new food, new work and working conditions. Without formal education, he found it difficult to express himself in the words of a newly-heard language which included sounds that did not occur in his native tongue. However, his manner of compromising these sounds became one of his strongest characteristics and as the Negro dialect evolved, it softened or eliminated the harsh sounds of American speech in a way that contributed to the beauty and charm of early Negro songs. The remarkable development of rhythmic qualities in Afro-American music probably has its sources in the African use of drums for communication. Drums not only beat out a primitive morse code,

* For insight into the background of Negro culture and an appreciation of the African heritage, I highly recommend the following reference books to supplement this material: LeRoi Jones, *Blues People* (New York: William Morrow, 1963); and Ralph Ellison, *Shadow & Act* (New York: Random House, 1963).

but conveyed a phonetic reproduction of words. In this way, the Africans developed a keen rhythmic sense, an awareness of tonal variation and sound inflection which was not readily recognizable to the Western ear. Their subtle musical devices also included an elaborate system of using percussion instruments of different timbres to produce harmonic contrasts while playing two, three, or more separate rhythm patterns to support the same melody.

The melodic characteristics of African music came not only from the arrangement of notes, but from the singer's vocal interpretation. The notes do not conform entirely to the traditional well-tempered scale, and the tense, slightly hoarse-sounding vocal techniques of work songs and the blues are rooted in West African musical tradition. In African languages, the meaning of a word can be altered by changing its pitch or by changing its stress. The Western listener is often critical of the hoarse shrill quality of Negro singers and attributes it to their lack of proper vocal training, but it comes from a conscious desire to produce a calculated effect. The Western concept of voice cultivation is foreign to true Afro-American music.

The natural musical talent of the Negro was mentioned by Thomas Jefferson in his *Notes on Virginia*, written in 1774. He told of the singing of Negroes on the plantations and how it was listened to with interest. Serious consideration of their songs, however, did not come until after the Civil War.

Early in the nineteenth century, the patterns of Negro minstrelsy began to take shape. At first, the movement had little to do with music. The performer was not a singing troubadour. He was an improvising entertainer who specialized in eccentric dancing; music was just one of his tricks. James Weldon Johnson describes the origins of minstrelsy in this way:

> Every plantation had its talented band that could crack Negro jokes, and sing and dance to the accompaniment of the banjo and the bones—the bones being the actual ribs of a sheep or other small animal, cut the proper length, scraped clean and bleached in the sun. When the planter wished to entertain his guests, he needed only to call his troupe of black minstrels.

Negro minstrelsy came to the American stage about 1830. It came in the form of a counterfeit imitation of the Negro bands by white actors in blackface. When the Negroes themselves came onto the stage twenty-five years later, the mold was too set to be radically changed. They had to accept the performance patterns which had been worked out and laid down by the white imitators. Professional minstrelsy was both popular and profitable during much of the nineteenth century. The movement that had been launched by white comedians who imitated the Negro ended, ironically, with the Negroes imitating the whites.

Two of the greatest minstrel troupes were Lew Johnson's Plantation Minstrel Company and the Georgia Minstrels, who were organized in 1865 as the first all-Negro company. These and other Negro troupes of their day furnished the first real employment of Negro entertainers and brought talent and artistry to the minstrel movement, which greatly raised its musical standards. In 1882, after three highly successful European tours, the Georgia Minstrels were at the height of their success. They were an organization of twenty-one performers, most of them trained musicians who so dignified the tradition that they played in concert halls and attracted the attention of the cultivated musical public. They introduced serious music on their programs, working it into the stereotyped minstrel program. Minstrelsy began with burlesque and ended with the circus. In between there was a romantic period in a romantic century when the great Negro artists took part in programs of clean comedy, a pleasant type of often nostalgic folk music and a display of virtuosity on a variety of musical instruments.

The two greatest geniuses to furnish music for this period—one white and one Negro—were Stephen Foster (Chapter 22) and James Bland. Both of these talented but irresponsible troubadors played a large part in establishing the undeserved glorification of the slavery regime. Until recently few whites questioned their ideas—the sun was always shining, the magnolia trees were always in bloom, and everyone was happy down South. James Bland is best known for his songs: "Carry Me Back to Old Virginny," "In the Evening by the Moonlight," "Oh Dem Golden Slippers," and "In the Morning by the Bright Light," but as in the case of Stephen Foster many of his songs were given away or sold for a few dollars and published under another name. Richard Milburn, a Negro barber in Philadelphia, who played guitar and was a marvelous whistler, was another victim of song stealing. "Listen to the Mocking Bird" was published under his name in 1855, but later editions were credited to his mother, Alice Hawthorne, or to Septimus Winner, who re-arranged some of the words.

Negro singing in a formalized style first became known to the country at large through the travels of Negro singers, first from Fisk University, then from Hampton, Tuskegee, and other industrial schools. Fisk University, founded in Nashville, Tennessee, in 1866, was a pioneer institution dedicated to educating the freed slaves. Since this type of project was not altogether popular at the time and financial support was difficult to obtain, George L. White, music director at the school, started on a concert tour in 1871 with thirteen members of his choir. Three years later, when the tour was finished, they had raised more than $150,000, mostly in voluntary contributions from their audiences. More important for the cause of music, however, the songs of the Negro had been presented artistically and received enthusiastically throughout all of America and much of Europe. The Fisk Jubilee singers, as they were called, were well received by Queen Victoria of England and the Emperor of Germany.

The best evidence of the warm welcome accorded Negro composers is in the membership of the American Society of Composers, Authors, and Publishers (ASCAP). All but a few Negro composers and lyricists are enrolled, and the Society boasts proudly of such men as William C. Handy, Louis Armstrong, James Weldon Johnson, William Grant Still, Harry T. Burleigh, Sheldon Brooks, Thomas (Fats) Waller, and many others. When ASCAP was founded fifty years ago, its charter members included Dr. James Weldon Johnson and Dr. Harry T. Burleigh, two Negroes who had already achieved doctorates and high recognition for compositions in the field of symphonic and concert music. Doctor Johnson had attained such prominence as a musicologist, journalist, poet, and educator that President Theodore Roosevelt appointed him to the diplomatic corps as a consul. Doctor Burleigh had a fine baritone voice and successfully toured the concert halls of the United States and Europe. He was twice summoned to command performances for King Edward VII of England. He is probably best remembered as the composer of "Deep River," one of the greatest spirituals of all times.

When emancipation came, the Negro reached out for perfection in the highest types of Western music. Within two decades after the Civil War, Negroes were enrolled in conservatories, studying the great masters and displaying talent for composition of all forms of music. Many Negro composers wrote popular songs as well as serious concert music; others, such as William Grant Still, confined their efforts to the classical forms. Doctor Still, winner of several fellowships and holder of honorary degrees, spent some time in arranging and conducting popular music for radio and television but remained steadfast in his classical ambitions. Among his works are four symphonies, three ballets, several symphonic poems, and a wealth of chamber music and concert songs.

The most forceful impact of Negro composers has been on the music of the masses, music with something to say to everyone. Few seemed better able to say it than William Handy. Born in Florence, Alabama, in 1873, he received a good education from his clergyman father, and taught school for a time. Later, he played the trumpet professionally and starred at the Chicago World's Fair in 1893. His greatest ambition was to compose music. Early in his career, he composed songs distinctive enough to win public favor; after introducing "Beale Street Blues," "Memphis Blues," "Harlem Blues," and above all, "St. Louis Blues," the well-deserved title Father of the Blues was bestowed upon him.

William Handy was blind in the last years of his life, but he devoted himself to the W. C. Handy Fund for the Negro blind. At his death there was mourning all over the nation, but especially in Memphis, where a public square was dedicated to him. Of course, William Handy was not the first to create works in the "blues" mode, but more than any other man, he set the form and passed it on to the people. In so doing, he paved the way for the advent of American jazz.

Jazz was born of the musical experience of Negro people in America and into it went the complex rhythms and musical conceptions of their African heritage. The background of jazz was strange to white people whose musicians and critics were steeped in the traditions of Western European music and they had little or no patience with new sounds and techniques that rebelled against the things they had been taught. But despite everything the critics of jazz could do, it prospered and grew and became not only the music most representative of America but of all sections of the world influenced by American culture. Negroes had been playing their kind of music since the early 1890's, but it was not generally recognized until twenty years later when a group of white players known as the Original Dixieland Jazz Band moved North and established themselves in Chicago. At that time, however, there were probably a dozen Negro bands in the South that were superior to this white group. Modern jazz developed directly from the blues of the American Negro, from their ages-old songs of protest and rebellion. The subject matter ranged from love to politics, current events, and race relations to working conditions. Whether they are comically satirical or deadly serious, they are always realistic and sincere in their intent, never maudlin or superficial.

"The blues have a distinctive tonal scale in which the third and seventh tones tend to be lowered. The degree varies so these 'blue' notes cannot be reproduced accurately on any instrument of fixed pitch such as the piano. On a keyboard instrument, the blues effect is produced by striking two keys near the desired tone which creates a dissonant sound. The form consists of twelve bars of music in common time instead of the usual sixteen (see Chapter 24).

Negro bands such as those of Duke Ellington, Fletcher Henderson, Bennie Moten, Louis Armstrong, Jimmy Lunceford, Don Redman, and others played a swinging style of jazz for years, but it was not accepted by white America until after the First World War when Benny Goodman based the sounds of his big white band on traditional Negro style.

The spirituals of the American Negro were his own creation and it was proper that he should sing them. However, it was a tragedy that Negroes were relegated to singing Negro spirituals only. Until recently, few people saw these songs as "art," and even fewer imagined that the voice singing them might also sing grand opera.

Thirty years before the New York Metropolitan Opera House was opened in 1883, an ex-slave was presented and accepted in London as a great singer. Elizabeth Taylor Greenfield—later known as the Black Swan—was said by English critics to equal the great Jenny Lind in the beauty and technical proficiency of her voice. Thomas Bowers displayed such vocal talent that he was called the American Mario, after the great Italian tenor. Madam Sisseretta Jones, like Bowers, had a great voice which was compared to that of Adelina Patti, the leading singer of the times. The comparison was so favorable she was known as the Black Patti and performed in the principal cities of Europe during the 1890's. Madam Jones established her own musical company known as the Black Patti Troubadours and remained at its head for nineteen years. America obviously recognized the talents of these singers but it never allowed them to push open the operatic door for Negroes.

The historic aid for the Negro singer has been the church, which often develops singers through a choir program with performances of excellent music. Ellabelle Davis, a church soloist, serves as an example of this sort of training. She made her operatic debut in an opera called *The Chaplet* without having had formal training. Later, with five years of study she stunned Mexico City in 1946 with an exceptional performance of *Aïda*.

It is difficult for a young singer to gain early experience in opera. To offset this disadvantage, Negroes organized their own opera companies. The first of these was the Colored Opera Company, established in 1873. This was a company composed entirely of amateurs, but they were so expertly trained that a Philadelphia newspaper, in reviewing a performance of the Company, said that though "the opera, *The Doctor of Alcantara,* has frequently been given previously by various English companies, we venture to say, never so perfectly in its ensemble as by this company."

The Drury, another early company, was established in 1900. It was named for Thomas Drury and was primarily a touring company appearing in New York, Philadelphia, Boston, and Providence.

Other Negro opera companies were the American Negro Opera Company and the Harlem Opera Workshop. These companies built admirably upon the foundation laid by the Negro church, but they presented too few performances, lacked permanent houses to work in, and were constantly in need of funds.

In 1919, thirteen young musicians, feeling a need to help themselves and other musicians, organized the National Association of Negro Musicians. They wanted their organization to encourage the development of musical talent through scholarships for needy students; they wanted it to enrich the careers of professional musicians through workshops, seminars, and conferences; they wanted it to be a showcase for the cultural contribution of the Negro in music. These were worthwhile aims and it is a tribute to its founders that this organization continues to play an active role in music. It gave Marian Anderson her first scholarship and, in 1953, awarded Grace Bumbry, a brilliant mezzo-soprano, similar aid.

In spite of what the Negro community did to sustain its opera singers, there was much more to be done. Young voices, professionally trained, had few places to perform where they could gauge their potential artistry. The old saying that a prophet is not without honor save within his own country was never more true—most Negro singers who aspired to opera found their best opportunities in Europe.

Lillian Evanti was one of the brilliant young singers to be well received in France. After being there six months, she made her operatic debut in *Lakmé* with the Nice Opera Company, and was successful in the major roles of *La Traviata, Romeo and Juliet, Lakmé,* and *Lucia di Lammermoor.* Even in Europe, however, color seems to have been a barrier for the Negro singer. In spite of her success, she did not perform in the major European opera houses.

In 1930, Caterina Jarboro, a young singer from Wilmington, North Carolina, made her debut as *Aïda* at the Puccini Opera House in Milan. Her success was immediate, and after Milan she performed with the Paris Opera. She returned to America in 1933 and signed a contract with the Chicago Opera Company. When she performed *Aïda* in July of that year, she was the first Negro to perform with an American company. The debut was an artistic success and two more performances of *Aïda* were given in Chicago, after which the door was once more closed to the Negro. Jarboro returned to a career in Europe and has never performed with an American Opera Company again.

After Jarboro's success, no Negro appeared with an American Company until 1945. In that year, Todd Duncan, already celebrated for his portrayal of Porgy in *Porgy and Bess,* was contracted to play the part of Tonio in *Pagliacci* at the New York City Center Opera Company. One year later, Camilla Williams, a brilliant young soprano, was contracted to play the lead in *Madame Butterfly.* This was followed by other roles and a permanent place for her with the New York City Center Company. The New York Center has also given opportunities to other Negro singers. In the late forties, Lawrence Winters and Margaret Tynes appeared there and both have since become international stars.

In 1955, Marian Anderson made her debut—and the debut for the Negro—at the Metropolitan Opera Company. Shortly afterward, she was joined by Robert McFerrin, a first-prize winner in the Metropolitan auditions and the first Negro to enter the Metropolitan's opera training course. The success of Marian Anderson represents the triumph of genius over the great obstacle of race prejudice. She was born in South Philadelphia in 1908. Her family had only a meager income and the death of her father in 1920 brought still greater financial difficulties, but her rare talent was recognized and through the cooperation of her family, friends, and church, she was able to study music with first-rate teachers.

The climax of her lifelong struggle against race prejudice came when her manager tried to hire Constitution Hall in Washington, D. C., for a recital in February, 1939. Because the Daughters of the American Revolution looked with disfavor on the appearance of a Negro in Constitution Hall, the theater was barred to her. Such calculated discrimination evoked a chorus of protest throughout the country. Musicians, statesmen, clergymen, and writers vehemently denounced the DAR, and Mrs. Franklin D. Roosevelt resigned from that organization. Secretary of the Interior Harold L. Ickes then invited Miss Anderson to give her concert at the Lincoln Memorial. She consented, offering to sing for nothing to whoever cared to come to listen. On April 9, an audience of 75,000 assembled before the Memorial, among them Supreme Court Judges, Congressmen, Cabinet members. Another audience of several million listened over the radio as she sang lieder and Negro spirituals. Before her stretched an enthusiastic throng which was paying homage in no uncertain terms to a great artist. Beyond her loomed the massive and benign figure of Abraham Lincoln, seeming almost to serve as spiritual godfather to the proceedings. This concert, incidentally, is the subject of a mural design decorating the new Department of the Interior building, in Washington, D. C.

One week later when Marian Anderson came onto the stage at a concert in Carnegie Hall, a capacity audience rose spontaneously to its feet and gave her one of the most impressive demonstrations ever to be seen there. Here, surely, the Daughters of the America Revolution had their answer and Marian Anderson had proved herself to be one of the great artists of all time.

Leontyne Price, one of the great dramatic sopranos in opera today, was born in Laurel, Mississippi, where she began to show musical talent at an early age. From there she went to Central State College in Wilberforce, Ohio, and later, on a scholarship, to the

Julliard School of Music in New York. In 1952, as Mistress Ford in a Julliard production of *Falstaff*, she first received wide critical notice, with the result that she was chosen to sing Bess in a revival of Gershwin's *Porgy and Bess*. This production had a triumphant tour of Europe and a long Broadway run. In November, 1954, Miss Price made her recital debut in New York's Town Hall; in the three years following, she appeared with the NBC-TV Opera, successively as Tosca, as Pamina in *The Magic Flute,* and in the television premiere of Poulenc's *Dialogues of the Carmelites.* This last she sang with the San Francisco Opera in 1957 at the time of her first performance in *Aïda.* European engagements followed and in the fall of 1959 she made her debut with the Chicago Lyric Opera. Miss Price had the great honor of opening the Metropolitan at its new home in the Lincoln Center for the Performing Arts in 1966, as Cleopatra in *Antony and Cleopatra,* an opera written especially for her.

After World War II, there was a shortage of singers in Europe and many young Negro musicians, like their predecessors Evanti and Jarboro, made their way there. Some of the talented Negro Americans who have made successful operatic debuts are Vera Little, Gloria Davy, Kathleen Crawford, Leonora Lafayette, Grace Bumbry, and Gwendolyn Simms.

In the history of American opera companies, eleven Negroes have appeared with the Metropolitan, eleven with the San Francisco, fifteen with New York Center, five with the Lyric of Chicago, seven with Boston, and one with Pittsburgh. The total number of different Negro singers to have appeared in all American opera companies is thirty-four, and most of these have appeared since Marian Anderson's debut at the Metropolitan in 1955.

Although the works of Negro composers are not commonly heard on symphonic concerts, several have established themselves as first-rate artists. Ulysses Kay's *Sinfonia in E* has been performed by the Cleveland Orchestra under George Szell; *Of New Horizons,* by the New York Philharmonic under Thor Johnson; and *Serenade for Orchestra,* by the Louisville Orchestra. Another composer to gain recognition is Howard Swanson, whose *Short Symphony* was played by the New York Philharmonic under Dimitri Mitropoulos and won a New York Music Critics' Circle Award. Hale Smith's *Contours* was premiered by the Louisville Orchestra and later performed by the Cleveland Orchestra, the Symphony of the New World (New York) and the Cincinnati Orchestra. His *Music for Harp and Orchestra* was commissioned and played by the Symphony of the New World.

Under the direction of Newell Jenkins, Julia Perry's *Stabat Mater* was performed by Clarion Concerts (New York), with mezzo-soprano Betty Allen singing the leading role; Coleridge Taylor Parkinson's *Concerto for Viola and Orchestra* was performed at Philharmonic Hall under the auspices of the National Association of Negro Musicians, with Selwart Clarke as soloist. John Carter's *Requiem Seditiosam,* dedicated to the memory of Medgar Evers, was premiered by the Symphony of the New World.

In addition to the great artists already mentioned, the leading concert singers today are soprano Adele Addison, mezzo-soprano Shirley Verrett, mezzo-soprano Betty Allen, and baritone William Warfield. The spectacular success of pianist André Watts opened heretofore closed doors to Negro instrumentalists. Several years ago, Natalie Hinderas became the first Negro pianist to join the roster of Columbia Artists, a major management company. She worked with two other highly gifted pianists, Armenta Adams and Eugene Haynes, who are now with major concert managements. Other instrumentalists who are building major careers are cellist Kermit Moore, violinist Sanford Allen, flutist Harold Jones, and violist Selwart Clarke. In the field of conducting, Dean Dixon has an international reputation, Everett Lee is permanent conductor of an orchestra in Sweden and Henry Lewis is building a solid career on the West Coast.

Forces of change that came at the close of World War II brought new opportunities in television for the Negro musician, who has always played a major role in the American entertainment field. A change in the attitudes of producers and directors regarding the use of Negroes is evident, but it has come about slowly. No longer is the Negro restricted to servant roles or character parts which show him as an uneducated, happy-go-lucky member of lower-class society, but there are still limitations to the role he may expect to play. Both the television and the moving picture industry have tended to perpetuate stereotypes of the Negro and although highly rated and welcomed in television programming, he has for some hard-to-explain reason been largely relegated and even limited to guest spots on variety shows.

Nat "King" Cole and Sammy Davis, Jr., have had their own network programs. Harry Belafonte as actor and producer has won several awards for his hour-long specials, but these represent only a small token of the rich Negro potential. Lena Horne, who has been called the greatest of all night-club singers, has had to go to England to make television specials, as has Eartha Kitt. The place of the Negro in American society is changing rapidly and it is beyond the scope of this brief survey to do more than list some of the representative Negro artists in the field of musical entertainment, but we may expect greater recognition for them in the future.

In female vocal groups, the most popular singing trio to emerge in the 1960's has been The Supremes, closely followed by The Ronettes, The Chiffons, and Marvelettes. In men's vocal groups, the Ink Spots have been favorites for years, along with the Mills Brothers. More recently organized are: The Contours, The Temptations, The Four Tops, and the Drifters. There is a very long list of popular vocalists who have reached the top in their field, but some of the most representative are: Billie Holliday, Paul Robeson, Pearl Bailey, Ella Fitzgerald, Lena Horne, Sarah Vaughan, Dorothy Dandridge, Carmen McRae, Nina Simone, Nancy Wilson, Diahann Carroll, Leslie Uggams, and Eartha Kitt. Other musicians who represent a lengthy list of master entertainers are: Nat "King" Cole, Ray Charles, Billy Eckstine, Louis Armstrong, and Sammy Davis, Jr. Finally, two of the great band leaders of all times are Duke Ellington and Count Basie. There is always the question of how contemporary jazz musicians should be evaluated. We cannot know how long the current trends of today will last, nor can we know in what directions they will lead toward new musical concepts. However, artists currently representative of the *new jazz* are Charles Lloyd and the Charles Lloyd Quartet; John Handy and the John Handy Quintet.

Looking toward the future of American television, we will undoubtedly see an increasing number of Negroes assuming key roles as producers, directors, performers, and technicians. How can it be otherwise with so great a wealth of talent?

Summary

1. The natural musicality of the Negro was recognized and noted by American and European writers before the Revolutionary War, but factual information before 1850 is scarce.
2. Minstrelsy came to the stage as an imitation of plantation Negroes by white actors and musicians.

3. When the Negroes came into stage minstrelsy, they adopted the patterns already set.
4. Two of the greatest ministrel troupes were Lew Johnson's Plantation Minstrel Company and the Georgia Minstrels.
5. The greatest Negro songwriters of the period following the Civil War were James Bland and Richard Milburn.
6. The Jubilee Singers of Fisk University gave formal presentations of Negro songs in 1871. They were followed by choirs from Hampton, Tuskegee, and other industrial schools.
7. Negroes are well represented in the membership of the American Society of Composers, Authors and Publishers. Dr. James Weldon Johnson and Dr. Harry T. Burleigh were charter members.
8. William C. Handy is known as the Father of the Blues, the form which served as a basis for twentieth-century jazz.
9. Among the Negro bands which first played the swinging style of music later known as jazz were: Duke Ellington, Fletcher Henderson, Bennie Moton, Louis Armstrong, Jimmy Lunceford, and Don Redman.
10. The Colored Opera Company was organized in 1873, followed by the Drury Opera Company, the American Negro Opera Company, and the Harlem Opera Workshop.
11. Early operatic singers went to Europe to avoid the strict race barriers.
12. Marian Anderson and Leontyne Price have been eminently successful in the operatic field and have done much to open the door for Negro singers.
13. Negro composers are not commonly heard on symphonic concerts, but Ulysses Kay, Howard Swanson, Julia Perry, Coleridge-Taylor Parkinson, and John Carter have established themselves as first-rate artists.
14. Leading Negro symphony conductors are Dean Dixon, Everett Lee, and Henry Lewis.
15. Negro entertainers have always rated high in America. It is hard to explain why they seem to be limited to guest spots on television variety shows.
16. Looking toward the future, we will undoubtedly see an increasing number of Negroes assuming roles as producers, directors, and performers in the television and moving-picture industries.

Examples of Music

1. Price, Leontyne, *A Program of Song*, Faure, Poulenc, Strauss and Wolf. RCA Victor (LM 2279).
2. Anderson, Marian, *Spirituals*. RCA Victor (LM 2032).

3. Anderson, Marian, *Best Loved Schubert Songs*. RCA Victor (Red Seal LM 98).
4. Anderson, Marian, *Alto Rhapsody*, Op. 53 (Brahms); *Kindertoten-lieder* (Mahler). RCA Victor (1146).
5. Warfield, William, *Ancient Songs of the Church* and *Karl Loewe Ballads*. Columbia (ML 4545).
6. Bibb, Leon, *Love Songs*. Vangard (9037).
7. Swanson, Howard, *Seven Songs*. American Recording Society by the Ditson Musical Foundation.
8. Kay, Ulysses, *Sinfonia in E* (1950). Composer's Recordings, Inc. (Oslo Philharmonic).
9. Perry, Julia, *Short Piece for Orchestra* (1952). Tokyo Imperial Philharmonic (Schwam Catalog, June, 1967).

The New Music of Jazz

10. Coleman, Ornette, *This Is Our Music*. Atlantic (1353).
11. Coleman, Ornette, *The Shape of Jazz to Come*. Atlantic (1317).
12. Coltrame, John, *My Favorite Things*. Atlantic (1361).
13. Coltrane, John, *Meditations*. Impulse (A-9110).
14. Taylor, Cecil, *Looking Ahead*. Contemporary (M-3562).
15. New York Art Quartet. *New York Art Quartet*. (ESP 1004).
16. Lloyd, Charles, *Forest Flower, Charles Lloyd at Monterey*. Atlantic (SD 1473).
17. The Charles Lloyd Quartet, *Journey Within*. Atlantic (SD 1493).
18. The John Handy Quintet, *The 2nd John Handy Album*. Columbia (CL 2567).
19. Simone, Nina, *Nina Simone Sings the Blues*. RCA Victor (LSP 3789).

Glossary

A cappella Choral music without instrumental accompaniment.

Action The mechanism of a keyboard instrument.

Adagio "Comfortable, easy." A slow tempo.

Agnus Dei "Lamb of God." A section of the Mass.

Allegro "Cheerful." A lively, brisk tempo.

Andante "Going along, moving." A very moderate tempo.

Anthem A sacred choral composition with English words.

Antiphonal Singing or playing by alternating groups.

Aria A lyrical song in opera; a solo with instrumental accompaniment.

Art song An independent composition, a song for solo voice and piano.

Atonality, atonal Without tonality; pertaining to music which has no key center.

Ballet An art form consisting of group dancing with musical accompaniment.

Baritone voice The male voice range between tenor and bass.

Baroque Period roughly between 1600 and 1750.

Basso ostinato "Obstinate bass." A constantly repeated bass line.

Bel canto "Beautiful song." A style of singing associated with Italian schools of the seventeenth and eighteenth centuries.

Benedictus Second part of the Sanctus section of the Mass.

Bourrée A quick dance of French origin, often included in Baroque suites.

Buffa "Comic." As in *opera buffa,* comic opera.

Cadence The melodic, harmonic, and rhythmic formulas used at the end of a piece of music (or at the end of a phrase, period, or section within it) to create an impression of conclusion.

Cadenza An improvisatory passage for an unaccompanied solo instrument, usually in a concerto near the end of a movement.

Canon A polyphonic composition in which two or more instruments have the same melody starting at different times.

Cantata A composite vocal form with instrumental accompaniment, usually in several contrasting sections.

Chamber music Instrumental ensemble music performed with one player on each part.

Chant Gregorian chant, plain chant, plainsong. Monophonic, unaccompanied, liturgical vocal music.

Choir A group devoted to singing sacred music. A group of instruments of the same family.

Chorale Hymn tune of Protestant churches.

Chord Three or more tones sounding together.

Chromatic scale A scale composed entirely of half-steps.

Clavichord A fifteenth-century keyboard instrument, developed from an earlier instrument called the *monochord*.

Clavier A keyboard instrument with strings, e.g., clavichord, harpsichord, piano.

Coda "Tail." The concluding section of a music form.

Concertino (1) Diminutive of concerto; (2) A group of soloists in a *concerto grosso*.

Concerto Composition for solo instrument with orchestra.

Concerto grosso A multimovement form featuring a small group of solo instruments with a larger body of accompanying instruments, usually string orchestra and a keyboard instrument.

Consonance Combined sounds with simple vibrating ratios. Agreeable concords. Inactive harmonies.

Continuo The bass line figuration in Baroque music which was played by a keyboard instrument and one or more melody instruments.

Contrapuntal Polyphonic. Employing counterpoint.

Counterpoint The art and study of combining melodies.

Credo "I believe." The longest section of the Mass.

Cyclic The principle of using common themes in different movements of multimovement works.

Dampers The mechanism which terminates the vibration of the strings in pianos and similar instruments.

Dissonance Combined sounds with complex vibrating ratios. Discord. Active harmonies.

Dixieland A style of jazz.

Dominant The fifth degree of the scale, or the chord built on it, or the key starting on the fifth note of the original tonic.

Dynamics Variations of loudness and softness.

Episode A passage between main structural divisions in a form. In fugues, a passage between statements of the subject.

Etude "Study." A piece of music designed to give practice in instrumental technique.

Exposition In sonata form, the first large division in which the themes are "exposed." In fugues, the sections in which the subject is present.

Figuration The consistent use of a melodic or harmonic pattern.

Figured bass A bass part provided with numerals and symbols to indicate harmonies.

Form The structure and organization of musical ideas.

Fugue A polyphonic form in which each of a specified number of voices enters with a subject.

Gloria "Glory." The second section in the ordinary of the Mass.

Grand opera Opera on a lavish scale. The term came from nineteenth-century French opera.

Ground bass A short melodic phrase repeated continuously in the bass.

Half-step The smallest interval in Western music.

Harmony Simultaneous sounding of different musical pitches. Progressions of chords.

Homophonic, homophony Music with a predominant melody supported by a subordinate accompaniment.

Impromptu A title applied by early Romantic composers to a short piece for piano.

Interlude Music suitable to be played between acts of a play or opera.

Invention A type of instrumental composition of which Bach's *Two Part Inventions* are the prime example.

Key The tonal center of a work or passage, indicated by the key signature and often included as part of the title. Keys are identified by letter names.

Keyboard The visible part of the mechanism that is touched by the player of the piano, organ, harpsichord, etc.

Keynote Tonic. The principal note of the key. The first degree of the scale in tonal music.

Kyrie "Lord have mercy." The first part of the Mass.

Leitmotif (Leitmotiv) "Leading motive." In Wagnerian music dramas, musical motives associated with characters, objects, emotions, or ideas.

Libretto The text, or words, of any dramatic musical work.

Lied (pl., *Lieder*) "Song." Used as a general designation for art songs as opposed to folk songs.

Linear Pertaining to lines. Used to emphasize the horizontal (contrapuntal) aspect of music in contrast to the vertical (harmonic) aspect.

Lyric Song-like. Expressive of inner feelings. Not epic or dramatic.

Madrigal A secular form, usually for unaccompanied voices in four to six (most often five) parts with a lyrical poem as text.

Major scale A seven-note scale pattern characterized by a major third between the first and third degrees and half-steps between the third and fourth and between the seventh and eighth degrees.

Mass A solemn rite of the Roman Catholic Church commemorating the sacrifice of Christ.

Mazurka   A Polish folk dance in triple time, with the second beat generally accented.

Meter   The pattern of accents and note values in a measure of music.

Metronome   A mechanical device for measuring units of time.

Minuet   A French dance of rustic origin in triple meter and a moderately fast tempo. The customary third movement in the symphony of the Viennese Classical period.

Mirliton   A fifteenth-century wind instrument. Also known as the "eunuch flute." Present-day Americans call it a "kazoo."

Mode   Pertaining to major or minor, or to one of the scale patterns of early ecclesiastical music.

Monophony   Music consisting of a single, unaccompanied line.

Motet   A sacred vocal form, usually for unaccompanied voices and in polyphonic style.

Motive   The smallest recognizable unit of music.

Movement   The complete and comparatively independent divisions which together form suites, sonatas, symphonies, and other works.

Musicologist   One devoted to the scientific study of music, particularly its history and literature.

Mute   A device for softening, muffling, or modifying the tone of string and brass instruments.

National music   Music with peculiarities of style that arise from the cultural heritage of a country.

Neo-Classicism   A twentieth-century movement which reverts to the ideals of the Viennese Classical and Baroque periods.

Nocturne   "Night song." Chopin used the name for piano pieces with a smooth-flowing melody.

Octave   An interval comprising eight scale degrees. The two tones of an octave have a vibrating ratio of 1:2.

Opera   A drama wholly or mostly sung, with orchestral accompaniment, and presented on stage with appropriate costumes, scenery, and action.

Opus (abbrev. *Op.*)   "Work." Applied especially to musical compositions. Opus numbers are assigned to a composer's works in order of publication, and are often included with the title and key as an added means of identification.

Oratorio   A large dramatic composition, usually on a sacred theme, for soloists, chorus, and orchestra, consisting of many contrasting sections. Presented without staging.

Overture   The instrumental introduction to operas and stage works. The first movement of compositions in the suite form. Independent, one-movement compositions for orchestra or band.

Partita   A suite. A group of dance movements.

Period   A unit of musical form which presents a complete musical idea, usually in two or more phrases, and which ends with a complete cadence.

Phrase   A unit of musical form which presents an incomplete musical idea and ends with a cadence.

Pizzicato   "Plucked." A manner of producing tone on string instruments.

Plectra   Plucking devices used in playing certain string instruments.

Polonaise   A stately and festive dance of Polish origin; in moderate triple meter.

Polyphony   Music conceived as a combination of melodies. Polyphony and counterpoint are virtually synonymous.

Polytonality   The presence of two or more tonalities (keys) at the same time.

Prelude   Properly, an introductory piece or movement intended to precede the body of a work. Also applied to independent works, especially brief pieces for piano.

Presto   "Very fast."

Recapitulation   The third major section in sonata form, in which all the themes return in the tonic key.

Recitative   A passage in declamatory style for solo voice with simple harmonic accompaniment.

Register   A portion of the pitch range of voices and instruments.

Requiem   Mass for the dead.

Rhapsody   A freely constructed musical composition, often of nationalistic character.

Ripieno   The full orchestra as distinct from a group of soloists in a *concerto grosso.*

Romantic music   Music which is primarily subjective, with emphasis on imagination, emotion, and freedom of expression.

Rondo   A type of musical form in which a constant thematic element alternates with contrasting sections.

Sanctus   "Holy." A section of the Mass.

Scale   A stepwise arrangement of the tones of a given key and/or mode.

Scherzo   "Joke, jest." A piece or movement characterized by vivacious rhythm and brusque humor. Scherzos often supplant minuet movements in the sonatas, quartets, and symphonies of Beethoven and later musicians.

Schottisch   "Scottish." A round dance of the polka variety, but somewhat slower.

Score   A composite of all the parts of a composition. Scoring is the art of arranging music for a specific medium.

Seventh chord   A four-note chord constructed of alternate scale tones.

Shawm   Any of several wind instruments played with a double reed.

Sonata   A multimovement composition for a solo instrument or for a solo instrument with piano.

Sonata form   The complete plan, in three or four movements, of sonatas, trios, quartets, symphonies, etc.; more specifically, the structure of the first movement of such compositions, consisting basically of three main sections: exposition, development, and recapitulation.

Subdominant   The fourth degree of the scale, or the chord built on it, or the key associated with it.

Suite   A set or series of movements, often a group of dances or selections from a stage work.

Symphonic poem   A programmatic work for orchestra, usually in one extended movement.

Symphony   A large orchestral composition in three or four movements. A complete sonata for orchestra.

Te deum   Hymn of praise.

Tetrachord   A tone series within the interval of a fourth.

Text   The words of a musical composition.

Texture   The disposition and relationship of the various components in the musical fabric. The types of texture are: monophonic, polyphonic, and homophonic.

Thorough bass   See *Figured bass.*

Timbre   Tone color or quality.

Toccata   A brilliant, freely constructed composition; originally for keyboard instruments, but now sometimes applied to works for other mediums.

Tonality   Key and mode.

Tone poem   See *Symphonic poem.*

Tone row   A series of all twelve tones of a chromatic scale played in a specific order, with none repeated.

Tonic   The keynote. The first degree of the scale, or the chord built on it.

Triad   A three-note chord constructed of alternate scale tones.

Twelve-tone system   A technique of composition devised by Arnold Schönberg, based on a *tone row.*

Unison   Two or more tones with the same pitch.

Variations   A type of composition based on one or more constant elements.

Whole-tone scale   A six-note scale with no half-steps.

Index